SELLING DIVERSITY

SELLING DIVERSITY

Immigration, Multiculturalism, Employment Equity, and Globalization

◆◆

Yasmeen Abu-Laban
Christina Gabriel

broadview press

NATIONAL LIBRARY OF CANADA CATALOGUING IN PUBLICATION DATA

Abu-Laban, Yasmeen, 1966-
Selling diversity: immigration, multiculturalism, employment equity,
and globalization/Yasmeen Abu-Laban, Christina Gabriel.

Includes bibliographical references and index.
ISBN 1-55111-398-8

1. Canada—Emigration and immigration—Government policy.
2. Canada—Emigration and immigration—Economic aspects.
3. Multiculturalism—Canada.   4. Multiculturalism—Economic aspects—Canada.
5. Affirmative action programs—Economic aspects—Canada.
6. Globalization—Economic aspects—Canada   I. Gabriel, Christina, 1961-
II. Title.

FC104.A28 2002   305'.0971   C2002-902398-X   F1035.A1A28 2002

BROADVIEW PRESS, LTD.
is an independent, international publishing house, incorporated in 1985.

North America
Post Office Box 1243,
Peterborough, Ontario, Canada K9J 7H5

3576 California Road,
Orchard Park, New York, USA 14127
TEL (705) 743-8990; FAX (705) 743-8353

www.broadviewpress.com
customerservice@broadviewpress.com

United Kingdom and Europe
Plymbridge North (Thomas Lyster Ltd.)
Units 3 & 4a Ormskirk Industrial Park,
Old Boundary Way, Burscough Rd,
Ormskirk, Lancashire L39 2YW
TEL (1695) 575112; FAX (1695) 570120; E-MAIL
books@tlyster.co.uk

Australia
UNIREPS University of New South Wales
Sydney, NSW 2052
TEL 61 2 9664099; FAX 61 2 9664520
infopress@unsw.edu.au

Broadview Press gratefully acknowledges the support of the Ministry of Canadian Heritage through the Book Publishing Industry Development Program.

Cover design by Zack Taylor and Liz Broes.
Typeset by Liz Broes, Black Eye Design.

Printed in Canada

10 9 8 7 6 5 4 3 2 1

To Claude Couture and Zachary Jericho Couture, with love.
Y A-L

To William Walters, with love.
CG

CONTENTS

Acknowledgements 9

ONE   Diversity, Globalization, and Public Policy
in Canada 11

TWO   Immigration and Canadian Citizenship 37

THREE   Contemporary Directions:
Immigration and Citizenship Policy 1993–2001 61

FOUR   Multiculturalism and Nation-Building 105

FIVE   Employment Equity 129

SIX   Selling (Out) Diversity in an Age of Globalization
165

Selected Bibliography 181

Index 195

ACKNOWLEDGEMENTS

Many people have supported and encouraged this project from its initial stages as an idea through to the writing of the book. We are very grateful to them all.

We would like to begin by thanking our publisher Broadview and in particular Michael Harrison and Suzanne Hancock for supporting and guiding this manuscript. We were also aided by the comments from anonymous external reviewers.

We wish to acknowledge the Department of Political Science, University of Alberta and its Chair, Janine Brodie, for stimulating the lively intellectual environment that initially provided the impetus for this project. In particular, Christina Gabriel's holding of an Izaak Walton Killam Post-Doctoral Fellowship at the University of Alberta between 1998 and 1999 was instrumental to fostering a collaboration that ultimately grew to span Edmonton to Peterborough to Ottawa.

Our thanks also go to our many colleagues and friends who graciously and kindly read drafts of all or parts of this manuscript: Pat Armstrong, Claude Couture, Lise Gotell, Eric Helleiner, Andy Knight, Rianne Mahon, Steve Patten, Miriam Smith, Daiva Stasiulis, William Walters, and Reg Whitaker. We have greatly benefited from your valuable comments and observations.

At the University of Alberta, thanks, as well, go to Patience Akpan and Md Nuruzzaman for their extremely capable and timely research assistance, and to Alice Lau for library assistance. It was much appreciated. Financially this project also benefited from Trent University, Peterborough.

Finally, and most importantly, we would like to thank William and Claude for their unreserved support and encouragement of this project and for tolerating the somewhat frequent absences that proved necessary for the completion of this project.

chapter ONE

Diversity, Globalization, and Public Policy in Canada

In 2001 the City of Toronto hosted the International Olympic Committee (IOC) in its effort to secure the 2008 summer games. The grand finale of the IOC visit was an evening dinner gala where Prime Minister Jean Chrétien won a standing ovation for his endorsement of the bid by stressing that Toronto's advantage, as opposed to other contender cities, was its "diversity."[1] In an apparent attempt to emphasize this, the evening's festivities included Cirque du Soleil-like acrobats, Slavic and Celtic dancers, hip-hop artists, First Nations drummers, a black choral group, and a conga line dancing to the lyrics "Hot, hot hot," all of which left the head of the IOC's inspection panel musing that it was "impressive" that diversity seemed to "work" in Canada.[2]

Prime Minister Chrétien's marketing of Toronto and the collage of cultures packaged as entertainment for the consumption of IOC members capture in microcosm a broader trend we call "selling diversity." The selling of diversity finds expression in recent developments in the three public policies that are examined in this book: immigration, multiculturalism, and employment equity. Immigration policy has been one major means by which the state has historically controlled membership in the Canadian political community by selecting who would be (and who would not be) eligible for entry, residence, and citizenship in Canada. Multiculturalism policy, first articulated by the federal government of Liberal Prime Minister Pierre Elliott Trudeau in 1971, has been an important means by which ethnic minorities (i.e. non-British, non-French, non–Aboriginal Canadians) were represented in the official symbolism of the Canadian nation. Employment equity, a policy first introduced by the federal Conservatives of Prime Minister Brian Mulroney in 1986, has been a key policy aimed at ameliorating discrimination faced in employment by visible minorities, women, Aboriginal peoples, and people with disabilities. The purpose of this book is to examine these three important policy areas, which reflect on how Canadian citizenship has been granted to immigrants and the ways in which diverse citizens can seek symbolic representation and equality in Canadian institutions and society.

Our central argument is that despite the different rationales that informed the introduction and historical evolution of immigration, multiculturalism, and employment equity policies, today each policy is affected by new rationales that put stress on the language of business. Thus an emphasis on markets, efficiency, competitiveness, and individualism has been central to recent rearticulations of the three policy areas. This we suggest is a direct response by Canadian policy-makers to the perceived exigencies of globalization—namely, capturing global markets and enhancing Canada's competitiveness. This interpretation of, and strategy of response to, globalization has resulted in a selling of diversity, whereby the skills, talents, and ethnic backgrounds of men and women are commodified, marketed, and billed as trade-enhancing. In this context, certain notions of "diversity"—those which pertain to competitiveness—are viewed favourably, both at home in Canada and globally. As a result a commitment to enhance justice and respect in a diverse society, while not abandoned entirely, has been muted. This development, we suggest, should be viewed with caution. On its own terms selling diversity may "work," but it does not necessarily guarantee greater equality between Canadians.

In this chapter we outline the key concepts and themes which structure our critical examination of selling diversity. First, we address the idea and relevance of diversity for understanding social power and the state. Second, we outline current discussions of the impact of globalization on a world configured in nation-states. Third, we consider the impact of globalization on public policy. Fourth, we examine the relevance of a gender analysis of social diversity and public policy. We conclude with a brief overview of what each of the subsequent chapters contains.

THE CANADIAN STATE, DIVERSITY, AND THE POLITICS OF IDENTITY

"Diversity" can reflect a number of points of difference among people. These might include gender, age, place of birth, ethnicity, culture, education, physical ability, social class, religion, sexual orientation, language, place of residence, citizenship status, political ideology, domestic relationships, and personal style and attributes. Indeed, the list could be endless if we consider how every person is unique. However, while there are potentially endless points of diversity, not all of them are necessarily implicated in forms of collective political mobilization or in the way power and resources are divided at any given moment. Nor are all possible points of difference necessarily implied when the term "diversity" is employed. For this reason it is important to examine the differences denoted or connoted when the term is used—be it by public figures, politicians, or academics.

In this book, unless otherwise stated, we use the term diversity to describe socially constructed differences relating to gender, race/ethnicity, and class. As social constructions, these forms of difference are not inherently and biologically given, but rather take on historically specific meanings as a result of human action. Our focus on gender, race/ethnicity, and class is not exhaustive of all forms of difference that might be usefully examined in understanding the policies of immigration, multiculturalism, and employment equity. Nonetheless, the emphasis on these three intersecting social relations is not simply arbitrary. We see these points of difference as crucial because of the part they have played in the (uneven) distribution of power and resources in Canadian society, historically and in the contemporary context. These points of difference are also important to the way that groups mobilize and make claims today and are frequently featured in current political debates of the three policies. Indeed, the very introduction of a policy like employment equity was a response to claims made by groups such as ethnic minorities (non-British, non-French, non-Aboriginal immigrants and their descendents), women, and Aboriginal peoples for greater inclusion and equity.

The collective mobilization around points of difference is central to what is termed the politics of identity, and in this process the state exercises considerable power. Drawing from the understanding of Max Weber,[3] the state is traditionally defined by social scientists as a set of institutions, including the government of the day, parliament, the bureaucracy, courts, and the military; the state is the highest authority of, or has sovereignty over, a given territory. When it comes to the politics of identity, the state is a key player in determining which identities and identity claims are taken into account and how they are represented in actions or policy, and conversely which ones are downplayed or even ignored.[4] To further understand this power of the state and the complex way in which social relations relating to gender, race/ethnicity, and class may interact together, consider Prime Minister Jean Chrétien's appointment of Adrienne Clarkson to the post of Governor General of Canada.

In October 1999, Adrienne Clarkson became the first member of a visible minority to be appointed Governor General. As a child in 1942, Clarkson had immigrated to Canada from China—a fact stressed by Chrétien in highlighting the symbolic value of his choosing her to play the ceremonial role of the Queen's designate.[5] Indeed, in the fanfare surrounding her appointment the Prime Minister argued that "her appointment is a reflection of the diversity and inclusiveness of our society and an indication of how our country has matured over the years."[6] Clarkson also used her appointment to highlight the same theme, stating that "I am the first immigrant, I am originally a refugee, and I think this is a very important evolution for Canada."[7]

In this discussion, the emphasis placed on Clarkson's symbolic value as an immigrant does indeed relate to certain evolving demographic trends which have had implications for identity politics. Canada is a settler-colony founded on French and British immigration and the expropriation of land from Aboriginal peoples. The project of European settler-colonization dating from the seventeenth century played out very differently by the close of the twentieth century. According to the 1996 Census, immigrants constitute 17.4 per cent of the Canadian national population, with urban concentrations of 42 per cent of the population in Toronto, 35 per cent in Vancouver, and 18 per cent in Montreal.[8] Since the 1970s, there has been a steady decline in immigrants arriving from European countries and an increase in immigrants arriving from countries in the Caribbean, Central and South America, Africa, the Middle East, and Asia. Thus, while prior to 1961 about 90 per cent of immigrants arrived from European countries, between 1991 and 1996 only 19 per cent came from European countries, with 57 per cent coming from countries of Asia.[9]

This has had an impact on the way Canadians describe their ethnic heritage(s). According to the 1996 Census, 17 per cent of the population reports a British Isles-only ancestry; 9 per cent report a French-only ancestry; and 28 per cent a single origin other than British-Isles, French, or just Canadian.[10] Some 36 per cent of Canadians reported more than one origin in the 1996 Census.[11] Also reflecting the shift towards immigrants arriving from countries outside of Europe is the growing number of visible minorities in Canada. Visible minorities are defined in state policy as "persons other than Aboriginal peoples, who are non-Caucasian in race or non-white in colour."[12] Whereas in 1986 visible minorities made up 6.3 per cent of the total Canadian population, in 1996 they represented 11.2 per cent of the population.[13] Thus, the appointment of Clarkson may be read as an attempt on the part of the Chrétien government to give symbolic recognition and representation to recent immigrants who are racial minorities, a collectivity which has since the early 1980s mobilized around themes relating to racism, inequality, and under-representation in institutions of power.[14]

Clarkson and Chrétien may have framed her appointment as important in relation to the diversity stemming from contemporary immigration. However, it is notable that a further interrogation of discussions surrounding this appointment reveals how a complex and intersecting set of social relations relating to gender, race/ethnicity, and class are implicated in power in Canada—even if the post Clarkson assumed is ceremonial rather than overtly and actively political.[15] Thus, for example, an analysis of the media coverage of Clarkson's appointment suggests that there was an unusual and critical focus on her personal life, including her relationship with spouse and writer John Ralston Saul (who was billed as useful because he could advise her); her purported estrangement from the two daughters of her "failed" first marriage; and a general depiction of Clarkson as cold, rich, and uppity and, thus, unfit for the role of "mother of the nation."[16] The intense and hyper-critical focus on Clarkson's domestic relationships was gendered in that this kind of scrutiny is not normally done with male public figures; additionally, it tapped into some popular stereotypes about class-privileged Asian women.[17]

The example of Clarkson serves to draw our attention to how understandings of diversity are relevant on a number of fronts. For the government of the day headed by Jean Chrétien, Clarkson's status as an immigrant and visible minority was underscored as important to her appointment, a feature that feeds more broadly into the power played by the state in determining which points of diversity are named and taken (or not taken) into account. The broader popular and media commentary surrounding this appointment also reveals a complex set of issues that reflect on how Clarkson's appointment challenged the traditional vesting of power (ceremonial or not) with white, class-advantaged males in Canada. Ultimately, the underlying message, that Clarkson was somehow unfit for the role of Governor General, is suggestive of how both social forces and the state are involved in contestations over diversity, identity politics, and power in Canada.

Today, issues relating to the state, diversity, and identity need also to be examined in relation to globalization. Many posit that the sovereign power of the state might be eroding as a result of globalization: this contention has captured the attention of contemporary analysts because it confronts the traditional understanding that the state is the highest authority of a given territory and population.

GLOBALIZATION AND THE STATE

As a force serving to shape the contemporary world, globalization suggests the erosion of state sovereignty in the face of a world-scale reorganization of economic, technological, and cultural activities or flows.[18] The term globalization came in vogue during the 1980s among scholars attempting to understand the socio-economic changes affecting industrialized countries in the West, as well as issues that had global impact (e.g., possible nuclear Armageddon or environmental crisis).[19] Since that time, it has been frequently invoked in the media, in business, and in finance. In fact, in all of the world's major languages, there is a term for globalization.[20] The result is that globalization is a trendy concept that is often not clearly defined,[21] rendering it a "cliché of our times."[22]

To give definition to the concept, it is most useful to highlight some of the issues that are signalled in discussions of the economic, technological, and cultural changes brought about by globalization. From the vantage point of economics, globalization can be defined as the "shift in investment, production, and trade decisions from serving national markets to serving world markets."[23] Specifically this shift involves 1) an enlargement and extension of markets; 2) the greater mobility of capital; and 3) production processes that allow for final products to be assembled from many different units, made in a large number of countries, and flexibly produced to fill specialized market niches.[24] In terms of markets and trade, an example might be how the American-based McDonalds hamburger chain has franchises in a host of countries including Russia, South Africa, and Korea. The British magazine *The Economist* publishes annual cross-national figures on the cost of a Big Mac to illustrate comparative purchasing power in a simple and even digestible way for readers.[25] In terms of finance, there is now a greater mobility of capital, as illustrated by how economic units like currencies, stocks, or shares have become more mobile as a result of new information technology.[26] The growing trend of flexible production can be exemplified by the Italian chain store Benetton, which pioneered the use of computer technology to control the design and amount of clothing produced according to daily computerized sales returns.[27]

In addition, globalization has technological and cultural implications. Global cultural flows include the flow of information, images, ideas, and even people.[28] The flow and dissemination of electronic images and information has been enhanced by increased technological ability—through satellites and the Internet, for instance. For example, in 1999 not only Americans but people in countries throughout the world were able to see President Bill Clinton questioned about his personal relationship with intern Monica Lewinsky and to access the final report of the grand jury's deliberations, all on the World Wide Web. The flow of ideas, especially ones emerging from the Enlightenment world view like "freedom," "rights" (including private property rights), and "democracy," is also apparently global and often symbolized by images:[29] Chinese university students at Tiannamen Square erected a replica of the Statue of Liberty to symbolize the "democracy" they were calling for in 1989.

Thus the technological and cultural flows associated with globalization serve to connect peoples and countries around the world; moreover, events and activities in one part of the world can have consequences for individuals and communities in distant parts.[30] Demonstrating such global repercussions, in May 2000 a Filipino university student caused computers around the globe to crash when he sent out the "love bug" virus. This not-so-innocent "love letter" caused computer problems for the Canadian Parliament, the British House of Commons, the White House, the U.S. State Department, and the American military, among others.[31]

One specific stream within global cultural flows that pertains to our discussion is the movement of men and women within and between countries of the developing South and industrialized North. The movement of peoples across national borders is one of the most evident forms of globalization today and a major source of greater diversity.[32] People who cross national boundaries might be those whom states explicitly seek to fill labour market positions (guest workers, temporary workers, and immigrants). But they might also be refugees, the family members of immigrants or citizens, illegal immigrants, international students, exiles, and even tourists. The movement of people across national boundaries brings with it the possibility of ongoing cultural intermixing—be it religious, ethnic, linguistic, or other. This is why some have suggested that globalization appears to challenge the dominance of a single national cultural identity in favour of other forms of identity, including shifting and even new hybrid (or mixed) ones.[33]

While these examples are useful in illustrating the sorts of processes and issues that have captured the attention of analysts, it is nonetheless the case that globalization is a highly contested concept within the social sciences and humanities today. Major debate rages over how globalization is to be understood, its impact as a force affecting the power of individual states, and its influence in relations between countries of the North and South in the modern world.

To simplify this debate, it is helpful to think of the differences in terms of a continuum. At one end of the spectrum are the analysts who use the term globalization to suggest that the period since the 1980s represents a massive break in human history.[34] Proponents of this view see globalization—specifically, economic transformation—as challenging the traditional economic power balance between countries of the North and South, eroding the sovereignty of the state as a governing unit, and heralding the emergence of a possible new, global society.[35] From this vantage point, globalization means that the site of authority, power, and politics is located outside the state.

At the other end of the spectrum are those that suggest that there is nothing new today that warrants the label globalization and that the economic interdependence between states today is no different than in other eras, such as during the nineteenth century.[36] From this position, globalization is basically a myth that masks the way that states continue to hold considerable power and sovereignty over their borders and internal affairs.

We suggest that the most appropriate understanding of the economic, cultural, and technological changes associated with "globalization" falls somewhere in the middle of the spectrum and should be historically sensitive. From this perspective, the processes associated with globalization today are not entirely new and do not represent a radical break from the past. This perspective acknowledges that for centuries goods, ideas, and even people have crossed state borders or other political barriers.[37] However, while globalization processes may not be new, what makes the contemporary era unique is the intensification of economic, political, cultural, and technological processes that transcend, but do not necessarily supercede, the state.[38]

Of course a "middle position" does not settle the matter; we expect the broad debate on these aspects of globalization will continue to attract scholarly attention. We would further suggest, therefore, that the phenomenon of globalization (contemporary or historic) cannot be fully addressed either in terms of abstract social theory or empirically based generalizations of groups of nation-states. Rather, a fuller comprehension of globalization also requires attending to empirical evidence gleaned from specific countries, specific actions, and specific policy discussions engaged in by state actors. This is why employing a country case study attendant to policy and policy discussions is useful.

GLOBALIZATION, NEO-LIBERALISM, AND PUBLIC POLICY

Country case studies can illuminate another feature of globalization worthy of attention: the way in which globalization is a *discourse* (or framework of language, ideas, references, and understanding which shapes power relations). Looking at the British context, it has been suggested by Colin Hay and Matthew Watson that there is a dominant discourse of globalization which has been "promoted to the point at which it now seems to be 'almost everywhere' at least in part because it privileges the political interests of an ascendant social class to the exclusion of others."[39] Similarly, in Canada, some feminist scholars have suggested that certain policy responses have emerged from a particular understanding of globalization by decision-makers. They have drawn attention to how the result of globalization is not neutral when it comes to disadvantaged groups (especially women, workers, and minorities).[40] Thus, for example, Marjorie Cohen avers that:

> ... both globalization and [economic] restructuring [wrongly] are terms which imply a kind of inevitability to the policy changes which are occurring.... In this sense restructuring appears apolitical and outside the purview of social analysis dealing with gender, class and racial issues.[41]

As noted earlier, since the 1980s the term globalization has gained increasing currency. To what extent do references to the term or to processes associated with globalization enter into discussions (including policy discussions) in government circles? To answer this requires also addressing what policy-makers say in the name of "globalization," as well as what they do. Our analysis will show how the discourse of globalization employed by Canadian policy-makers is informed by the language, ideals, and references of neo-liberalism, particularly those ideals which emphasize efficiency and global competitiveness, as opposed to global community or global responsibility.

Our analysis of immigration, employment equity, and multiculturalism assesses how contemporary processes of globalization and globalization discourse have affected domestic policy-making in these three areas. In examining these areas we emphasize the specificity of the "national" or domestic dimensions—that is, the degree to which processes of globalization have affected the workings of the Canadian nation-state and its institutions. Recent policy shifts within the areas of immigration, employment equity, and multiculturalism also need to be considered against the broader reorientation of the state.

The post-war period saw the emergence of what is termed the welfare state.[42] The work of economist John Maynard Keynes provided some of the guiding assumptions of the welfare state in many anglo-American countries.[43] Keynes argued that states could use their taxing and spending powers to actively intervene in the economy to promote full employment and economic growth. Essentially governments were to borrow and spend during economic downturns to keep the economy afloat. In theory, deficits accrued during these times would be paid down by funds generated during times of economic growth. These ideas were applied to a greater or lesser extent by policy-makers in Canada and elsewhere. Additionally, a welfare state was constructed through a series of redistributive programs including unemployment insurance, social assistance payments, family allowance, universal health care, and access to education. Taken together, these public policy measures were designed to ensure that the risks, economic insecurity, and inequalities associated with a competitive market economy were minimized (although by no means entirely eliminated). These policy measures granted new social rights that permitted citizens to meet their basic needs.[44]

The post-war Keynesian state was more than a set of social entitlements. It also embodied a particular set of expectations and understandings about the role of the state; the relationships between state, market, and family; and the nature of citizenship. It was accepted, for example, that not only could the state intervene in the economy but also that it should. Also, the state was viewed as a champion of social justice.[45] Canadians were members of a national community of citizens where their citizenship rights embodied more than "having a set of formal 'negative' constitutional rights of 'life, liberty and security of person' [but also embraced] 'positive' social welfare rights"[46] that people could claim as members of a community—on the basis of being Canadian. All these premises were built around the idea that the post-war state exercised sovereignty over a given national territory that defined the boundaries for both "economic exchange and for political community."[47]

Increasingly, these understandings are being destabilized and challenged as the post-war Keynesian welfare state is being reconfigured in complex and uneven ways. Among the questions scholars debate is the extent to which welfare state policies and practices are eroded, the degree of convergence between changing national economies, the nature and scope of the state's withdrawal from the public realm, and how the changing international political economy is implicated in the reconfiguration. The various labels attached to the emergent state form to distinguish it from the Keynesian welfare state include, but are not limited to, neo-liberal,[48] lean,[49] and competitive.[50] These labels signal an attempt to differentiate the post-war Keynesian welfare state from more current, and often uncertain, configurations of the state.

The term "neo-liberal" is frequently used as a catch-all, signalling a set of assumptions—frequently presented as common-sense truths—that frame many recent changes around political discussion and public policy. These assumptions include a more limited role for the state and, consequently, an emphasis on cutting back state policies and programs; a greater stress on individual self-sufficiency; and a belief that free markets are efficient allocators of goods and services. Consequently, among the values that are extolled by neo-liberal ideals are competitiveness, efficiency, choice, and consumerism.

Neo-liberal assumptions have also influenced new and narrower understandings of citizenship. As Canadians are told that they as individuals and/or families are responsible for their future, the social rights attached to the Keynesian welfare state come into question. Increasingly, for Canadians "the market and their own worthiness will determine not only whether they succeed or fail but whether they live their lives with dignity or in fear of poverty."[51] Neo-liberal assumptions have also influenced, in part, the vigorous ideological attack on social solidarity and collective political action. Today, women, racial minorities, and the poor are often depicted as "special interests" grouped against the wishes and concerns of "ordinary Canadians." As a result, many of the equality struggles of such disadvantaged groups are undermined.[52]

Neo-liberal policy prescriptions are frequently touted as the only possible response to the exigencies of globalization. And yet, it just may be that these prescriptions "allegedly necessary for participation in the global economy permit more degrees of freedom than is commonly thought," and there are considerable cross-national variations in responses.[53] Moreover, the way in which governments choose and shape their responses is predicated on earlier, national development strategies. Some scholars have described this phenomenon as the "bio-diversity" of states, arguing that such variance finds its origin in differing historical traditions and institutional capacities.[54] In this respect distinct national histories and institutional capacities play an important role in the policy process, which only underscores the need to examine public policies more carefully in relation to specific countries.

One of the key lines of enquiry in this book is to consider the degree to which policy changes in the three areas of immigration, multiculturalism, and employment equity have been informed by neo-liberal assumptions, values, and changing conceptions of citizenship. In turn, what role does a globalization discourse play in justifying the adoption of neo-liberal prescriptions? In the case of each policy area, we also provide an overview of historical developments, since recent reforms—whether inspired by neo-liberal rationales or not—are usually imposed upon previous incarnations of the policy and existing institutional arrangements.[55] In other words, existing policy commitments and goals are not necessarily completely abandoned in favour of market-orientated ones, but may well be transformed. As a result, the exact consequences of policy changes may be uncertain and even contradictory.

New policy directions, whether in immigration, multiculturalism, or employment equity, are not simply imposed from the top down. Policy debates in each area are framed not just by state officials but also by other members of the policy community, including non-state actors such as advocacy groups, academics, research think-tanks, and other interested parties.[56] Whatever assertions to the contrary, neo-liberal prescriptions—framed as responses to globalization—do not necessarily enjoy across-the-board support. There are groups and individuals who contest policy changes and new directions. These actors may themselves be part of new transnational networks and organizations that supercede national boundaries.

It has been suggested that one of the outcomes of globalization is the potential to widen the context of domestic policy-making in two specific ways. First, non-state actors might use international bodies, such as the World Trade Organization and the European Court of Justice, to seek solutions that transcend the boundaries of the nation-state and, as a consequence, affect national decision-making. Second, it is argued that the boundaries between domestic and external policies have become much less clear.[57] These developments have led some scholars to speak of the internationalization of public policy.

But what is meant by internationalization? In the words of one assessment, internationalization refers to "a process by which various aspects of policy or policy-making are influenced by factors outside national territorial boundaries."[58] This assessment makes an important point when it stresses that the internationalization of various policy fields proceeds at an uneven pace and that many policy areas may be characterized by weak or strong variants of internationalization.[59] As with globalization, the internationalization of public policy—including the transfer of policy ideas, arrangements, or institutions across borders—is not necessarily entirely new: in the nineteenth century, European powers coercively imposed institutions, legal codes, and forms of bureaucratic organization on their colonies.[60]

Our examination of immigration, multiculturalism, and employment equity considers the degree to which contemporary Canadian domestic policy concerns are enmeshed with processes of internationalization, and we are sensitive to the way in which this process may be reciprocal. As noted above, analysts have drawn attention to transnational forums and G7 and other international agreements, such as the UN Conventions, as examples of an increasingly internationalized policy infrastructure. But it should also be pointed out that analysis of specific policy areas in terms of how policy developments and concerns generated in Canada find resonance in debates and policy discussions abroad and vice versa[61] has been somewhat uneven. This aspect of the internationalization of public policy may be thought of as the "export" of policy ideas and arrangements.[62]

DIVERSITY, GENDER ANALYSIS, AND PUBLIC POLICY

This study of the changing nature of immigration, multiculturalism, and employment equity is structured around the premise that policy outcomes, such as those that flow from the espousal of a globalization discourse stressing neo-liberalism, do not affect all groups of people in the same way. Feminist scholarship has raised the question, "What difference does difference make in power relations?,"[63] generating a body of work that emphasizes how unequal relations of power find expression within public policy and public policy outcomes. Indeed, some of the richest contributions to policy studies come from feminists who have examined gender assumptions within public policy and the way in which policy outcomes may affect men and women differently—for example, how the sexual division of labour and women's consequent location in the workforce ensures that many policy outcomes will have gender-specific effects. But gender analysis provides insights into the differential effects of policy on groups other than men and women because it "opens up space for a critical treatment of other forms of exclusion and marginalization.[64] For this reason a gender analysis is a useful starting point for an examination of the three policy areas in relation to diversity.

Feminism and gender analysis is sometimes mistakenly believed to have relevance only to those policy areas that have to do with so-called women's issues.[65] Yet, as Sandra Burt astutely points out using the example of childcare, a "women's issue" is not as clearcut as it would first appear. Burt's argument is that gender relations underpinning the rights and duties associated with childcare have varied considerably since Confederation, and as a result identifying childcare as a "'women's issue' is in some dispute."[66] In 1867, for example, fathers had absolute guardianship rights over their children, while today many national childcare advocacy groups construct childcare as a "parental issue" to underscore that both parents share responsibilities. Burt's point is that, when viewed through an historical lens, responsibility for childcare as primarily a "women's issue" is problematic. Moreover, Canadian feminists have recently offered assessments of a wide range of policy domains, which seem at first glance to have little to do with gender but which in fact are gendered insofar as their assumptions and implications affect men and women differentially: economic restructuring, labour market regulation, and regional trade agreements like the North American Free Trade Agreement.[67]

Feminist scholarship in the area of policy analyses has offered a number of important insights. Chief among these has been the identification of androcentrism within public policy and policy analysis.

> Androcentricity is essentially a view of the world from a male perspective.... From an androcentric perspective, women are seen as passive objects rather than as subjects in history, as acted upon rather than as actors; androcentricity prevents us from understanding that both males and females are always acted upon as well as acting, although often in very different ways.[68]

At its most superficial level a gendered analysis counts women in—it demands that data be disaggregated, for example. Thus, early studies of women in political life attempted to address the exclusion of women from inquiry by examining how women participated in decision-making.[69] But contributions to developing a feminist policy framework have moved far beyond this. Indeed, it has been suggested that using gender as a category of analysis allows for a much fuller analysis.[70] Susan Phillips argues, firstly, that a gender perspective helps to refocus attention on activities that have been rendered marginal or invisible in traditional policy studies. For instance, two typically neglected areas are the issue of women's unpaid labour in the domestic sphere and that of women's political activities in spaces not commonly considered the domain of "official politics of legislatures" such as community activism.[71] Secondly, a gender analysis confronts dominant, but flawed, assumptions. It highlights how concepts and terms themselves may be gendered, having drawn on experiences typically associated with men, not women, to establish the norm. Thirdly, gender analysis poses new research questions and challenges existing conceptualizations.[72] Feminist scholars have suggested that traditional policy studies have neglected to consider the "gender basis" of whole policy fields. One review of feminist policy studies highlights how feminist scholars have demonstrated the degree to which social policy is premised on particular assumptions about the gender roles of men and women.[73] The welfare state's social provisions, for example, have been constructed around an assumption that men are breadwinners/workers, who are active in the realm of politics and the economy, while women are dependants, associated with the domestic realm of family life. This gendered division has been characterized as the public-private dichotomy—a dichotomy that is central to our analysis of selling diversity.

Various definitions of what is "public" and what is "private' have informed the study of politics for centuries. Whereas much traditional literature has treated the "private realm" as beyond the scope of regulation, state action, or public scrutiny, feminist contributions have problematized the dichotomy and emphasized that politics occurs in both realms. This understanding underpins the famous slogan of the second wave of the women's movement, "the personal is political."[74] Feminist contributions have used this dichotomy—characterized as "an ideological marker that shifts in relation to the role of the state in particular historical moments in particular contexts, and in relation to particular issues"[75]—as an analytical tool to focus attention on the gendered organization of the two spheres. It has been argued that lines can be drawn between the public and private spheres in a number of ways. These public/private lines include state/market, state/family, and market/family.[76] Feminists have emphasized that the relation between the spheres of public and private, however defined, is not "so much in opposition to one another, but rather in *reciprocal connection with* one another."[77] Additionally, they have identified how these ideological boundaries are constantly being negotiated and renegotiated, pointing out that in this act "not everyone stands in the same relation to privacy and publicity; some have more power than others to draw and defend the line."[78] Where the line is drawn has political consequences for different groups of people.

We find it useful to examine policies and policy discussion in relation to what they reveal about particular constructions of the public/private. For instance, constructions that focus on the changing relationship between state and market are silent, more often than not, on the consequences for the realm of familial relations; they have implications for how we understand state activities (e.g., whether they are expanding or shrinking) and for how we understand power relations. For example, it is argued that the adoption of particular neo-liberal policy prescriptions will lead to a shrinking of the public domain as governments attempt to shift responsibility from the state to the private realm. In this understanding, analysts suggest that public provisions such as health care might be transformed into goods and services that the market can provide and might be downloaded onto community-based organizations or into the realm of private households.[79] The responsibility for risk—constructed as a shared responsibility under the terms of the welfare state's social programs—appears to have shifted to the volunteer sector, individuals, and families. Yet, which individuals in our society are most frequently called upon to undertake activity formerly provided by the state, such as care of the sick? Invariably the answer is women, who undertake caring work and unpaid labour.[80] Thus, we see the terms under which the lines between the public and private are being renegotiated in neo-liberal policy prescriptions as gendered.

To some extent the federal government of Canada has recognized the merits of using gender as a category of analysis. At the Fourth United Nations World Conference on Women held in Beijing, September 1995, the Canadian government unveiled *Setting the Stage for the Next Century: The Federal Plan for Gender Equality*. This plan outlines eight objectives, the first being to implement gender-based analysis throughout all federal departments and agencies. The report also highlights how gender-based analysis is the key to developing effective policy analysis and cites a New Zealand definition:

> Gender analysis is based on the standpoint that policy cannot be separated from the social context, and that social issues are an integral part of economic issues. Social impact analysis, including gender analy-

sis is not just an add-on, to be considered after costs and benefits have been assessed, but an integral part of good policy analysis.[81]

Within the federal bureaucracy, Status of Women Canada has also published an implementation document called *Gender-Based Analysis: A Guide for Policy Making*. This document outlines eight stages of the policy development process and provides suggestions to assist analysts at each of juncture. For example, to ensure gender is incorporated in identifying and defining a particular policy issue, the guide suggests that analysts consider:

> defining issues and target groups so that the diverse and different experiences of women and men are taken into account. In what ways were these definitions influenced by your gender? When a cultural practice falls outside the dominant society, what steps have you taken to define what is, from a cultural and gender perspective, acceptable and/or different?[82]

Gender Based Analysis also explicitly acknowledges that inequality is rooted in attitudes and conventions not only "about women but also about race, age, sexual orientation, disability, colour, etc."[83] In addition, it calls for actions and strategies that recognize "differences in experiences and situations between women and men, and among women."[84] Taken together the guide and the *Federal Plan for Gender Equality* offer an important starting point for a consideration of gender within the policy process.

The increasing recognition of the complexity and variety of women's experiences has prompted many feminists to question the viability of policy frameworks predicated on the belief that there are "natural" differences between men and women. For example, it has been argued that essentialist conceptions premised on "innate characteristics" should be abandoned in favour of a conception of identity that is viewed "in relation to external and constantly shifting contexts that include a network of other players and structural factors such as economic conditions, cultural dimensions and political institutions."[85] In a similar vein, it has been suggested that feminist interventions do not necessitate a singular focus on women but "rather the goal is to reveal the networks of power that are formed by the web of social relations."[86] In this way, feminist policy studies, as Susan Phillips has stated, has been concerned with "identity and voice"; for this reason, policy concerns cannot be treated as absolute but are "perspective dependent." Consequently, "policy design must be examined for its differential effects based on gender, class, race, age ... and these effects need to be evaluated and understood from the lived experience of those groups or communities affected."[87]

Despite this goal it would appear a "perspective dependent" approach remains underdeveloped in the growing feminist public policy literature within Canadian political science, a discipline which has been central in the development of the multidisciplinary fields of public policy and public administration. As noted by Ship:

> Feminist scholarship has yet to challenge the dominant conceptions and social constructions of ethnicity and "race" in the Canadian context that are shaped by the preoccupation with the Anglo-French division, punctuated by the occasional reference to the political struggles of First Nations peoples—limitations it also shares with much of Canadian political science.[88]

As a result, gender analysis of Canadian public policy has not sufficiently interrogated the consequences of policy for ethnic minority and racialized women.[89]

Our examination of immigration, multiculturalism, and employment equity policy attempts to redress this deficiency by addressing the differential impact of public policy on particular social groups. Immigration and multiculturalism are frequently presented as gender neutral and are not areas around which the mainstream English-Canadian women's movement has traditionally mobilized (although this has changed significantly in the last few years).[90] Employment equity has long been on the agenda of the women's movement, constructed as "a women's issue," but the degree to which assessments of employment equity have considered differential outcomes for groups of ethnic minority and racialized women is questionable.[91]

Additionally, our historical review of these three policy areas will consider the period from 1993 to 2001 in more explicit detail. This contemporary period coincides with the government's commitment to gender-based analysis. Our assessment considers the validity of the government's stated claim that the adoption of a gender-based analysis represents a "fundamental shift in the way government will think and act."[92] This assessment is pertinent now because the government's commitment to women's issues and gender equality is seen by some as more symbolic than material.[93]

PLAN OF THIS BOOK

This book assesses the historic and contemporary policy environment surrounding immigration, multiculturalism, and employment equity, with particular attention to the period from 1993 to 2001. In addition to a new government emphasis on gender-based analysis, this is an important marker of the current period in Canada because the Liberal Party, headed by Jean Chrétien, came to power in 1993 and has since that time won two other federal elections (1997 and 2000).

In what follows we suggest that the discourse of globalization that stresses and justifies neo-liberal ideals has profound implications for diversity and equality. With respect to diversity, as noted we pay special attention to race/ethnicity, class, and gender in relation to immigration, multiculturalism, and employment equity policies. Our analysis seeks to demonstrate how each policy is gendered by exposing how policy measures have differential effects on men and women (and different groups of men and women) and also by highlighting how gender assumptions inform policy frameworks and discussions. A central focus of our gender assessment is the ways in which the socially constructed dichotomy between the public and private spheres informs immigration, multiculturalism, and employment equity.

We conceive of equality as involving both *formal equality* (that is, that everyone has the same rights) and *substantive equality* (that is, that everyone is able to access the same opportunities by holding and actually exercising those rights). Issues relating to formal and substantive equality permeate debates over the extension of citizenship and citizenship rights, notions of national belonging, and conceptions of social justice. In Canada, as in many other countries, issues relating to citizenship, belonging, and justice have taken on renewed salience as a result of globalization. Policy areas such as immigration (which relates to the extension of formal equality rights through citizenship), multiculturalism (which relates to national identity and belonging), and employment equity (which relates to substantive equality) are sources of contention precisely because they are sites where these broader debates are played out.

In the following chapters we take up the impact of globalization discourse and the themes of equality and diversity in a detailed consideration of specific policy areas. Chapters Two and Three provide an assessment of the changing contours and development of Canadian immigration policy. Immigration provides an example of a policy that to some extent has always been internationalized. These chapters also examine the shifting construction of the "ideal" or "model" citizen—

a construction that is both gendered and racialized—from the beginnings of Canada as what has been termed a "white settler society" to the apparent repudiation of this model in post-war policy. Our analysis also addresses recent policy debates, including those around a proposed "Citizenship Act," an advisory committee report *Not Just Numbers*, and the proposals for an "Immigration and Refugee Protection Act" introduced in March 2001. In each case, we consider some of the broad implications of these measures for various groups.

In Chapter Four, we examine multiculturalism policy and nation-building with an eye towards how the policy has increasingly been the source of partisan and popular attack. The controversy over multiculturalism has brought out tensions over the role of the state in the area of culture and an argument that culture should be left in the "private" realm of the home and family. We trace multiculturalism policy from its roots in the 1970s to current incarnations of multiculturalism which increasingly emphasize the commodification of "minorities" and "minority culture." We pay specific attention to the consequences of these changing policy directions for women and people of colour. We also highlight the role that multiculturalism policy has played in constructing a particular vision of a "national community," which subverted earlier visions premised on anglo-conformity, and the manner in which Canadian multiculturalism has been upheld as a model for other countries.

Chapter Five provides a detailed look at the development of employment equity at the federal level and in the one province that adopted even more comprehensive employment equity measures than the federal government—Ontario. Employment equity was justified as a means of attaining social justice for particular disadvantaged groups. Responses to employment equity, especially at the provincial level in Ontario, have been very negative. Our analysis will also show that in this case that there has been a retreat by the state from labour market regulation and equity. Instead, influenced by American developments, businesses are being encouraged to take up "diversity" as a business strategy to capitalize on markets.

We conclude in Chapter Six by revisiting each of the case studies, firstly to draw out some of the findings for broader debates around globalization and public policy and diversity and, secondly, to raise questions about the future of the Canadian political community. We also make some observations about the implications of broad policy directions for disadvantaged groups and their status within Canadian society.

◆ NOTES ◆

1 "TO-Bid Made City Proud—Gala a Fitting Finale for Games Pitch," *The Toronto Star*, 13 March 2001 (*Dow Jones Interactive*, University of Alberta Library System, 8 April 2001): 1.

2 "TO-Bid Made City Proud" 1-2. Ultimately the bid failed, and the 2008 Summer Games will take place in China.

3 Weber defined the state as "a human community that (success-fully) claims the monopoly of legit-imate use of physical force within a given territory." From *Max Weber: Essays in Sociology*, ed. and trans. H.H. Gerth and C. Wright Mills (New York: Oxford University Press, 1958) 78, as cited in Ronald H. Chilcote, *Theories of Comparative Politics*, 2nd ed. (Boulder: Westview Press, 1994) 98.

4 Jane Jenson, "Understanding Politics: Concepts of Identity in Political Science," *Canadian Politics*, 3rd ed., ed. James Bickerton and Alain Gagnon (Peterborough: Broadview Press, 1999) 44-45.

5 As quoted in "Clarkson Lauds Canadians for Tolerance," *Globe and Mail*, 8 October, 1999. A3.

6 "Voices," *The Toronto Star*, 9 September 1999: A7.

7 William Walker, "Clarkson Reflects Canada's Profile," *The Toronto Star*, 9 September 1999: A7.

8 Canada, Statistics Canada, *1996 Census: Immigration and Citizenship* <http://www.statcan.ca/english/census96/nove4/naliss.htm> 2-13.

9. Canada, Statistics Canada, *1996 Census: Immigration and Citizenship* 1-2.

10 Canada, Statistics Canada, *1996 Census: Ethnic Origin, Visible Minorities* <http://www.statcan.ca/Daily/English/980217/d980217.htm> 1-3.

11 Canada, Statistics Canada, *1996 Census: Ethnic Origin, Visible Minorities* 3.

12 Canada, Statistics Canada, *1996 Census: Ethnic Origin, Visible Minorities* 8.

13 Canada, Statistics Canada, *1996 Census: Ethnic Origin, Visible Minorities* 10.

14 Yasmeen Abu-Laban, "The Politics of Race, Ethnicity and Immigration," Bickerton and Gagnon 468-72.

15 Andil Gosine, "Presenting Adrienne Clarkson: Gender, Nation and a New Governor-General," *Canadian Women's Studies* 20.2 (Summer 2000): 6-10.

16 Gosine 6-10.

17 Gosine 6-10.

18 Yasmeen Abu-Laban, "The Future and the Legacy: Globalization and the Canadian Settler-State," *Journal of Canadian Studies* 35.4 (Winter 2000-2001): 262-76.

19 Anthony McGrew, "A Global Society?," *Modernity: An Intro-duction to Modern Societies*, ed. Stuart Hall *et al.* (Oxford: Blackwell Publishers, 1996) 470.

20 David Held *et al.*, *Global Trans-formations: Politics, Economics and Culture* (Stanford: Stanford University Press, 1999) 1.

21 Henk Overbeek, "Towards a New International Migration Regime: Globalization, Migration and the Internationalization of the State," *Migration and European Integration: The Dynamics of Inclusion and Exclusion*, ed. Robert Miles and Dietrich Thränhardt (London: Pinter, 1995) 21.

22 Held *et al.* 1.

23 David Crane, *The Canadian Dictionary of Business and Economics* (Toronto: Stoddart, 1993) 276.

24 Hélène Pellerin, "Global Restructuring in the World Economy and Migration: The Globalization of Migration Dynamics," *International Journal* XLVIII (Spring 1993): 241; and David Jary and Julia Jary, *The Harper Collins Dictionary of Sociology* (New York: Harper Collins, 1991) 197.

25 See "Big MacCurrencies," *The Economist*, 29 April 2000: 75.

26 David Held, "The Decline of the Nation State," *New Times: The Changing Face of Politics in the 1990s*, ed. Stuart Hall and Martin Jacques (London: Verso, 1990) 193.

27 Robin Murray, "Benetton Britain: The New Economic Order," Hall and Jacques 57.

28 Appadurai names and discusses the cultural flows of people, images, and ideas as "ethnoscapes," "mediascapes," and "ideoscapes," respectively. See Arjun Appadurai, "Disjuncture and Difference in the Global Cultural Economy," *Global Culture: Nationalism, Globalization and Modernity*, ed. Mike Featherstone (London: Sage, 1990) 295-310.

29 Appadurai 295-310.

30 McGrew 470.

31 Lily Nguyen, "Love bytes world .com," *The Toronto Star*, 5 May 2000: A1.

32 Yasmeen Abu-Laban, "Reconstructing an Inclusive Citizenship for a New Millennium: Globalization, Migration and Difference," *International Politics* (December 2000).

33 Stuart Hall, "The Question of Cultural Identity," *Modernity: An Introduction to Modern Societies*, ed. Stuart Hall, David Held, Don Hubert, and Kenneth Thompson (Cambridge: Polity Press, 1995) 596-634.

34 Gordon Laxer, "Introduction," *The Canadian Review of Sociology and Anthropology* (Special Issue: Globalization) 32.3 (August 1995): 248.

35 Held *et al.* 3-5.

36 Held *et al.* 5-7.

37 Luis Roniger, "Public Life and Globalization as Cultural Vision," *The Canadian Review of Sociology and Anthropology* 32.3 (August 1995): 260.

38 Held *et al.* 7-9.

39 Colin Hay and Matthew Watson, "Globalisation: 'Sceptical' Notes on the 1999 Reith Lectures," *Political Quarterly* 70.4 (Oct.-Dec. 1999): 418-26. *Academic Search Elite*, University of Alberta Library System, (April 10, 2001): 2.

40 Christina Gabriel, "Restructuring at the Margins: Women of Colour and the Changing Economy," *Scratching the Surface: Canadian Anti-Racist Feminist Thought*, ed. Ena Dua and Angela Robertson (Toronto: Women's Press, 1999) 128-33.

41 Marjorie Griffin Cohen, "From the Welfare State to Vampire Capitalism," *Women and the Canadian Welfare State*, ed. Patricia M. Evans and Gerda R. Wekerle (Toronto: University of Toronto Press, 1997) 30.

42 It should be noted that in many other countries welfare-type programs were in place from the late nineteenth century on. For a discussion, see, for example, Douglas E. Ashford, *The Emergence of the Welfare States* (Oxford: Basil Blackwell, 1986).

43 For a comparative discussion, see Grahame Thompson, "The Evolution of the Managed Economy in Europe," *Economy and Society* 21,2 (1992): 129-151.

44 Isabella Bakker and Katherine Scott, "From the Postwar to the Post-Liberal Keynesian Welfare," *Understanding Canada: Building on the New Canadian Political Economy*, ed. Wallace Clement (Kingston: McGill-Queens University Press, 1997) 286-310.

45 Jane Jenson, "Fated to Live in Interesting Times: Canada's Changing Citizenship Regimes," *Canadian Journal of Political Science* 30.4 (December 1997): 634.

46 Stephen McBride and John Shields, *Dismantling a Nation: Canada and the New World Order* (Halifax: Fernwood, 1993) 15.

47 Greg Albo and Jane Jenson, "Re-mapping the State in an Era of Globalization," Clement 216.

48 See for example, McBride and Shields, *Dismantling*; Janine Brodie, *Politics on the Margins: Restructuring and the Canadian Women's Movement* (Halifax: Fernwood, 1995).

49 Alan Sears, "The 'Lean' State and Capitalist Restructuring: Towards a Theoretical Account," *Studies in Political Economy* 59 (Summer 1999): 91-114.

50 See Grace Skogstad, "Globalization and Public Policy: Situating Canadian Analysis," *Canadian Journal of Political Science* 34.4 (December 2000): 805-28.

51 Albo and Jenson 233.

52 See Jane Jenson and Susan Phillips, "Regime Shift: New Citizenship Practices in Canada," *International Journal of Canadian Studies* 14 (Autumn): 111-35.

53 David Cameron and Janice Gross Stein, "Globalization, Culture and Society: The State as Place Amidst Shifting Spaces," *Canadian Public Policy* 26 (August 2000): s26.

54 Cameron and Stein s26.

55 For discussion see Skogstad 818-19.

56 For more on the term policy community see Leslie Pal, *Beyond Policy Analysis* (Scarborough: Nelson, 1997) 187-233.

57 Skogstad 821.

58 G. Bruce Doern, Leslie Pal, and Brian Tomlin, eds., *Border Crossings: The Internationalization of Canadian Public Policy* (Toronto: Oxford University Press, 1996) 3.

59 Doern *et al.* 4.

60 Diane Stone, "State of the Art: Learning Lessons and Transferring Policy Across Time, Space and Disciplines," *Politics* 19.1 (1999): 55.

61 Doern *et al.* 3-4.

62 Stone 57.

63 For a discussion see Anne Phillips, "Introduction," *Feminism and Politics*, ed. Anne Phillips (Oxford: Oxford University Press, 1998) 12-15.

64 Susan Ship, "Problematizing Ethnicity and 'Race' Feminist Scholarship on Women and Politics," *Women and Political Representation in Canada*, ed. Caroline Andrew and Manon Tremblay (Ottawa: University of Ottawa Press, 1998) 328.

65 For discussion see Susan Phillips, "Discourse, Identity and Voice: Feminist Contributions to Policy Studies," *Policy Studies in Canada*, ed., Laurent Dobuzinskis, Michael Howlett, and David Laycock (Toronto: University of Toronto Press, 1996) 242-44.

66 Sandra Burt, "The Several Worlds of Policy Analysis: Traditional Approaches and Feminist Critiques," *Changing Methods: Feminist Transforming Practice*, ed. Sandra Burt and Lorraine Code (Peterborough: Broadview Press, 1995) 369.

67 See for example individual contributions in Janine Brodie, ed., *Women and Canadian Public Policy* (Toronto: Harcourt Brace and Jovanovich, 1996); Susan Boyd, ed., *Challenging the Public/Private Divide: Feminism, Law, and Public Policy* (Toronto: University of Toronto, 1997); and Linda Briskin and Mona Eliasson eds., *Women's Organizing and Public Policy in Canada and Sweden* (Montreal: McGill-Queens University Press, 1999).

68 Magrit Eichler, *Nonsexist Research Methods: A Practical Guide* (Boston: Unwin Hyman, 1988) 5.

69 For discussion see Burt 358-59.

70 Phillips.

71 For discussion see Jill Vickers, *Reinventing Political Science* (Halifax: Fernwood, 1997) 33.

72 Phillips 250-51.

73 Mary Hawkesworth, "Policy Studies Within a Feminist Frame," *Policy Sciences* 27 (1994): 106.

74 Joan Landes, "Introduction," *Feminism, The Public, and The Private*, ed. Joan Landes (Oxford: Oxford University Press, 1998) 1.

75 Susan Boyd, "Challenging the Public-Private Divide: An Overview," Boyd 4.

76 Boyd, "Challenging" 8-9.

77 Boyd, "Challenging" 13, emphasis in original.

78 Joan Landes, citing Nancy Fraser, in Joan Landes, "Introduction" 3.

79 Pat Armstrong, *et al.*, *Exposing Privatization: Women and Health Care Reform in Canada* (Toronto: Garamond, 2002) 8-9.

80 See for example, Armstrong *et al.*; Sheila M. Neysmith, *Restructuring Caring Labour* (Toronto: Oxford, 2000) 1-28.

81 Canada, Status of Women Canada, *Setting the Stage for the Next Century: The Federal Plan for Gender Equality* (Ottawa: Ministry of Supply and Services, 1995) 16.

82 Canada, Status of Women Canada, *Gender Based Analysis: A Guide for Policy Making* (Ottawa: Ministry of Supply and Services, 1996) 13.

83 Canada, Status of Women Canada, *Gender Based Analysis* 13.

84 Canada, Status of Women Canada, *Setting the Stage* 10-11.

85 Phillips 252.

86 Isabella Bakker, "Introduction," *Rethinking Restructuring*, ed. Isabella Bakker (Toronto: University of Toronto Press, 1996) 9.

87 Phillips 243.

88 Ship 328.

89 Ship 318.

90 Daiva Stasiulis and Yasmeen Abu-Laban, "Unequal Relations and the Struggle for Equality: Race and Ethnicity in Canadian Politics," *Canadian Politics in the 21st Century*, ed. Michael Whittington and Glen Williams (Scarborough: Nelson Thomson Learning, 2000) 343-44.

91 An exception to this is Abby Bakan and Audrey Kobayashi, *Employment Equity Policy in Canada: An Interprovincial Comparison* (Ottawa: Status of Women Canada, 1999).

92 Status of Women Canada, *Perspectives* 9.1 (Spring 1996)

93 Sandra Burt, "Looking Backward and Thinking Ahead: Toward a Gendered Analysis of Canadian Politics," *Canadian Politics in the 21st Century*, ed. Michael Whittington and Glen Williams (Scarborough: Nelson Canada, 2000) 323.

chapter TWO

Immigration and Canadian Citizenship

As a country founded on settler-colonization, immigration has been central to the history and the evolution of Canada. Immigration policy is an important policy area because of its clear and inherent connection with the question of whether or not formal citizenship is granted to potential immigrants.[1] Canadian immigration policy consists of the acts, regulations, and practices that affect which foreigners are allowed to come to Canada and, ultimately, which ones are granted Canadian citizenship.[2] While immigration is an area of shared provincial and federal responsibility,[3] the purpose of this chapter is to examine Canadian immigration and citizenship policies historically, from 1867 to 1993, at the federal level. We suggest that immigration policy from its inception has been heavily tied to economic criteria, specifically the perceived needs of the Canadian labour market. In addition, immigration policy has been both explicitly and implicitly tied to a vision of who is an "ideal" or "model" Canadian citizen.

IMMIGRATION AND CITIZENSHIP 1867-1967

When it comes to the history of immigration policy in Canada, two issues have been of central importance.[4] The first relates to cultural considerations of religion, race, and ethnicity. While historically both British- and French-origin groups asserted dominance over the indigenous population, Britain, with the conquest of New France in 1760, was able to impose control over most of North America. The intention of the British settlers was to develop the country as a "white settler colony."[5] Not surprisingly, after Confederation in 1867, the newly self-governing Canadian state continued to reflect ethnic and racial hierarchies. As a result, for much of Canadian history immigration policy explicitly favoured white, particularly British-origin, Protestants, who were viewed as "model citizens."

The second issue which historically has affected immigration policy-making is the perceived needs of the labour market, which at times required the admission of immigrants viewed as "not ideal" (non-British and non-Protestant). For example, between 1880 and 1884, when the Canadian Pacific Railway was being constructed, Chinese (male) labourers were recruited specifically to work on the most dangerous and least well-paid jobs. Then, following the completion of the railway in 1885, the Chinese Immigration Act was passed. This Act introduced the infamous "head tax" system by which Chinese admission to Canada was made progressively more expensive and prohibitive, until it was completely banned by further legislation in 1923. Chinese women and children were not allowed admission into the country.[6] These policies were intended to discourage permanent settlement[7] and prevent the increase in the size of the "alien" population.

Although Chinese and Asian men were allowed to enter the country as "cheap" labour, women from these communities were actively discouraged from coming to Canada. The concern for racial purity that was the cornerstone of much of English Canadian nation-building and immigration policy meant that it was not desirable that women from the so-called "lower races" reproduce.[8] Elaborate racial hierarchies were in place, and the most despised groups were Asians and blacks. These groups were frequently constructed as morally depraved.[9] Thus, Prime Minister John A. Macdonald assured anti-immigration campaigners that with the recruitment of Chinese labourers there need be "no fear of a permanent degradation of the country by a mongrel race."[10]

Whereas state practices actively excluded Chinese women from entering Canada, the migration of women from "preferred groups" was encouraged. Throughout the late nineteenth and early twentieth century the state encouraged the immigration of white British women to Canada. This group was actively sought after, including domestic workers to fulfill a specific labour market need. But they were also recruited "for their future or potential roles as wives and mothers of the Canadian nation, and thus as nation builders and civilizers."[11] It has been pointed out that this role as "daughters of the empire" and "mothers of the nation" did not necessarily insulate them from the unfavourable conditions of domestic work. But it did allow them to change employers, exit domestic work for other types of work, or marry. These choices were not as readily available to women from the "least desirable" backgrounds.[12]

The gendered nature of recruitment patterns was also evident in Interior Minister Clifford Sifton's famous policy of "settling the west" in the early twentieth century by attracting agricultural workers. For the first time, Canada turned heavily to countries of southern and eastern Europe for its immigrants. The reigning assumption was that male agriculturalists would till the soil and women would produce the offspring necessary to further populate the west of Canada. In a famous statement, in which Sifton said he favoured as a good quality immigrant a "stalwart peasant in a sheep-skin coat" with a "stout wife" who would breed children, he went on to signal the relative insignificance of British-origin urban workers:

> A Trades Union artisan who will not work more than eight hours a day and will not work that long if he can help it, will not work on a farm at all and has to be fed by the public when work is slack is, in my judgment, quantity and very bad quantity. I am indifferent as to whether or not he is British born. It matters not what his nationality is: such men are not wanted in Canada.[13]

Sifton's statement notwithstanding, at the same time as the Canadian government was attempting to attract Southern European and Eastern European settlers to the relatively unpopulated West it was working to discourage American blacks from entering.[14] When a group of black settlers from Oklahoma proposed to farm in Western Canada the reaction was swift: the Athabasca Landing Board of Trade wrote to the Minister of the Interior in 1911, "Canada is the last country open to the white race. Are we going to preserve it for the white race, or are we going to permit blacks free use of large portions of it?"[15] In response to widespread and virulent racism the federal government undertook a number of measures to discourage the entry of American blacks.[16]

A distinct form of exclusion that became evident in the early decades of the twentieth century was tied to political or ideological criteria. This form of exclusion often overlapped with discrimination based on race/ethnicity. As Reg Whitaker notes:

> The Bolshevik Revolution in 1917 and the Winnipeg General Strike and sympathy strikes in other Canadian cities in 1918 together provided a new source of alarm to the Canadian state and to Canadians with property: the "dangerous foreigner," the alien as Red revolutionary, anarchist, or labour agitator.[17]

By the 1920s, the perceived threat posed by Communism resulted in the state's efforts to either prevent the entry of entire groups (such as Finns, Ukrainians, and Russians) perceived as potentially Communist or (and this was mostly the case) to prevent the naturalization of those immigrants already in Canada deemed similarly undesirable, an effort which sometimes led to deportation.[18]

During the Depression and World War II, immigration was effectively halted due to the high unemployment rate. It was only after 1945, in the context of Canada's post-war boom, that immigration began anew. However, Prime Minister Mackenzie King made it quite clear that immigrants from outside of Europe were to be avoided. Since King's 1947 statement effectively shaped immigration policy well into the 1960s, it is worth quoting at length

> The policy of the government is to foster the growth of the population of Canada by the encouragement of immigration....
>
> ... With regard to the selection of immigrants, much has been said about discrimination. I wish to make it quite clear that Canada is perfectly within her right in selecting the persons whom we regard as desirable future citizens. It is not a "fundamental human right" of any alien to enter Canada. It is a privilege. It is a matter of domestic policy.
>
> ... There will, I am sure, be general agreement with the view that the people of Canada do not wish, as a result of mass immigration, to make a fundamental alteration in the character of our population. Large-scale immigration from the orient would change the fundamental composition of the Canadian population. Any considerable oriental immigration would, moreover, be certain to give rise to social and economic problems of a character that might lead to serious difficulties in the field of international relations. The government, therefore, has no thought of making any change in immigration regulations which would have consequences of the kind.[19]

Thus it was clear that immigration was perceived by King primarily as a matter of domestic policy and was to be treated as such. As well, immigration from "the orient" (meaning everything in the Eastern hemisphere outside of Europe)[20] was not desired in Canada.

As a result, a series of reasons could be legally used to keep those immigrants deemed undesirable out. These included not only the nationality, ethnic group, occupation, or class of the applicant but the "unsuitability with regard to climatic, economic, social, industrial, educational, labour, health, or other requirements," and the "probable inability to become readily assimilated or to assume the duties and responsibilities of Canadian citizenship within a reasonable time after admission."[21]

In addition, after World War II, in the context of the Cold War, returning concern over the ideological or political leanings of potential immigrants led to the emergence of even more refined security controls within the Canadian state. While the United States overtly erected barriers to immigrants, and even visitors, who might have communist sympathies, in Canada the RCMP along with senior bureaucrats established screening mechanisms to bar immigrants and refugees on grounds of national security in a similar but somewhat less open manner.[22] Reg Whitaker suggests that this came about not so much because of direct pressure from American officials on Canada to preserve the world's longest unprotected border by having similar immigration criteria, but rather because many Canadian officials carried the same views as American officials.[23]

In a settler society, such as Canada's, immigration policy plays an important role in determining membership of the national community because immigrants are always, whether wilfully or not, prospective citizens. To be a citizen is to enjoy formal membership—with its specified rights and duties—in a nation state. People commonly acquire nationality in a number of ways:

- *jus solis* is the rule under which nationality is acquired by the mere fact of birth within the territory of the state ...
- *jus sanguinis* provides that nationality is acquired by descent wherever the child is born ...
- *naturalization* ... is the process by which a person who was formerly an alien becomes a subject or citizen of the state.[24] ...

But the concept of citizenship embraces wider notions of belonging, identity, and loyalty. The question of "who does and does not belong— is where the politics of citizenship begins."[25]

In Canada, as in many other countries, what constitutes full citizenship has been continuously debated. A formal definition of Canadian citizenship was established in 1947. Prior to this, terms such as "Canadian national" or "British subject" were in use.[26] As it has been pointed out, a working definition of citizenship was in place in 1910, and distinctions were made "between immigrants and non-immigrants categories that could be based on nationality occupation and country of origin. Privileged status was given to "agriculturalists, British subjects, and USA citizens."[27]

Such distinctions in the understanding of citizenship are intimately linked
to processes of nation-building. Frequently, these processes are reduced
to economic requirements, such as the construction of an infrastructure
or the imperatives of the labour market. But immigration policies, it is
argued, are also integral to the other aspect of nation building: "the development of a morally and physically healthy settler population and later a
citizenry based on 'love and loyalty to Canada and the British Empire.'"[28]
Historically, people were welcomed who best conformed to the "ideal
citizen" of a white settler society whose very identity was underwritten
by a shared order of being. This commonality was premised on imperi-
alistic racial hierarchies, British values, and British institutions. Consequently,
while immigration policy worked on a supposed "open door" policy—
as we discussed earlier—there were always those who because of their
"race" were castigated as "inassimilable" and as a result faced many obstacles in acquiring access to settler status and citizenship rights.[29]

One of the most basic citizenship rights is the franchise. The political right to vote and run for office was a right denied to many people
in Canada's history. Most Aboriginal peoples did not have the franchise
because, living on reserves, they were constructed as wards of the crown
under the Indian Act (1876) and its subsequent amendments. Those who
wished to exercise this political right lost their status as well as any benefits received under the Act. This provision was not changed until
1960.[30] Additionally, prior to 1947, through a number of provincial
and federal regulations, members of certain groups, including the
Chinese, East Indians, and Japanese, were excluded from the basic
political right of voting. The denial of the franchise had wider implications. In British Columbia, for example, it acted to bar Chinese from
entry into certain professions, such as law and pharmacy.[31] These exclusions "embodied common prejudices in law while affirming the popular conviction that these minorities were less than full citizens" and their
persistence underscored the extent to which racial and ethnic origins
influenced admission to the national political community.[32]

Similarly, at this time gender also underwrote many dimensions of
citizenship. Women, too, were denied the right to vote, run for office,
or be appointed to the Senate because they were not "persons." The
franchise was eventually extended to women in an uneven fashion.
Between 1916 and 1917 women won the right to vote from five
provinces. By 1918 the vote was extended by the federal government
to most women, on the same basis as men. Women did not receive the
right to vote in provincial elections in Quebec until 1940. In addition
the exclusions that applied to minorities discussed above meant that many

racial-minority women were not enfranchised until after World War II.[33] Through public policy and law the state worked to uphold women's inequality and constructed them as second-class citizens.

The introduction of the Canadian Citizenship Act in 1947 marked the beginning of a period when many of the explicit barriers to the formal rights of citizenship were removed; between 1947 and 1949 the provisions which disenfranchised Chinese, East Indians, and Japanese Canadians came to an end. The Act also represented an attempt to stimulate a "distinctive sense of Canadian citizenship"—clearly distinguished from a British identity.[34] Liberal MP Paul Martin Sr., the architect of the legislation, stated that

> Citizenship means more than the right to vote; more than the right to hold and transfer property; more than the right to move freely under the protection of the state; citizenship is the right to full partnership in the fortunes and future of the nation.[35]

Despite this definition of citizenship, to be a Canadian citizen in 1947 was a somewhat ambiguous thing. Canadian citizens exercised political rights in Canada, but owed allegiance to the British crown.[36] Canadian citizens remained British subjects, and the new Citizenship Act did not change this in any decisive way, either practically (only British subjects were not required to appear in a citizen's court and be examined like other immigrants)[37] or in the minds of such elements as those who objected to the Act's providing "Slavs" the same status as "Britons" in Canada.[38]

IMMIGRATION AND CITIZENSHIP 1967-1993

It was not until 1967 that the explicit racial and ethnic discrimination that had imbued Canadian immigration policy up to then was removed, and a new system of evaluation put into place: a "point system" which assesses all immigrants on the same skills- and training-related criteria. The point system, which is still in place today, sets out a maximum number of points an applicant may receive for factors such as level of education, vocational preparation, knowledge of one or both official languages, and occupational demand in Canada. Initially, applicants had to earn at least 50 points out of a possible 100.[39] Subsequent changes in the early 1990s tied the system more closely to the needs of the Canadian labour market and raised the standard to 70 points for a "pass mark."[40]

The introduction of the point system was premised on the need to correlate immigration planning and employment policy, for a "selective immigration policy today must be planned as a steady policy of recruitment based on long-term considerations of economic growth."[41] To this end, specific, high-demand occupations are placed on a list, with an eye towards meeting the particular needs of employers through immigrant selection. In many ways the occupations list is premised on an understanding that the state can play a role in anticipating and meeting the labour market needs of the country.

In 1976 the federal government introduced a new immigration act, which formally recognized the point system. Through this Act, three categories of immigrants were highlighted:

- *family class* (where Canadian citizens and permanent residents older than 18 can sponsor certain relatives who wish to immigrate to Canada);
- *refugees* (those people who, according to the United Nation's definition, have a well-founded fear of persecution in their homelands);
- *independent immigrants* (these include assisted relatives, retirees, entrepreneurs, and self-employed persons).

Of these categories, independent immigrants are the only ones who are explicitly assessed on the points system.

Also in the late 1970s the Canadian Parliament reviewed the Citizenship Act and introduced a number of changes. A key reform replaced "British subject" status with that of "Commonwealth citizen." The latter has no significant obligation or privileges. Essentially the reforms placed all those seeking Canadian citizenship on an equal footing.[42] The explicit preferences for British immigrants as prospective citizens that had marked much of Canada's immigration policy were no longer sustainable.

The concept of citizenship, as we noted, entails more than a legal definition of access. It also includes rights and duties. The extent of these rights and duties is the outcome of political contestation. British sociologist T.H. Marshall has offered an important analysis of citizenship that concerns the content of rights and duties and how they may be realized in the context of economic-based inequalities. Marshall divided citizenship into three elements, civil, political, and social. Civil rights include "liberty of person, freedom of speech, thought and faith, the right to own property ... and the right to justice." Political rights for Marshall included the right to vote and the right to run for political office. The institutions he associated most closely with these first two elements were the courts and Parliament.[43] But Marshall was also concerned with social rights—"the right to a modicum of economic welfare and security ... according to the standards prevailing in society"—and he viewed the welfare state as the institutional mechanism for the distribution of these rights.[44] Through the welfare state, provisions are made for public education, universal health care, and public housing and income security programs. Thus, social rights make possible a fuller expression of citizenship for those groups who would be disadvantaged in terms of resources and power and, hence, would suffer most acutely from the insecurities generated by a market economy. "Without social rights, gross inequalities would undermine the equality of political and civil rights inherent in the idea of citizenship."[45]

In Canada, a particular conception of social citizenship found expression in the post-World War II welfare state. The Canadian state began to play an important redistributive role, implementing a series of social programs with the intention of providing a minimum (national) standard of provision to members of the political community. While the nature of what is an appropriate "minimum" was and is much debated, the 1960s and 1970s marked a period of social-program expansions. Medicare was introduced, an unemployment insurance program was constructed, and post-secondary education was expanded.[46] As a result, for many Canadians the idea of Canada—and what makes a Canadian—was linked to the welfare state. For example, it became common for Canadians to distinguish themselves from Americans by reference to social programs such as health care. And it was during this time that two other features also come to the fore. First, there was a growth of "state support for intermediary organizations, which might represent citizens to and in the state."[47] Through the Secretary of State, the government gave funding to women's organizations, ethnocultural organizations, and minority language associations.[48] Second, ideas of equity and social justice prevailed.[49] To some extent these found expression in the area of immigration and particularly refugee intake.

The 1980s—The Politicization of Immigration Issues

During the first mandate of the Conservative government headed by Brian Mulroney (1984-88), immigration emerged as a highly politicized issue, especially in the area of refugee intake. Outside Canada, refugees are not assessed by the points system; nevertheless, when they are selected in camps abroad, a series of questions about suitability (e.g., knowledge of official languages, educational levels) are asked, which suggests that an informal points system is in place. When refugees arrive in Canada and make a formal claim, however, the international (United Nations) agreements Canada has signed mean that the validity of a refugee claimant's fear of persecution, and not other criteria, forms the basis of selection. In 1986 and 1987 the refugee claims of Tamils and Sikhs aboard boats arriving on Canada's east-coast shores were called "false" and "bogus" in the media and in popular circles. At the time a special recall of Parliament set the stage for the minister of immigration to demand "legislation to protect against the influence of ships of fortune about to disembark clandestine cargoes of humanity on Canadian shores" and in so doing further pushed the issue onto the public agenda.[50] Indeed, it has been suggested that there was a "seeming manipulation" of the "refugee crisis" to garner support for tougher legislation.[51] These circumstances led to heightened political tensions centered not only on refugees but indirectly on immigration in general. The government passed new and more restrictive refugee legislation in 1987.

> These bills restricted the scope of the refugee route greatly shortening the period for hearing claims, provided sanctions against ships bringing illegal immigrants to Canadian shores and against voluntary groups assisting individuals to make refugee claims, and—most controversially—made provision for quicker and easier deportation for those whose claims were rejected.[52]

The Mulroney government's attempt to address the refugee issue did not win supporters either in the pro- or anti-immigration camp. For the latter, the government had not taken a tough enough position. Many of the former saw the new measures as a retreat from Canada's international commitments.[53] The fact that Canada was not immune from global migratory movements was also underscored. The worldwide refugee crisis meant the numbers of official (United Nation's definition) refugees doubled from 8 million in 1980 to 16 million by 1990.[54] By the

1990s, there was an even greater politicization of immigration, and Canada proved itself to be even more tied to international developments in determining who could or could not be a citizen.

However, it should also be noted that under the Mulroney government, the family-class intake (where the so-called dependent spouse and offspring are to be found) was the largest category. In fact, despite rising unemployment rates during the late 1980s and early 1990s the Mulroney Conservatives kept the family-class category proportionately higher than the others, partly in the hopes of winning voters from minority communities, partly because of their feeling that immigration was good for the economy.[55] Annual immigration levels actually increased. Nonetheless, it has also been shown that popular opposition to immigration in Canada, as measured in public opinion polls, is related to the unemployment rate; that is, the higher the level of unemployment, the greater is the hostility towards immigration.[56] In 1988, national opinion polls indicated that 30 per cent of Canadians felt there were too many immigrants. By April 1993 this figure had risen to over 45 per cent. And by 1994 polls reported more than half of all Canadians were of the opinion that there were too many immigrants in the country.[57] As we discuss in Chapter Three, it was within this highly charged political environment that the Liberal government, under Jean Chrétien, embarked on immigration reform.

POST-WAR IMMIGRATION POLICY—DIFFERENTIAL AND UNEQUAL EFFECTS

The Immigration Act of 1976 became the key legislation guiding Canadian immigration policy and programs and an important marker of the removal of overt racial and ethnic bias from selection. While there was an official rejection of the explicit restrictions and preferences that framed earlier policies, the 1976 Immigration Act itself is built upon a set of assumptions and practices that nonetheless produce unequal outcomes for different groups of people. In many ways this belies the stated intent of the policy. Indeed, when the Liberal government of Prime Minister Lester B. Pearson introduced the point system in 1967, the understanding was that this system was to involve no discrimination on the basis of "race, colour or religion," and was to be "universally applicable."[58] Here, we examine how implicit hierarchies and assumptions about women and gender roles frame the categories of the 1976 legislation.

As noted, independent applicants are assessed on the points system, which is presented as "universal," "objective," and a "fair" method of selecting potential Canadian citizens.[59] However, the point system is not a neutral instrument of selection and "discrimination in less obvious forms persisted."[60] Scholars, for example, have drawn the connection between the location of immigration offices abroad and administrative delays in processing applications as key factors in accessibility to Canada.[61] For example, in the 1960s it was noted that

> Canada's immigration services "were reasonably adequate for the normal volume of the applicants" in the United States, the British Isles, and northern and western Europe. By contrast, in southern Europe and the rest of the world, Canadian facilities did not begin to match the interest shown in Canada as an emigration destination.[62]

However, examining the 1980s, Alan Simmons noted, the staffing situation was a little more complex. On one hand, there were very few offices in Africa and some parts of South Asia. On the other hand, the Caribbean and Hong Kong were relatively well served, as was Europe. Simmons suggests that

> Staffing is allocated to countries with medium-high to high levels of education and occupation skills, capacity in English or French, a history of institutional and cultural contact and a high level of interest in emigration to Canada.[63]

Consequently, in his view, Hong Kong and the Caribbean, which are not European-origin countries, nevertheless do well in terms of access to services because of the legacy of colonial institutions, education, and language, as well as the fact that the socio-economic situation in Hong Kong and countries of the Caribbean prompted an interest in emigration to Canada.[64] On the other hand, other areas of the world are not equally serviced, despite the officially non-discriminatory nature of the policy. Thus, there are "sanctioned practices that act in a discriminatory manner with respect to the geographic location and, hence, the ethnic/racial background of potential immigrants."[65]

As described earlier, the points system awards points for education, vocational training, occupation, and work experience. This model privileges those people who can access and/or pay for appropriate, formally recognized education and training. Additionally, as the Canadian Council on Refugees has noted, recognition of prior learning can produce differential impacts, insofar as:

> People who are trained in Western scientific or knowledge systems in the South are not given the same recognition as if they were trained in the North. People who are trained within non-western educational worldviews or scientific traditions experience great difficulty in gaining recognition for their training and skills.[66]

Consequently, in practice, the point system tends to favour applicants from countries with extensive educational opportunities, thereby indirectly favouring certain countries over others.[67] Thus, there are class and geographic (hence, racial/ethnic) biases within the point system.

Class-based hierarchies are more apparent when the business program of the selection model is examined. Business immigrants are assessed on the points system, but not on all the criteria (for example, they are not assessed on occupational demand). While the favouring of immigrants with money can be dated back to the years immediately following World War II, when potential immigrants were viewed as especially meritorious if they could bring in enough capital to start a business,[68] the formalization of the business program did not occur until 1978. Initially, the program's emphasis was on attracting entrepreneurs who could provide a job for at least one Canadian and on self-employed persons. However, the program was given new emphasis in 1986 by Mulroney's Conservative government with the introduction of the investor stream of immigrants. Investor immigrants must have a net worth of at least CD$500,000 and commit to investing their money within Canada for a certain number of years. Trevor Harrison notes that the investor program addressed the desire of Michael Wilson (the finance minister during the Mulroney years) for Canada to have more millionaires.[69] This strategy, in addition to showing a decided class preference, also coincided with the fears of many Hong Kong residents about the shift in status of Hong Kong from a colony of (capitalist) Britain to (communist) China in 1997; indeed, the majority of people filling the business category during the 1980s and 1990s were from Hong Kong.[70] The business class epitomizes the complex ways in which class, race/ethnicity, and gender intersect. This category has thus far been dominated by wealthy Hong Kong Chinese men, we might add, since men are more likely than women to meet the criteria for the business immigration program.

Gender hierarchies play out within the selection model, though this is not always acknowledged. Canadian immigration policy itself is underpinned by the public/private dichotomy. This dichotomy has been termed by some as the "notion of separate male and female spheres"[71] and others "visions of masculine and feminine."[72] In either case what is being highlighted are processes which construct men as active agents who migrate accompanied by a dependent (female) spouse. In this respect it has been suggested that immigration policy can be seen as part of an institutional framework of state policies that "assume and sustain female dependency."[73] This analysis emphasizes that it is not the result of overt discrimination on the basis of sex but rather the ways in which rules, regulations, and practices produce different outcomes for men and women.[74]

The gender dynamics of the Canadian selection model need to be more closely considered in terms of the public/private division between paid work and economic activity/domestic labour. First, the points system places emphasis on formal educational and vocational training and occupational experience. In other words, the emphasis is on activity in the public realm. Women typically may have more difficulty than men in meeting this criterion.[75] And it is in this respect that the gender relations in the country of origin come into play. To the extent that women's roles are confined to the domestic realm and women's access to education and training is limited, men rather than women will be able to meet immigration requirements for independent applicants.[76] Criteria used in the points system favour the "public work" typically performed by men.

Second, the supposedly objective standard of skill at the centre of the points selection process needs to be interrogated. There is an emphasis on choosing applicants with the "right" skills to meet changing labour market demands. But

> … skills are historically rather than biologically or technologically constructed and that social construction is part of the process by which unequal social relations are reproduced. Such relations may reflect not only the unequal structures of class power but potentially all other differences including race, ethnicity, language and sex.[77]

The social construction of skill is intimately tied to the sexual division of labour. What counts as "women's work" in the public sphere is frequently associated with women's domestic labour in the private realm (service jobs such as cleaning, caring, teaching, and food processing).[78] Such jobs are frequently defined as unskilled or semi-skilled—and undervalued—because it is assumed that women's work embodies some natural female capacity. The popular perception "women have talents while men have skills,"[79] finds expression in the masculine view of skill embodied within the points system criteria.

Third, the gender dynamics of the selection model are illustrated by the fact that the points-based selection offers no points at all for women's unpaid work, despite the fact that domestic labour is integral to social reproduction. The devaluation of women's work—both paid and unpaid—produces negative consequences for women.

> The defect in the point system is not simply that it devalues the skills utilized in domestic work, but also that it uses this determination to reduce or eliminate the points available to applicants under other criteria.... For example, experience in a "high skill" occupation is worth more than the same length of experience in a "low skill" occupation; "low skill" occupations in high demand (such as domestic work) will attract no points whatsoever under the "occupational demand" category.[80]

The points system favours the "high-skilled" work typically performed by men because points are awarded on the basis of formal skills and education. The model reflects and reinforces the gendered construction of a public/private dichotomy—a male breadwinner, a female dependant. And in fact, women who enter Canada as immigrants typically do so as the "dependent spouse" of a male applicant.[81]

In Canada, according to Citizenship and Immigration, "the family class defines a list of relatives who may be sponsored for immigration to Canada by a citizen or permanent resident,"[82] and analysts have recognized that these provisions do provide women with an avenue of migration.[83] This is important given the difficulties that many women may experience in meeting points-based criteria. But the process of sponsorship (in which a sponsor pledges to financially support immigrating family members so that the latter do not require support from the state), according to one analysis, "can introduce unequal power dynamics in relationships [and] can promote and accentuate dependency and other unequal power relations within newcomer families."[84]

Relations of dependency are inscribed within the category in a number of ways. The entry provisions of the family class affect substantive citizenship rights insofar as the terms of entry define the ability of women to access certain social rights. For example, analysts and community groups have argued that entry status has a negative impact on women's ability to obtain language training. Through the 1980s many federally-funded language-training programs, such as those offered through the Department of Employment and Immigration, were directed to those "destined for the labour market," effectively excluding family-class immigrants. One 1987 assessment of this provision noted:

> The idea of labour-destined skilled workers being eligible for sub-sidies and in fact being preferred, is … just the latest version of immigration policies' preference for men. It used to be the head of the family that would get access to these programs. Today, this has changed, because it was disreputable and could expose [the Department of Employment and Immigration] to a Charter chal-lenge, so it changed to labour destined workers. The labour-des-tined worker is almost always a man. It is an old problem with a new coat.[85]

Changes in the delivery of language training in the early 1990s attempted to address some of these issues.[86]

The outcomes of women's dependency under family class provisions are heightened in cases of domestic abuse, where "women face a 'choice' of breaking sponsorship and risking deportation or staying silently within an abusive marriage."[87] The Canadian Council of Refugees has stated that "women in the process of being sponsored remain in abusive rela-tionships because of the threat of sponsorship being withdrawn and their deportation following."[88] In 1984, government reforms precluded automatic deportation in cases where it could be demonstrated that the sponsorship arrangement had been severed.[89] However, it has been pointed out that many women may be unaware of these provisions and may be threatened with withdrawal of sponsorship if the abuse is reported.[90] As well, while sponsored immigrants who have been abused are eligible for welfare and public assistance, there are barriers to access-ing these provisions.[91]

The family class is very much framed by relations of dependency. These relations rest on particular assumptions about men and women's gender roles. Within the immigration selection model there is an idealized con-struction of a heterosexual, nuclear family form—familism, which is

> … a set of ideas which characterize the "normal" or "ideal" family form as one where the man was the main breadwinner and his wife's main contribution to the family was through her role as mother, carer, and housewife, rather than as wage earner, and

who was therefore, along with her children, financially dependent upon her husband.[92]

This ideology prevails, despite the diversity of family forms and changing social relations.[93]

The entrenchment of familism in the form of the nuclear family—a form commonly associated with North America—is particularly problematic. Cultural, social, and religious norms play a role in the way in which "family" is defined. For many people in countries of the Third World, for example, the notion of family goes beyond the nuclear family and would include an extended family (grandparents, aunts, uncles, cousins, etc.). Family class provisions did not adequately address this issue. Many ethno-cultural advocacy groups continue to point out that despite the ostensibly multicultural nature of Canada there is "little recognition of, or tolerance for, diversified conceptions of family."[94]

Among the family forms not explicitly recognized under the provisions of the family class are those that include same-sex couples. Indeed, from 1952 to 1976 "homosexuals" were considered members of "an inadmissible class" and excluded from immigrating to Canada.[95] In the early 1990s Christine Morrisey, a Canadian, tried unsuccessfully to sponsor her partner Bridget Coll as a spouse. Morrissey took the case to court in 1992 and argued that immigration laws contravened the Canadian Charter of Rights and Freedoms. Immigration Canada granted Coll residence as an independent applicant before the case was settled.[96] Subsequently, Immigration Canada has used a regulation that "recognized separating couples could result in 'undue hardship'" as grounds for allowing same-sex partners entry on humanitarian and compassionate basis, case-by-case.[97] Lesbian and gay advocacy groups have pointed out that not everyone seeking entry is aware of this measure, nor do immigration staff routinely provide information.[98] The fact that same-sex relationships are not recognized under provisions of the family class is indicative of how a person's sexual orientation restricts access to citizenship rights. As long as "spouse" presumes "of the opposite sex," lesbians and gays cannot—despite possible exceptions—secure Canadian citizenship for their foreign partners on the same basis as heterosexuals, because within immigration provisions the definition of family is associated with particular gender roles and norms.

It should be noted that women do dominate in one non-family class category, domestic workers. Women who enter Canada under this category hold a very precarious relationship to formal Canadian citizenship. Under the 1981 Foreign Domestic Movement Program (FDM) and its successor, the 1992 Live-in Care Caregiver Program (LCP), terms were established for the recruitment of women to Canada under a system of temporary permits. The LCP is relatively small and made up predominantly of women from countries of the Third World who do domestic and childcare work in a Canadian citizen's home, after which they have the opportunity to apply for landed immigrant status and eventually Canadian citizenship. In contrast, other immigrant categories (like the family class or independent immigrants) enter Canada with landed status. Domestic workers in Canada have referred to their role as "the Third World in our living rooms."[99] Notably, the domestic worker program is a separate program not assessed on the point system. This graphically shows how domestic work—performed mostly by women—is not considered skillful in the same way as the work assessed on the point system.

CONCLUSION

There is a way in which immigration, by definition, has long been a feature of globalization. This is because the movement of peoples across state borders for purposes of settlement is a process that always involves more than one state. In addition, in the context of being a settler-colony, Canada's historical construction and patterns of migration were interwoven with Europe (France and particularly Britain). The policies of Britain in the context of Empire were important in shaping Canada as a "white settler colony" controlled by the British crown, and these impacted the development of immigration and citizenship policies in Canada, the boundaries of the Canadian nation-state, and the nature of the "model" or "ideal" citizen. In addition, throughout the twentieth century issues of national security have been implicated directly in developments and events both inside and outside of Canada's borders, starting with the perceived threat of communism. Thus, determining who could be legitimately included or excluded from entry into the country and/or to citizenship has also been tied to historically specific definitions of security.

In effect, immigration and citizenship policies have made (and still make) important statements about inclusion and exclusion. Throughout the period from 1867 to 1993 economic criteria have played a predominate, albeit shifting, role in determining preference. But immigration has not been solely about economics. This is why during the Cold War period immigrants or refugees who might be deemed sympathetic to communist views faced obstacles entering Canada, though this was not always directly stated or evident to the Canadian public. Up to the 1960s, ethnic and racial preferences were overtly at play, and state officials like Mackenzie King insisted that immigration was purely and mainly a "domestic" matter.

Reform after 1960 saw the abandonment of these explicit policies of racial and ethnic discrimination. Through the points system immigration remains tied to the needs of the Canadian labour market. The effect of the reforms is apparent in terms of the shift in the composition of immigrant groups. Before 1978 a full 70 per cent of newcomers came from Europe and only 11 per cent from Asia.[100] By 1993 immigrants from Asia accounted for 51.08 per cent of newcomers while those from Europe comprised only 18.19 per cent.[101] Nevertheless, as we illustrated above, the policies and practices associated with the new immigration act in the 1970s also contained a set of implicit hierarchies in class, gender, and race, which produce unequal outcomes for certain groups of people.

By the early 1990s immigration had emerged on the political agenda as a highly charged issue. In 1993, the newly elected Liberal government pledged to overhaul both immigration and citizenship policies. The new minister of immigration, Sergio Marchi, tabled *A Broader Vision: Immigration and Citizenship Plan, 1995-2000* in the House of Commons, calling the document "a fundamental change to Canada's immigration program," a forward-looking strategy that would both "make the immigration and citizenship program more affordable and sustainable" and respond to a "world characterized by sweeping and rapid change."[102]

The Liberals embarked on this task in a context in which the welfare state was undergoing significant and profound structural changes, while policy-makers and elected officials were attempting to respond to processes of globalization and economic restructuring. The understanding that the government has a pivotal role to play in insulating citizens against the vagaries of the market was and is under considerable dispute.[103] As we shall see in the next chapter, increasingly public officials addressing immigration have not stressed that immigration is a domestic matter, the way Mackenzie King did. Rather, they have stressed that immigration and a new economy must take into account the larger international and globalizing context.

◆ NOTES ◆

1 Yasmeen Abu-Laban, "Reconstructing an Inclusive Citizenship for a New Millennium: Globalization, Migration, and Difference," *International Politics* 37.4 (December 2000): 509-26. See also Yasmeen Abu-Laban, "Keeping 'em Out: Gender, Race, and Class Biases in Canadian Immigration Policy," *Painting the Maple: Essays on Race, Gender, and the Construction of Canada*, ed. Veronica Strong Boag (Vancouver: University of British Columbia Press, 1998) 70-72.

2 Abu-Laban, "Keeping 'em Out" 71.

3 Some provinces play a more active role than others. Since the 1960s, the province of Quebec has achieved the most control in the area of immigration and immigrant selection owing to the desire of successive provincial governments to have French-speaking immigrants in Quebec. However, the Quebec selection system mainly mirrors the federal system except for greater weight being accorded to speaking French.

4 Abu-Laban, "Keeping 'em Out" 71.

5 Daiva Stasiulis and Radha Jhappan, "The Fractious Politics of a Settler Society: Canada," *Unsettling Settler Societies: Articulations of Gender, Race, Ethnicity, and Class*, eds. Daiva Stasiulis and Nira Yuval-Davis (London: Sage, 1995) 96-99.

6 Lisa Jakubowski, *Immigration and the Legalization of Racism* (Halifax: Fernwood, 1997) 14.

7 Abu-Laban, "Keeping 'em Out" 71-72.

8 See Mariana Valverde, *The Age of Light, Soap, and Water* (Toronto: McClelland and Stewart Inc., 1991).

9 Valverde 110-19.

10 Valverde 111.

11 Sedef Arat-Koc, "From 'Mothers of the Nation' to Migrant Workers," *Not One of the Family, Foreign Domestic Workers in Canada*, ed. Abigail Bakan and Daiva Stasiulis (Toronto: University of Toronto Press, 1997) 54.

12 Arat-Koc 55.

13 Sir Clifford Sifton, "The Immigrants Canada Wants," *Maclean's Magazine* 35.1 (April 1922), cited in Mary Vipond, "Nationalism and Nativism: The Native Sons of Canada in the 1920s," *Canadian Review of Studies in Nationalism* 9 (Spring 1982): 82.

14 R. Bruce Shepard, "Plain Racism: The Reaction Against Oklahoma Black Immigration to the Canadian Plains," *Racism in Canada*, ed. Ormand McKague (Saskatchewan: Fifth House Publishing, 1991) 15-31.

15 Shepard 27.

16 Shepard 30-31.

17 Reg Whitaker, *Double Standard: The Secret History of Immigration* (Toronto: Lester and Orpen Dennys, 1987) 13.

18 Whitaker, *Double Standard* 14.

19 Mackenzie King, Hansard (Thursday May 1, 1947) as reproduced in Canada, Manpower and Immigration, *A Report of the Canadian Immigration and Population Study, Volume Two: The Immigration Program* (Ottawa: Information Canada, 1974) 201-07.

20 Freda Hawkins, *Canada and Immi-gration: Public Policy and Public Concern*, 2nd ed. (Montreal: McGill-Queen's University Press, 1988) 94.

21 *Canada Year Book 1957-1958*, as cited in G.A. Rawlyk, "Canada's Immigration Policy: 1945-1962," *Dalhousie Review* 42.3 (1962): 293.

22 Whitaker *Double Standard* 21-54.

23 Whitaker *Double Standard* 21.

24 William Kaplan, "Who Belongs? Changing Concepts of Citizenship and Nationality," *Belonging: The Meaning and Future of Canadian Citizenship*, ed. William Kaplan (Kingston: McGill-Queens University Press, 1993) 250.

25 Stuart Hall and David Held, "Citizens and Citizenship," *New Times*, ed. Stuart Hall and Martin Jacques (London: Verso, 1989) 175.

26 Paul Martin Sr., "Citizenship and the People's World," Kaplan 67.

27 Glenda Simms, "Racism as a Barrier to Canadian Citizenship," Kaplan 337.

28 Stasiulis and Jhappan 97.

29 Stasiulis and Jhappan 111-12.

30 Frances Henry, Carol Tator, Winston Mattis, and Tim Rees (eds.), *The Colour of Democracy, Racism in Canadian Society*, 2nd ed. (Toronto: Harcourt Brace, 2000) 130.

31 Henry et al. 73.

32 P. Kenneth Carty and W. Peter Ward, "The Making of a Canadian Political Citizenship," *National Politics and Community in Canada*, ed. P. Kenneth Carty and W. Peter Ward (Vancouver: University of British Columbia Press, 1986) 74.

33 Linda Trimble, "The Politics of Gender," *Critical Concepts: An Introduction to Canadian Politics*, ed.

Janine Brodie (Scarborough: Prentice Hall, 1999) 310.

34 Carty and Ward 68.

35 Martin Sr. 73.

36 Martin Sr. 74.

37 Martin Sr. 74.

38 Carty and Ward 66.

39 Knowles 158.

40 Lorne Foster, *Turnstile Immigration: Multiculturalism, Social Order, and Social Justice in Canada* (Toronto: Thompson Educational Press, 1998) 72.

41 Canada, Manpower and Immigration, *White Paper on Immigration* (Ottawa: Queen's Printer, 1966) 12.

42 Carty and Ward 69.

43 T.H. Marshall, "Citizenship and Social Class," *Citizenship and Class*, ed. T.H. Marshall and Tom Bottomore (London: Pluto Press, 1991) 8.

44 Marshall 8.

45 Ruth Lister, *Citizenship: Feminist Perspectives* (London: MacMillan Press, 1997) 17.

46 See Isabella Bakker and Katherine Scott, "From the Postwar to the Post-Liberal Keynesian Welfare State," *Understanding Canada: Building on the New Canadian Political Economy*, ed. Wallace Clement (Kingston: McGill-Queens University Press, 1997) 286-310.

47 Jane Jenson and Susan Phillips, "Regime Shift: New Citizenship Practices in Canada," *International Journal of Canadian Studies* 14 (1996): 118.

48 Leslie Pal, *Interests of State: The Politics of Language, Multiculturalism, and Feminism in Canada* (Montreal and Kingston: McGill-Queen's University Press, 1993).

49 Jenson and Phillips 117-19.

50 Robert Holton and M. Lanphier, "Public Opinion, Immigration and Refugees," *Immigration and Refugee Policy Australia and Canada Compared*, ed. Howard Adelman, et al. (Toronto: University of Toronto Press, 1994) 129.

51 Daiva Stasiulis, "Symbolic Representation: And the Numbers Game: Tory Policies on 'Race,'" *How Ottawa Spends 1991-1992*, ed. Frances Abele (Ottawa: Carleton University Press, 1991) 238.

52 Reg Whitaker, *Canadian Immigration Policy* (Ottawa: Canadian Historical Association, 1991) 22.

53 Janine Brodie and Christina Gabriel, "Canadian Immigration Policy and the Emergence of the Neo-Liberal State," *Journal of Contemporary International Issues* 1.11: 9-10 <www.yorku.ca/research/cii/journal/issues/vol1no1/article_3.html>

54 "Refugees," *The Courier* 121 (May-June 1990): 65.

55 John Veuglers, "State-Society Relations in the Making of Canadian Immigration Policy During the Mulroney Era," *Canadian Review of Sociology and Anthropology*, 37.1 (February 2000): 95-111.

56 Douglas L. Palmer, "Determinants of Canadian Attitudes toward Immigration: More than Just Racism?" *Canadian Journal of Behavioural Science* 28.3 (July 1996): 180-92.

57 *Globe and Mail*, 10 March 1994, cited by Brodie and Gabriel.

58 Canada, Manpower and Immigration, *White Paper on Immigration* 6.

59 Jakubowski, 17-18.

60 Jakubowski 20.

61 See for example Jakubowski 20; Anthony Richmond, *Global Apartheid* (Toronto: Oxford University Press, 1994) 131; Stasiulis and Jhappan 117.

62 Valerie Knowles, *Strangers at Our Gates* (Toronto: Dundurn Press, 1997) 159.

63 Alan Simmons, "Racism and Immigration Policy," *Racism and Social Inequality in Canada*, ed. Vic Satzewich (Toronto: Thompson Educational Publishing, 1998) 103.

64 Simmons, "Racism" 103.

65 Abu-Laban, "Keeping 'em Out" 78.

66 Canadian Council for Refugees, *Report on Systemic Racism and Discrimination in Canadian Refugee and Immigration Policies* (Montreal: CCR, 2000) 12. <www.web.net/~ccr/antiracrep.htm>

67 Abu-Laban, "Keeping 'em Out" 76-77.

68 Trevor Harrison, "Class, Citizenship and Global Migration: The Case of the Canadian Business Immigration Program, 1978-1992," *Canadian Public Policy* XXII.1 (1996): 9-10.

69 Harrison 13.

70 Harrison 16-17.

71 Stasiulis and Jhappan 119.

72 Ruth Fincher, Lois Foster, Wenona Giles, and Valerie Preston, "Gender and Immigration Policy," Adelman.

73 Monica Boyd, "Migration Policy, Female Dependency, and Family Membership: Canada and Germany," *Women and the Canadian Welfare State*, ed. Patricia Evans and Gerda Wekerle (Toronto: University of Toronto Press, 1997) 142.

74 Boyd, "Migration Policy," 155.

75 For discussion of women's access to education and training, see Susan Bullock, *Women and Work* (London: Zed Books, 1994) 87-99.

76 Monica Boyd, "Migration Regulations and Sex Selective Outcomes in Developed Countries," *International Migration Policies and the Status of Female Migrants, Proceeding of the UN Expert Group Meeting on International Migration Policies and the Status of Female Migrants* (New York: United Nations, 1995) 84.

77 Jane Jenson, "The Talents of Women, the Skills of Men," *The Transformation of Work: Skills, Flexibility and the Labour Process*, ed. S. Wood (London: Routledge, 1989) 142.

78 Bullock 73-74.

79 Jenson 151.

80 Audrey Macklin, "Foreign Domestic Workers: Surrogate Housewife or Mail Order Servant?," *McGill Law Journal*, 37:3 (1992), cited by Ad Hoc Committee on Gender Analysis of the Immigration Act, National Association of Women and the Law, *Gender Analysis of Immigration and Refugee Protection Legislation and Policy* (Ottawa: NAWL, 1999) 11.

81 Boyd, "Migration Policy" 153-154.

82 Citizenship and Immigration Canada, *Building on a Strong Foundation for the 21st Century* (Ottawa: Minister of Public Works and Government Services, 1998) 22.

83 UN Secretariat, "The International Migration of Women: An Overview," Department for Economic and Social Information and Policy Analysis Population Division, *International Migration Policies and the Status of Female Migrants, Proceeding of the UN Expert Group Meeting on International Migration Policies and the Status of Female Migrants* 9.

84 Ad Hoc Committee on Gender Analysis of the Immigration Act, (NAWL) *Gender Analysis* 5.

85 Mary Eberts, "Language training policy under the Charter of Rights," *Report of the Colloquium: Equality in Language and Literacy Training,* cited by Vijay Agnew, *Resisting Discrimination* (Toronto: University of Toronto Press, 1996) 175.

86 Boyd, "Migration Policy" 156-157.

87 Tania Das Gupta, "Families of Native People, Immigrants, and People of Colour," *Canadian Families: Diversity, Conflict, and Change*, ed. Nancy Mandel (Toronto: Harcourt Press, 1995), cited by Abu-Laban, "Keeping 'em Out" 77.

88 Canadian Council For Refugees (CCR), *Canadian NGO Report on Women and Children Migrants* (February 2000) 4. <www.webnet/%7Eccr/womench.htm>

89 Agnew 199-200.

90 Agnew 200.

91 CCR 4.

92 Fiona Williams, *Social Policy: A Critical Introduction* (Cambridge: Polity Press, 1986) 6.

93 Meg Luxton, "Feminism and Families: The Challenge of Neo-Conservatism," *Feminism and Families: Critical Policies and Changing Practices*, ed. Meg Luxton (Halifax: Fernwood, 1997) 12-13.

94 Jakubowski 77.

95 Equality for Lesbians and Gays Everywhere (EAGLE), "Brief to the Immigration Legislative Review Ministerial Consultations" March 11, 1998. np.

96 Lesbian and Gay Immigration Task Force (LEGIT), "Brief to the Legislative Review Ministerial Consultations, Appendix 1: The Immigration Journey of Lesbians and Gay Men in Canada, Same-sex Couples Are a Reality" March 1998.18-19.

97 LEGIT, "Brief to the Legislative Review" 20.

98 LEGIT, 'Brief to the Immigration Legislative Review Advisory Group," April 1997: 7.

99 Marie Boti and Sr. Florchita Bautista, as cited in Jennifer Hyndman, "Globalization, Immigration and the Gender Implications of Not Just Numbers in Canada," *Refuge* 18.1 (February 1999): 29.

100 Jane Badets, "Canada's Immigrant Population," *Social Trends*, ed. Craig McKie and Keith Thompson (Toronto: Minister of Supply and Services Canada and Thompson Educational Publishing, 1990).

101 Canada, Citizenship and Immigration Canada, *Facts and Figures: Overview of Immigration* (Ottawa: Ministry of Supply and Services, 1994) 5.

102 Canada, Citizenship and Immigration Canada. "Statement of the Honourable Sergio Marchi" (Ottawa: House of Commons, 1994), cited by Brodie and Gabriel 1.

103 See Stephen McBride and John Shields, *Dismantling a Nation* (Halifax: Fernwood, 1997).

chapter | THREE
Contemporary Directions
IMMIGRATION AND CITIZENSHIP POLICY 1993-2001

This chapter examines recent attempts to fundamentally overhaul Canada's immigration and citizenship policies. These initiatives have been undertaken at a time when processes of globalization have prompted Canadian policy-makers to respond to widespread international changes. Reforms have been pursued in a number of policy areas, immigration and citizenship among them. And it is within these two policy areas that questions of state sovereignty and state power become salient. Some social theorists have argued that while one aspect of state sovereignty—control over a territory—may be changing due to internationalization of markets and new technology, states play a key role in "the regulation of populations; people are less mobile than money, goods or ideas, in a sense they remain 'nationalized,' dependent on passports, visas, residence and labour qualifications."[1] But, as Saskia Sassen has argued, "it is no longer sufficient simply to assert the sovereign role of the state in immigration policy and design"; equally important is an examination of "the transformation of the state itself."[2] These insights provide a starting point for our assessment of the current directions of immigration and citizenship policy. Recent reforms, especially in the case of immigration policy and design, have been guided by the need to make the country more competitive. In making these reforms, however, the state has exerted power in new and different ways. As we show, control remains a key facet of state action.

Attempts to rewrite immigration and citizenship policy in the 1990s have placed immigration and citizenship policies at the forefront of the political agenda. Issues around belonging, difference, and national identity have played prominently in these policy debates, as has a globalization discourse that emphasizes global competitiveness, individual self-sufficiency, economic imperatives, and cost recovery. As we detailed in the last chapter, large numbers of immigrants have always been selected on the basis of their ability to contribute to the Canadian economy. This is accentuated and consolidated in current developments. In response to the perceived economic imperatives of globalization, the "best" immigrants, and by extension prospective citizens, are those whose labour-market skills will enhance Canada's competitive position in a world economy. Conversely, the "best" are countered with those less desired—the family class—because the latter are (erroneously) constructed as "non-contributors" to the economy and nation.[3] The contemporary construction of the model citizen is also taking place within a policy environment that increasingly emphasizes security and control.

Fundamental changes to Canadian immigration policy are being considered in the aftermath of the September 11, 2001 attacks on the World Trade Center and the Pentagon. While they are the outcome of more than 10 years of debate and consultation, many proposed and actual changes are being implemented now within an environment where security concerns, border control, and anti-terrorism measures have taken on a much larger public profile and policy salience. Additionally, there are growing demands that Canada adopt a security/perimeter approach and work to harmonize Canadian immigration and refugee policies with those of the United States. These demands are prompted by processes of economic globalization insofar as increasing continental integration has linked Canada more closely with the United States. For example, "more than CDN $1.5 billion of goods crosses the Canada-US border daily."[4] The tightening of the Canada-United States border immediately following September 11, 2001 cost Canadian businesses millions of dollars. This led business groups to pressure the Canadian government to reassure Americans that security concerns are being addressed.[5] The open-borders vision of an integrated North American economy is at odds with demands that the border be "secure" and "policed" against terrorism, smuggling of aliens, and drugs.[6] It is likely that anti-terrorism measures, border control, and a North American security perimeter will dominate policy debates into the foreseeable future, ensuring that immigration remains a prominent and highly charged issue.

The starting point of the assessment presented in this chapter is the 1993 election of Jean Chrétien's Liberal government. During the election campaign, the party's stated position on immigration was to balance Canada's demographic and economic needs with humanitarian considerations. Once in power the Liberals embarked on a series of public consultations to—in the words of then-Minister of Immigration, Sergio Marchi—"forge a comprehensive, forward looking, and progressive immigration framework to take Canada into the next century."[7] It would be seven years before the government would introduce new legislative proposals in the House of Commons. We detail and analyze some key milestones in this process: the initial consultation phase; regulatory changes (1995); and the subsequent publication of a government-commissioned Advisory Report, *Not Just Numbers: A Canadian Framework for Future Immigration* (1997). Together they foreshadowed the policy directions the government would pursue in legislation between 1999 and 2001. Specifically, the now defunct Bill C-16, "An Act Respecting Canadian Citizenship," and Bill C-11, "The Immigration and Refugee Protection Act,"[8] introduced in February 2001, passed in the Senate in the fall of 2001. The consultation process and debates around these measures have prompted Canadians to consider the nature of Canadian identity and the future of Canadian society. This chapter considers how a particular reading of processes of globalization which emphasizes neo-liberal ideals finds expression in current proposals, and, relatedly, considers how these directions reinforce or subvert existing gender, country of origin (and therefore race/ethnicity), and class hierarchies.

INITIAL PHASE: 1994-1995 CONSULTATION AND POLICY CHANGES

Early in 1994 the Liberal government announced a sweeping consultation process that would determine immigration policy directions for the next century. This consultation process took place in a period in which immigration and citizenship issues had become highly politicized. The emergence of the Reform Party in 1987, with its vocal anti-immigration stance, and its subsequent presence on the national stage played a significant role in bringing immigration issues to the fore. The Reform Party (now the Canadian Alliance) has consistently argued that immigration levels should not only be reduced but should be guided by economic needs, not by social or humanitarian imperatives. For example, Reform MP Art Hanger attacked immigration policy in 1994 on the basis that it neglected to consider the costs of immigration and added,

> ... [p]roblems will only be made worse if we accept the flood of immigrants proposed by the government, especially when those immigrants are chosen largely from the family or refugee classes and not as independent immigrants chosen for their human capital, chosen for their skills, their ability to quickly and independently

integrate into Canadian life as well as their ability to contribute to
the economic needs of the country.[9]

Reform Party members not only emphasized economic rationales
regarding immigration but called for stronger control to secure borders
against illegal migrants. They raised the spectre of "illegal immigrants"
and "bogus refugees" to further demonstrate their contention that
Canadian immigration policy and immigration regulations were too
lax.[10] The Reform Party's interventions in the immigration debates
both reflected some elements of public perception and helped to shape
public opinion against immigration. This led to one suggestion that:

> ... the party's biggest successes may not be measured tangibly
> through the ballot box, but to the degree that certain political
> discourses ... have become legitimized. Prior to the arrival of the
> party, there was little political debate about immigration and mul-
> ticulturalism.
> The Reform Party has re-politicized issues that in recent times have
> remained uncontested at the level of party politics.[11]

It is in this context that immigration consultations first took place.

The consultation process itself was sweeping. Indeed, Minister of
Immigration Sergio Marchi announced that the purpose of the consultation was to "move beyond traditional interest groups" and to
engage "Canadians in a discussion of shared goals and shared responsibilities."[12] A closed-door planning session in March 1994 kicked off an
eight-month policy review process. This initial meeting was designed
to identify key immigration themes to be discussed and the appropriate consultation method. In the summer a number of working groups
examined key themes and questions.[13] Following this, Citizenship and
Immigration Canada organized a series of public "town hall" meetings.
In all, 10,000 Canadians participated in consultations through "town hall"
meetings, study circles, and written submissions. The outcome of the
consultations, reported in November 1994, revealed a number of diver-
gent viewpoints on such matters as whether immigration levels should
be reduced or remain the same and whether immigration was or was
not good for the economy.[14] Despite the apparent commitment to a form
of participatory democracy, the government chose not to explicitly
evaluate the conflicting views.[15]

Instead, the Liberal government announced a series of changes to
immigration policy in November 1994. These changes emphasized

lowering immigration levels and selecting immigrants who could "contribute" to Canadian society and place less demand on state-financed integration services. According to Citizenship and Immigration Canada, "this means raising selection standards; ensuring that Canadians honour their responsibilities toward sponsored family members; and achieving the appropriate balance between the economic and family components of immigration."[16] There is an explicit economic focus embedded in this statement. The "ideal" immigrant/potential citizen is one who has the necessary skills and attributes to join the Canadian labour market and contribute to the globalizing economy. The "ideal" immigrant is also a self-sufficient one, one who will not make demands on the social programs of the welfare state. And if the "ideal" immigrant has a family or dependants, the "ideal" immigrant will be able to support them and bear the costs of their integration into Canadian society.

To some extent, the points system, with its so-called objective criteria and its link to labour-market occupation demand, has always sought the model immigrant/citizen. And in this respect, one analysis suggests that the points system can be read as treating immigrants as commodities. The outcome of this process of commodification, it is argued, "is that it leads to an evaluation of people's potential contribution to and value to the country solely on the basis of their expected place in the labour market."[17] This long-standing feature is further entrenched in the increasing emphasis placed within immigration policy documents, government statements, and popular debate on "human capital." Human capital theory, derived from economics, holds essentially that people's knowledge and skills are "a factor of production in the same way as physical capital (buildings, raw materials, machinery etc.)."[18] Skills and knowledge are acquired throughout an individual's lifetime through "investments" in formal education, on-the-job training (apprenticeships), and work experience. Such investments are linked to productive capability.[19] As outlined in Chapter Two, the emphasis on the labour market has always been present in Canadian immigration policy, but the 1994 changes mark a period in which this tendency becomes much more acute. The government subsequently reformed the points system to greater emphasize job experience and language skills. The increased emphasis placed on economic performance criteria, skills (especially transferable skills), and education continues through subsequent policy changes.

Thus, Citizenship and Immigration Canada's Annual Report to Parliament 1995-2000 indicated that, "beginning in 1996, the balance between economic, family, and other immigrant components will place greater emphasis on attracting those with the capacity to settle quickly and contribute to Canada."[20] Planned percentages in 1995 indicated 43 per cent in the economic category and 51 per cent in the family class. By 2000 planned percentages were 53 per cent economic and 44 per cent family class.[21] Under the proposal the levels for family class and refugee categories—those people not selected on the basis of the point system— were reduced. Members of the family class, mostly women, were viewed as "non-contributors" because contribution was measured narrowly in terms of economic criteria, namely, "providing their employers with a window on foreign markets; introducing knowledge and technological skills to the labour market; [and significantly] paying higher than aver- age taxes."[22] There was therefore a continuing and fundamental failure to recognize the value of women's work, whether both domestic work— unpaid work performed in the home—or any of the other forms of activity in which women might engage, such as work in a family-owned business or volunteer work in the community sector. Additionally, it has been argued that the distinction between those who contribute to the labour market and those who do not is "too simplistic and not empiri- cally validated" insofar as many immigrant women, in the family class, are often active members of the Canadian labour force.[23]

On the other hand the independent stream—skilled workers and business investors—was scheduled to increase in the same period. Citizenship and Immigration Canada reported that, "[i]mmigrants selected for their skills and abilities are more likely to earn higher incomes and help spur economic growth."[24] This privileges those from advantaged- class backgrounds, but neglects the fact that the economic self-suffi- ciency of an immigrant and the likelihood that he or she will make use of social and immigrant settlement programs, is just one measure of the worth of any immigrant.[25] It is important to note as well that immigrants do not necessarily acquire jobs in Canada that are commensurate with their actual "skills" because of a variety of structural barriers, including the lack of recognition of many foreign degrees and training.[26]

Changes to the composition of immigration streams are particularly gen- dered since the proportion of men in the independent categories that were valorized—skilled workers and business immigrants—is greater than that of women. In 1993 in the independent categories (independent applicants and business immigrants) aged 15-plus years, there were 18,723 males versus 13,840 females. In contrast, women were over-represented in the family class. Women aged 15-plus numbered 55,409 in the family class while men numbered 37,557.[27] Consequently, cuts to the family class impact women directly. But the implications of the changes go beyond the numbers. The increasing emphasis on economic criteria for selection ensures that the gender division within immigration policy, discussed in the previous chapter, remains intact. And for this reason, it is postulated that changes in selection criteria, coupled with the cuts to immigrant settlement services, which are part of the retrenchment of the welfare state, will render women much more dependent within family relationships.[28]

Throughout the consultation process in 1994 and the changes immediately introduced afterward, there was little or no discussion about the gendered nature of the family class, sponsorship, or its attendant relations of dependency.[29] What did emerge on the agenda, however, was the spectre of sponsorship default. The government cited a figure of 14 per cent for the rate of sponsorship default in the Toronto area. However, as one advocacy group pointed out, the government neglected to include other necessary qualifiers, including that "the rate of dependence on social assistance among households in Toronto headed by sponsored family class immigrants ... is slightly lower than the general rate of social assistance in the Census Metropolitan Area" and, further, that "the most common reasons for assistance were unemployment and desertion."[30] What was being emphasized here is that, in many cases of sponsorship breakdown, people's financial circumstances had deteriorated. The period under consideration, 1984 to 1994, was a time of recession, and this affected all people. The government's stated objective to "establish mechanisms to ensure that sponsors honour their obligations" and thereby make "a commitment to reduce the burden on Canada's social services that results from family sponsorship breakdown"[31] suggests a scenario of a "deadbeat" and "irresponsible" sponsor. There is no suggestion that the circumstances surrounding sponsorship default need to be considered. The state in this case—and through subsequent actions in the 1990s—would seek to reinforce "the neo-liberal value of 'self-sufficiency' or, reliance on the family, instead of the state."[32] Additionally, it should be emphasized that state power—in terms of increased regulation, scrutiny, and punitive measures—was being used in this case to enforce the apparent privatization of integration costs away from the state and onto immigrants themselves.

Cost recovery also came into play in the administration of immigration policy under the Liberal government. In its 1995 budget the government announced the introduction of a controversial new landing tax, known formally as the "right of landing fee"(ROLF), but referred to by some critics as a modern "head tax." Under its terms, each adult immigrant and refugee has to pay CDN$975 to enter Canada. The ROLF was coupled with additional fees for filing applications, introduced in 1992. To understand the implications of this, consider the example of a family of two adults and two children. They would incur a cost of CDN$1,950 in landing fees, plus a "processing fee" of $500 per adult and $100 per child.[33] On the surface these costs (which are extremely hefty for many new immigrants and pose an economic challenge) have been justified as a deficit-fighting measure. Revenues generated, according to the government, were to offset costs of integration. But there are deeper implications.

> The logic behind this justification clearly sets immigrants apart from the rights and benefits of Canadian citizenship. Unlike other public funded services, the costs of which are shared collectively by all Canadians through the tax system, this justification for head taxes involves a notion of user fees—a collective one shared by all immigrants.[34]

Insofar as settlement programs—housing, language training, education, and employment assistance—are measures of the social rights of citizenship, the imposition of fees coupled with government cutbacks in these areas erodes the social citizenship rights of immigrants. Further, any long-term benefit immigrants may bring to Canadian society is not acknowledged, nor is the fact that when immigrants enter the country they immediately pay taxes like any other Canadian.

But the implications of the ROLF go further yet. Its imposition has a differential impact on various groups. It imposes a new form of class, racial, and gender bias into the administration of Canadian immigration policy. This becomes apparent when one considers the wealth and pay differentials between the North and South as well as between men and women. For example, the fee is equivalent to six months' salary for many El Salvadorans, while it may account for 10 months' wages for a nurse in Sri Lanka.[35] The Canadian Council of Refugees (CCR) has pointed out that "given the relative costs-of-living, rates of currency exchange and average annual income, ROLF amounts to a regressive flat tax which affects disproportionately immigrants from the South."[36] One of the possible effects of ROLF, the CCR suggested, was that it might act as a barrier for notably, "economically disadvantaged classes of people and those from parts of the world with income levels markedly inferior to Canadian levels."[37] Similarly, the National Action Committee on the Status of Women stated that "given that we live in a world of great disparities between women and men; between rich and poor ... this head tax will make it difficult for many women, particularly women of colour, to enter or remain in Canada as permanent residents."[38] The landing fee also applied to refugees, who may arrive in Canada with very few financial resources, and CCR pointed out that one possible effect was that it would delay their applications for permanent residence—or they would simply be unable to apply because they had insufficient funds to do so.[39] In applying this measure to refugees, Canada became the only country in the world to charge fees to people seeking protection.[40] In February 2000, the Liberal government repealed the landing fee for refugees. However, it is still collected from other immigrants. Ottawa has projected that it will earn $120 million in revenues from this fee,[41] yet it has been reported that the funds have not been channeled to immigrant settlement services.[42]

The pronouncements of the Liberal government and the regulatory changes undertaken in the first stage of its mandate foreshadow the types of reforms in the new Immigration Act, intended to replace the one from 1976. In many ways the immigration changes introduced in the government's first mandate were structured by neo-liberal ideals of self-sufficiency, individualization, commodification, and, to some extent, a smaller role for the state in the area of social spending. The increasing emphasis on economic criteria within the selection model can be seen as an attempt to respond to a particular reading of economic globalization. Thus, in spite of the Liberal government's historical position of valuing immigrants and their contributions toward Canada's economic and social well-being, since taking office in 1993 they have, in the words of one analyst, "abandoned the field to their right-wing critics and political adversaries,"[43] such as the Reform/Alliance Party and members of the public critical of immigration.

NOT JUST NUMBERS: A CANADIAN FRAMEWORK FOR FUTURE IMMIGRATION 1997[44]

The Liberal government established an Advisory Group in November 1996 to review legislative provisions and policies regarding immigration, protection of refugees, and citizenship. The three members of the independent advisory group were Susan Davis, an immigration consultant; Roslyn Kunic, a partner in an economic consulting firm; and Robert Trempe, a former Quebec assistant deputy minister.[45] After extensive consultations, they produced an appraisal report: *Not Just Numbers: A Canadian Framework for Future Immigration*, released in January 1998. The report contained 172 recommendations. The discussion below highlights those proposals concerning citizenship, the family class, and independent applicants. It is important to emphasize that the report was not a statement of government policy but an effort (in the words of then-Minister of Immigration, Lucienne Robillard) to "initiate informed discussion."[46] *Not Just Numbers* is considered here because it was an important milestone in the Liberal government's attempt to chart new directions for immigration and citizenship policy. The report's proposals emphasize the trends already outlined above insofar as they valorize a narrow definition of "contribution," seek to ensure that immigrants bear the costs of their own integration, and do not address the gendered nature of the key immigration categories.

Not Just Numbers offers a brief statement of some of the nation's fundamental core values and principles. These include self-reliance, compassion leading to collective responsibility, investment (particularly in children), democracy, freedom, equality, and fiscal responsibility.[47] While these all may be laudable, an examination of the recommendations of the report suggests an overwhelming focus on self-reliance. This was noted in the consultation period. Calgary Immigrant Aid, an immigrant service agency, stated that,

> ... self-reliance ... [is] the most emphasized value ... and it appears to be a gloss for economic independence or self-sufficiency.... The emphasis on economic values to the detriment of other equally valid ones must be reduced.[48]

Indeed, *Not Just Numbers* takes a reading of globalization as one of its stated points of reference: "Of all the emerging tends, none is more dominant than what is loosely called globalization. Globalization is a code word for the breakdown of traditional boundaries among sovereign nations, economic markets, and individuals.... Globalization creates natural tensions that impact on immigration policy."[49] The report cites growing international competitiveness for both products and labour as well as increased fiscal constraints as factors to which contemporary policy-makers must respond.[50] Within this report, proposed directions for a new immigration policy are assessed using a specific cost-benefit rationale. Subsequent to the report's release, the government acknowledged that there was "some concern with the report's perceived economic and market-oriented focus" and "some criticism that the report was negative and problem-oriented in tone, and that proposed solutions were not always consistent with the declared values based approach."[51] And while the review acknowledges the need for a gender-based analysis, it admits this was not done, stating, "we were unfortunately unable systematically to check the effect of our recommendations on equality between the sexes."[52]

Not Just Numbers: The Family Class

In terms of the family class the report made some effort to address concerns raised about the definition of family by recommending the recognition of same-sex unions and common-law relationships as well as provisions that would have allowed the sponsoring of those with whom an applicant had a close, but not necessarily familial, relationship.[53] These proposals were welcomed by many as they challenged the valorized family form that has been at the heart of immigration policy—the heterosexual nuclear family—and acknowledged a conception of an extended family and other forms of family that might not be biologically based.

However, in making these recommendations the advisory group also stated:

> Canadians wish to be realistic about which costs and strains the social network can bear and who should bear them. Just as the government should not dictate all, neither can it provide for all needs.[54]

In this sense the advisory group signalled its support for a limited state role in the provision of immigrant settlement services. Indeed its authors refer to "tax fatigue" as an economic trend that structured their assessment.[55] Not surprisingly, then, they focussed on the short-term costs of integration, and many of their recommendations suggested that integration costs (specifically language training) be downloaded onto individuals and families. These additional costs would be added to the right of landing fees the Liberal government imposed in 1994; here, again, is the emphasis on integration costs being privatized, moved to individuals and their families and away from the Canadian state and all taxpayers.

The advisory group recommended that sponsors be required to pay for language training for all sponsored family members aged six and over who did not have proficiency in either of the two official languages. The language proposals were among the most contentious of the recommendations in the report. It has been pointed out that these types of language requirements would affect the source country of potential immigrants since immigrants from non-English and non-French speaking countries and those unable to afford and/or access language training would likely not be successful applicants.[56] The Metro Toronto Chinese and Southeast Asian Legal Clinic, for example, charged that

> [i]mposing a language requirement on family class immigrants is a way to achieve through the back door what the Government cannot do in an overt manner, i.e., to restrict the number of immigrants from certain developing countries. We all know that the top ten source countries ... are non-English speaking countries where the English language is available mostly to elites. Thus, regardless of the intent behind this proposal, the impact of the language requirement is clearly racist and classist.[57]

Calling the proposed language requirement racist and classist was a recognition that applicants whose sponsors can afford various fees, costs, and financial commitments are more attractive to Canada than those whose sponsors cannot. These costs impose a significant barrier to women and to people in low-income groups in Canada who wish to be reunited with their families from abroad. In the face of the considerable controversy generated by this particular proposal, the government moved to distance itself quickly from the language requirement.[58]

Not Just Numbers: Independent Applicants

As noted, those seeking admission to Canada are selected on the basis of a points system designed to measure related skills. Changes in 1986 and 1993 tied the system more closely to the needs of the labour market and raised the standard pass mark from 50 to 70.[59] Throughout the 1990s, immigration was viewed by many elements, such as the Reform Party, as one means to enhance Canada's competitive advantage. Through the selection of skilled workers, the nation could presumably augment its human capital base to compete in a global economy. Not surprisingly, immigration debates became infused with references to "human capital" and calls to build "Canada's skill base." Not Just Numbers states, for example:

> The movement towards a global economy has altered the nature of demand for human capital. Once blocked by both structural and institutional barriers, individuals now seek maximum return for their knowledge, skills, and experience, as well as their accumulated financial resources. Countries (and even large multinational corporations) are competing globally to attract people who can con-

tribute to economic development and growth. This global competition has exposed the shortage of highly skilled workers, crucial to the expansion of vital economic sectors.[60]

In another example, to facilitate the circulation of temporary skilled workers (e.g., in the high-tech industries) *Not Just Numbers* proposed streamlining the current process to allow companies with more than 20 employees to bypass existing immigration regulations. In this respect it acknowledged that it was "proposing a major shift in identification of labour market needs from government to the private sector."[61] It also proposed abolishing the points system but adopting a similar system of core standards for evaluation. These core standards emphasized official language skills, education, age (21 to 44 years), professional experience, and settlement arrangements. Settlement arrangements were defined as the holding of "liquid assets equal to six months low income cut off for family size"; without that, the prospective immigrant would have to be sponsored by a community group.[62] Despite this proposed abandonment of the points system, the Immigration Legislative Review failed to acknowledge the profoundly gendered nature of the points system, or of its own proposed changes. Its criteria, if adopted, would replicate and entrench the existing gender bias of the points system.

Not Just Numbers: Citizenship Provisions

Not Just Numbers embraced a concept of active citizenship in its recommendations, by valorizing the individual who discharges the responsibilities of citizenship privately through neighbourliness, voluntary work, and charitable gifts. This conception detaches citizenship "from its modern roots in institutional reform, in the welfare state and community struggles" and rearticulates social welfare in terms of charity, philanthropy, and self-help.[63] The report emphasized placing a higher value on citizenship and proposed citizenship criteria which would have made it more difficult for immigrants to access Canadian citizenship and social rights.

Not Just Numbers placed a requirement of "active participation" in Canadian society as a requisite for citizenship.[64] Applicants would need to demonstrate a measure of integration as demonstrated by two of the following conditions: employment, study, volunteer/community service, and family care. This proposal on active citizenship placed a criteria of citizenship not currently in place for people born in Canada. Moreover, the Ontario Council of Agencies Serving Immigrants (OCASI) pointed out that this type of requirement failed to recognize the responsibilities and hardships faced by immigrants in the settlement process,[65] including issues of domestic labour, difficulties in finding time to volunteer, and even the possible difficulty attendant in being accepted as a volunteer.

The proposals around citizenship also outlined additional "mandatory requirements" for citizenship that immigrants would have to meet. These included physical residence, knowledge of an official language, age, no serious criminal record, and fiscal responsibility. The latter would be demonstrated through the filing of income tax returns.[66] This recommendation linked the paying of tax to citizenship, imposing an obligation on landed immigrants that differed from that of other Canadian citizens. As one immigrant advocacy group representative pointed out, such an obligation is a "double standard" since the filing of tax returns "is not a requirement to maintain Canadian citizenship status."[67] On the one hand, this recommendation constructed immigrants—prospective citizens—as taxpayers. On the other hand, other proposals, notably those around language education, did not want immigrants to access existing social rights of citizenship funded by taxes. The tying of citizenship to filing of income tax returns or paying of taxes tends to valorize the neo-liberal individualistic constructions of a citizen as a "taxpayer" or "consumer."

In sum, it is important to emphasize that *Not Just Numbers* was a discussion document produced by independent consultants and commissioned by the Liberal government. As a discussion document, it is significant not just for the sweeping nature of its proposals but for the degree to which neo-liberal elements find expression in the framing of immigration and citizenship questions as well as in its recommendations. Public reaction to these contentious proposals was very mixed. The language proposals and core standards were the subject of considerable opposition. In the wake of the consultations around *Not Just Numbers*, the government chose a more moderate option of enacting reforms to the existing system.

NEW DIRECTIONS IN CITIZENSHIP AND IMMIGRATION 2000-2001

Between 1998 and 2001 the Liberal government moved to introduce new immigration and citizenship legislation. The proposed legislation is a retreat from the more controversial recommendations of *Not Just Numbers*, but does not appear to represent a significant break from past policy and practice. The government's attempt to redraft the legislation is framed, in part, by a recognition of globalization:

> Since Canada's most recent *Immigration Act* was proclaimed in 1978, the world has in many ways become a global village. In the intervening 20 years, technological change and the forces of globalization have brought about sweeping changes domestically and internationally.[68]

Similarly, in the parliamentary debate on the proposed Citizenship Act, one New Democratic Party (NDP) member told the House:

> ... many of us are looking at citizenship in a whole new light, given the global economy we currently live in.... Given the globalization of capital we are seeing borders disappear. Many say we are probably witnessing the beginning of the end of the concept of the nation-state.... The only way we can define ourselves and maintain our identity as Canadian is to ensure that the nation state of Canada survives ... and that the personification of that ... is by virtue of our citizenship.[69]

The Liberal government's proposals need to be considered in this context. The government's attempt was marked by a number of failed starts. Bill C-11, "The Immigration and Refugee Protection Act," was introduced in February 2001 and passed through the House of Commons and the Senate by October 2001. Its predecessor, Bill C-31 (which had similar provisions), died on the order paper when Jean Chrétien called the 2000 federal election. The government's proposed Citizenship Act, Bill C-16, suffered a similar fate. At present the Liberal government has not introduced a new citizenship bill. Bill C-11 received Royal Assent 1 November 2001.

New Immigration Act

Bill C-11, "Immigration and Refugee Protection Act," can be viewed as the end point of the long process of consultation and policy change that started shortly after the Liberals' first mandate. The bill will replace the 1976 Immigration Act, which had been amended more than 30 times since it was proclaimed in 1978. The Bill attempts a balance between two competing objectives, characterized in Minister Elinor Caplan's words as "opening the door" to the kinds of immigrants Canada desires while "closing the back door" to illegal migrants.[70] Bill C-11 has been criticized by a number of groups for going too far. The Canadian Bar Association told the Senate Standing Committee on Social Affairs, Science and Technology that "in its current form, Bill C-11 represents a fundamental and unacceptable shift in the way Canada treats immigrants and potential immigrants.[71] The Bill's passage through the Senate in Fall 2001 also coincided with the introduction of the government's new anti-terrorism measures and a climate in which security and border control have increasingly dominated the agenda. Indeed, some of the provisions in Bill C-11, such as identity cards for all permanent residents, have been fast-tracked as part of the government's fight against terrorism.

Following recommendations in *Not Just Numbers*, Bill C-11 is "framework legislation," detailing key principles while leaving the details of actual implementation and procedures to regulation. Advocacy groups and even the government's own members[72] have questioned the division of principle and procedure on a number of grounds. Firstly, the Bill's provisions tend to be weighted toward detailing the specifics of control, "closing the door" rather clearly, while leaving other important issues regarding "opening the door" to unspecified administrative regulation. The downloading of authority and power from the realm of legislation to that of regulation is a significant shift from existing immigration legislation, according to the Canadian Bar Association. Bill C-11 provides for an expansion of regulation power in a number of key matters, and this, in the Bar Association's view, significantly affects the rights and status of foreign nationals, permanent residents, and refugees.[73]

The concern raised here goes to the nature of framework legislation itself. On the one hand, it is recognized that such legislation allows for an immigration and refugee regime to be more responsive to changing conditions and circumstances.[74] Regulations that are necessary to operationalize and implement legislation can be introduced and amended quickly by the government of the day without legislative review. However, this downloading of legislation to regulation is problematic:

> First, important rights and processes now entrenched in the Act are removed and left undefined. The quality of these rights is left to the shifting policies of future Cabinets. Second, legislation can be extensively amended without Parliamentary scrutiny.[75]

Take the example of family reunification, which, under the provisions of Bill c-11, are left to the scope of regulation. In this matter, the group Equality for Gays and Lesbians Everywhere (EGALE) expressed its concern about framework legislation and regulatory power by stating:

> EGALE recognizes that the current government and administration are willing to affirm their constitutional responsibility to provide equality for same-sex families. It cannot be assumed, however, that future governments will be as supportive as this one. Enshrining the new provisions in the legislation will help to ensure that key concepts such as who qualifies under the family class are not subject to the vagaries of political change. Changing such a core concept should require a vote in Parliament, rather than a simple regulatory change.[76]

To some extent, the House of Commons' Standing Committee addressed these concerns by amending the Bill. Changes regarding

> ... examinations, rights, and obligations of permanent and temporary residents, loss of status and removal, detention and release, refugee eligibility, the pre-removal risk assessment, and transportation companies ...[77]

would be reviewed by Parliament. However, the Canadian Bar Association still expressed concerns that the proposed law left far too much to regulatory authority.[78]

Throughout the Liberal government's attempt to reform immigration policy (and citizenship policy) there has been limited interrogation of the key assumptions, gender or otherwise, that underlie each area or of what the desirable options to pursue might be, and why. Bill c-11 continues in this vein. The Maytree Foundation, a charitable organization, raised this issue directly in its brief to the Standing Committee on Citizenship and Immigration. Maytree posed a number of interesting questions:

> ... do we see immigration as being primarily about filling short-term labour market gaps, or meeting long-term economic strategies? Is it about reunifying families or supplying enough young workers to the labour (and tax-paying) pool to keep the health and pension benefits flowing for retiring baby-boomers?
>
> We often hear about Canada's need to compete with other countries for the world's best educated, most skilled, wealthiest immigrants. But why should we restrict "economic" migration to these; why not expand our focus to include anyone who truly wants to adopt this country as their home and who has the skills and ability to land on their feet? What responsibilities do we have to countries from which we draw immigrant professionals and trades people?[79]

In raising these questions Maytree was challenging the government and Canadians to engage in a much deeper discussion of the issues. In questioning both the premise that Canada is in competition with other states and the desirability of attracting skilled migrants, Maytree implicitly suggested that there are other options that could be considered in dealing with the consequences of economic globalization. However, the government proceeded on the assumption that the existing selection model (the points system) and the existing categories (independent, family, and refugee) only needed some fine-tuning. It embraced the need for highly skilled workers to help enhance the country's human capital base and by extension its ability to compete in the global market. It is not surprising, then, that the new Immigration Act as contained in Bill C-11 does not adequately address the differential and unequal effects that were the outcome of the policies and practices of the 1976 Immigration Act, discussed in the previous chapter. As the government moves to enact reforms in an attempt to respond to changes in the international realm, these effects become more acute.

Processes of globalization are explicitly invoked in the Liberal government's stated reasons for the new law. Take, for example, the following:

> As Canada enters the new millennium, poised to capitalize on the global economy and increase its wealth in the knowledge society, it needs immigration and refugee protection legislation that can respond quickly to a rapidly evolving environment ...[80]

And in terms of the focus, desirable immigrants—highly skilled ones—are seen as an important source of comparative advantage. Highly skilled workers are the reason to "open the door":

> The global labour force can benefit Canadians through job creation and the transfer of skills. Immigration legislation must be adapted to enhance Canada's advantage in the global competition for skilled workers.[81]

But simultaneously, Canada as a nation-state must respond to other aspects of globalization:

> Global migration pressures and the promise of significant profits from transporting and exploiting migrants have led powerful transnational criminal organizations to extend their activities to migrant smuggling and trafficking.... Canadians want to ensure they have the policy and legislative tools to deter migrant trafficking and punish those who engage in this form of modern slavery.[82]

Bill c-11's focus on control issues speaks to this concern. This said, the proposed Bill does not signal a wholesale abandonment of commitments and priorities established in the post-war period. What is evident is a reconfiguration of the terms of some of these commitments. For example, as discussed below, there are measures to expand the family class while enforcing sponsorship.

Bill c-11's proposals emphasize that Canada needs to attract more highly skilled workers to "grow and prosper in a new global economy."[83] Thus, the points system should be retained; however, there will be a greater emphasis on "sound and transferable skill sets," "skilled technical workers," and "tradespersons with good human capital attributes."[84] Transferable skills are those that are portable insofar as they have applicability to many different tasks, occupations, and workplaces. Examples of transferable skills include communication skills and analytical skills—data gathering and problem solving—as well as interpersonal skills. This selection model places a premium on the "flexibility" of individuals and makes the assumption that workers today will spend their careers in more than one job and, therefore, must be able to adapt quickly to changing labour market needs.

Additionally, this selection model speaks to a shift in the role of the state in managing the interface between immigration selection and labour market needs. In the immediate post-war period and through the

1960s and 1970s it was assumed that the state had an important role in the management of the labour market. Today, this assumption is questioned. The position of the government was summed up in a 1998 discussion document:

> The current [immigrant] selection system is premised on the capacity of governments to intervene significantly in the management of labour markets and to match the skills of foreign applicants to specific Canadian labour market shortages. However, in a world where technological change is the norm and industries appear and disappear almost overnight, it is no longer possible to micro-manage labour market supply and demand. For such an approach to be effective, very substantial resources would be required to continuously monitor labour markets, at a prohibitive cost to taxpayers.[85]

Thus, the government has moved away from the occupation-based model predicated on a list of occupations in demand to the emphasis on transferable skills and human capital as embodied in individual immigrants. Proposed changes in immigration selection speak to a broader trend of implicit and explicit withdrawal of the state from labour market regulation in the last decade.[86] It should be noted that this is not an absolute withdrawal, but it does indicate the changing role of the state.

The provisions around the temporary worker program are also indicative of the changing role of the state in terms of managing the labour market. Temporary foreign workers have to obtain employment authorizations to work in Canada. These authorizations are granted on a case-by-case basis. In each instance an employer makes an application to Human Resources and Development Canada and is required to show that he or she had made attempts to hire within Canada.[87] Bill C-11 is a move away from this process. The stated rationale is this: "to allow the immediate needs of employers to be met faster; to expand our access to the global labour market; to attract people who are skilled and on the move and to encourage them to make Canada their destination of choice."[88] Whereas formerly the state played the dominant role in the authorization of permits, it is now proposing to partner with business—both individual sectors and firms—to meet labour market skills shortages. This type of proposal is presented as less bureaucratic because it allows for a quick response at a time when the economy is rapidly changing.[89] As one document of Citizenship and Immigration Canada explains, the government is pursuing this option:

1. To stimulate Canada's economic development and growth through the retention or creation of permanent jobs, investment in infrastructure or capital infusion, and skills transfer or other enhancement of domestic human capital.

2. To provide flexibility and ensure that Canada retain its competitive advantage in the global economy.[90]

Additionally the state, in an effort to enhance competitiveness and address the "skills shortage" has been engaged in a number of pilot projects in the information technology sector. These proposals embody a shift from a form of statist regulation, the dominant role referred to above, to a more decentralized model—the partnership—but they do not indicate a withdrawal of the state from the management of immigration. The impetus behind such measures is economic globalization.

Bill C-11 also includes provisions for work authorizations for the spouses of skilled temporary workers, in order to make immigration in this class more attractive. The majority of temporary workers to Canada are male, with the bulk of those coming from the United States.[91] For this reason a spousal provision for temporary workers may benefit women especially by allowing them entry to Canada and work authorizations. However, this provision continues to entrench the dichotomy between constructed categories of "skilled" and "unskilled" workers insofar as exceptions to the provision, according to CIC, would include seasonal workers and live-in caregivers. While "seasonal workers" are mostly men coming to Canada from Mexico and Jamaica, "live-in caregivers"—again, an occupation considered "unskilled"—are predominantly women.

The emphasis on highly skilled workers, transferable skills, and human capital goes to the heart of Bill C-11's provisions around the independent class, and temporary worker provisions ensure that the gender, racial, and class biases of earlier incarnations of Canadian immigration policy will be replicated. Throughout the consultation process women's groups, for example, have repeatedly drawn attention to the fact that the points system is not gender neutral, but this issue is not well addressed in the provisions of Bill C-11.[92]

The government's proposals regarding the family class also consolidate some of the trends of the 1990s. While the premises that underwrite the family class are not questioned, the definition of family is expanded to include common-law and same-sex couples. Additionally, the government is proposing to raise the age for dependent children from under 19 to under 22. These changes have been welcomed. But, most significantly, the duration of sponsorship has been reduced for spouses, common-law partners, and same-sex partners from 10 years to three years.[93] This is particularly important for women, who are over-represented in this category. And, as pointed out in Chapter Two, sponsorship provisions may work to increase women's dependency and vulnerability. There remains more to be done, as the National Association of Women and the Law has summarized:

> Reducing the duration of sponsorship agreements is a positive, albeit very tentative, step towards the development of more just, equal and effective policy and legislation for immigrant families ... [but c]urrent research on the need to radically rethink the sponsorship system, moving away from reducing sponsorship obligations towards eliminating the sponsorship framework altogether must be explored and assessed by CIC.[94]

While reducing the duration of the sponsoring relationship, the government has moved to strengthen sponsorship obligations, thus keeping recommendations that were floated throughout the 1990s. In those situations where a sponsor defaults, the government is proposing new measures that will allow the state to recover costs by garnishment of wages, for example. Those people convicted of domestic abuse will not be allowed to sponsor, nor will individuals receiving social assistance (with the exception of those who receive it for reasons of disability). The latter provision has been criticized by some groups who view "family reunification as a fundamental right of everyone"; the measures are viewed as unacceptable because economic status should not be a bar to family reunification.[95]

The proposals around the selection model and the family class are characterized as within the realm of "opening the door." However, the other significant focus within Bill C-11, and one that has attracted considerable attention, is the measures around control and enforcement proposed to "close the door." Control has been characterized as involving the ability

- to deny selection and entry of individuals in the interests of preserving the health, security or economic interest of Canadians;
- to remove from Canada those who are without legitimate status; and
- to strip status and remove from Canada those whose conduct justifies our ultimate noncriminal sanction, exile from Canada through deportation.[96]

Indeed, it has been argued, "The heavy enforcement emphasis with which Bill C-11 was presented promotes negative stereotypes about refugees and immigrants and caters to xenophobia and racism in Canadian society."[97] Groups such as the Canadian Council For Refugees and the Canadian Bar Association have charged that Bill C-11 reduces the existing rights of immigrants and refugees. The Bill contains a number of important provisions regarding refugee determination. It is beyond the scope of this chapter, however, to analyze them in detail. However, some "tough" control measures proposed by the Liberal government should be noted. These measures took on greater salience following September 11, 2001 when former Minister of Immigration Elinor Caplan argued that speedy passage of the Bill was necessary because its provisions addressed concerns about security.[98]

The Bill lists the grounds immigration officers can use to bar individuals from Canada. Inadmissibility grounds include "security, human and international rights violations, criminality, organized crime, health, financial reasons, misrepresentation and non-compliance, inadmissible family members." Organized criminality (transnational activities such as people smuggling, trafficking in persons, and money laundering) and misrepresentation are new categories of inadmissibility.[99] Additionally, the terms "terrorism," "membership in a terrorist organization," and "security of Canada" are retained within Bill C-11, however, there is ongoing debate over defining these inherently political terms. For this reason, it is argued that the Bill "leaves refugees and immigrants impermissibly susceptible to unprincipled, arbitrary, and even unconstitutional decision-making with wholly inadequate opportunities for meaningful review or recourse."[100]

Permanent residents face losing their right of appeal to the Immigration Appeal Division "to review circumstances surrounding their loss of status or deportation when their case is based on broad grounds of inadmissibility, such as criminal acts."[101] "Serious criminality" defined as a crime is punishable in Canada by a sentence of at least two years. The Canadian Council for Refugees cautioned in its government brief that permanent residents can also be deported if found to be engaged in people smuggling, with no conviction required. It added, "thus a permanent resident could be deported without an appeal based simply on allegations of minimal involvement with smugglers to help a family member escape persecution."[102] This proposal has been criticized on the basis that it removes permanent residents from the sphere of "due process" under the law.[103]

Permanent residents would also be further distinguished from Canadian citizens through the introduction of a new status document. Bill c-11 includes provisions for what the government terms a "fraud resistant document indicating state-of-the-art security features including a tamper proof photo image";[104] other information included on the card would be "permanent resident's name, signature, date of birth, country of birth, country of citizenship, sex, eye colour, height, date of entry in Canada, place of landing, and immigrant category."[105] The government's initial position was that this measure would allow foreign carriers to recognize the bearer of the document as a permanent resident of Canada and thereby facilitate travel. But the introduction of identity cards raises a number of other issues and concerns. In August 2000, the Ontario Council of Agencies Serving Immigrants (OCASI), responding to the predecessor of Bill c-11 (Bill c-31) flagged a number of these issues. Firstly, OCASI argued that this type of document—renewable every five years—serves to underscore the "transitory nature" of permanent residence status. Additionally, OCASI pointed out,

> [t]here remains a lack of clarity about the type, amount of information or data that will be visibly or digitally stored on the card; who or which organizations will have access to this information and under what conditions; whether information will be disclosed/transferred between jurisdictions, government departments or enforcement bodies.[106]

The government's claims regarding the need for a reliable proof-of-status document are not unique. Identity cards are also associated with fraud control measures. In a 1999 newspaper column, writer Diane Francis extolled the virtues of a national identity card as a way to address what she saw as widespread abuses of Canada's social services. While she called for a card very similar to what the government proposed to be provided to each and every resident, her specific focus was very much on immigrants and refugees. She implied that all immigrants and refugees are counterfeiting and selling social insurance numbers and defrauding Ontario's Health Insurance Program (OHIP), and she accused "bogus" refugees of engaging in scams to access public housing and welfare.[107]

The control measures within Bill c-11 do little to dispel these negative stereotypes of refugees and immigrants as criminals, as threats to security, and as inappropriate drains on social service resources. In many ways these negative stereotypes have been reinforced by recent events. In the aftermath of the attacks on the World Trade Centre and the

Pentagon, the Liberal government moved quickly to introduce iden-tification cards before Bill C-11 passed through Parliament. As of June 2002, the "Maple Leaf Card" will be issued to new immigrants arriv-ing in Canada. Whereas initially the card was constructed as a "secure document" providing "easier identification by transportation compa-nies and clearer recognition of the rights associated with permanent res-ident status,"[108] it is now billed as an element of CIC's five-part security strategy. This strategy is part of the Liberal government's broader Anti-Terrorism Plan.[109]

Immigration Changes Post September 11, 2001

In fall 2001, the Chrétien government announced a package of measures designed to address national security and new global realities. Initial actions included the freezing of assets held by those believed to be linked to terrorists and the appointment of a cabinet committee to head Canada's anti-terrorist efforts. Subsequently, the government also introduced an omnibus anti-terrorism bill, $280 million targeted at technology upgrades and increased border control.[110] The Canadian Security and Intelligence Service (CSIS) received additional funding. Within these initiatives, $49 million was directed to Citizenship and Immigration Canada to fast-track the permanent resident card, for front-end security screening of refugee claimants, to increase deportation activity, and to hire 100 new staff to enforce upgraded security at ports of entry.[111] Security and control issues have always been an aspect of Canadian immigration policy, as detailed in Chapter Two; however, at the present time they have moved to occupy a much more prominent position in public debate.

Shortly after the events in New York and Washington, the *Globe and Mail* reported that Canadian border guards and customs officials were issued an internal alert to help them identify possible terrorists. In addi-tion to detailing employment and background characteristics, the bul-letin indicated that "particular attention should be given to any male between 16 and 50 who has traveled to at least two [of 16 listed] loca-tions." Almost all of the countries have "majority Muslim populations which it [the alert] describes as having the 'zones of conflict or terror-ist training centres.'"[112] This type of profiling invariably dispropor-tionately targets males from certain groups and raises concerns over equal treatment and civil rights. Moreover, this points to how processes of racialization may find expression in those deemed terrorist threats today (e.g., those of Arab origin, Muslims, and people of colour).

Canadian public opinion in the wake of September 11 appears to have swung towards favouring more stringent control and security.[113] Indeed, this has prompted some to suggest that public attitudes in the immediate aftermath of disaster are akin to the conditions that gave rise to McCarthyism in the U.S. during the 1950s and to the internment of Japanese Canadians during World War II.[114] In this climate the government also introduced an anti-terrorism bill in October 2001, which has generated much controversy. Provisions that would give law enforcement greater powers, including "preventive arrest of terrorism suspects" and "investigative hearing compelling witnesses to give secret evidence," have been criticized by many legal scholars for involving an unacceptable infringement on individual rights and liberties.[115] Additionally, the Canadian Council of Refugees, among others, has pointed out that definitions of "terrorist activities" and "terrorist groups" are too broad. They state that these terms "introduce vagueness, confusion, and politicization and [could] lead to arbitrary, inconsistent, and discriminatory decisions."[116] This type of legislation, according to critics, "could further stigmatize immigrants based on their ethnicity."[117]

GENDER BASED ANALYSIS AND IMMIGRATION POLICY 1993-2001

Over the 1990s gender-based analysis came to play a role within immigration policy development. During the Liberal consultations of 1994 gender did not figure prominently.[118] By the time independent consultants prepared *Not Just Numbers* in 1997, there was an explicit acknowledgement of the need to undertake a gender-based analysis, although the advisory group report neglected to do so. Nevertheless, a number of groups who appeared before the Minister of Immigration in 1998 during the public consultation process challenged the government to undertake a gender-based analysis of proposed immigration directions. These groups did play an active role in drawing the government's attention to the gender, race, and class-based hierarchies within the report's recommendations.[119] Subsequent assessments of *Not Just Numbers* also emphasized the lack of a gender-based analysis.[120] In other words, the government's stated international commitment—to implement gender-based analysis of future policies and legislation—provided a small space for groups to advocate for change and to take the government to task. Unfortunately, this was not immediately evident in the government's discussion paper on immigration, *Building on a Strong Foundation for the 21st Century* (1998). Both the advisory group consultation and the discussions around the white paper "featured little opportunity for public consultation and made little effort to elicit the expertise and experiences of immigrant and refugee women, or women's organizations at large, in developing new legislative frameworks."[121]

Building on a Strong Foundation for the 21st Century was however the subject of an independent gender analysis. In this case, the government, through Status of Women Canada, provided resources to the National Association of Women and the Law (NAWL) to

- ◆ facilitate broader involvement of women's organizations in analysis of current Canadian immigration and refugee law and policy; and
- ◆ To develop a document highlighting the action required to ensure that Canada's immigration and refugee legislation protects and promotes the equality of women.[122]

In March 1999 the NAWL's Ad Hoc Committee on Gender Analysis[123] produced its assessment. The report underscored the importance of developing a "perspective-dependent" approach by emphasizing that "gender analysis only addresses half the problem if not accompanied by race analysis of such legislation and policy."[124] It called on the government to actively increase the participation of women's groups in the policy development process.

> Good policy must respond to the realities of immigrant and refugee women's lives.... Effective participation of women's groups in immigration and refugee protection policy development would also benefit future legislation and women's groups in Canada by encouraging an exchange of knowledge and expertise on issues facing immigrant and refugee women, methods for conducting and reporting gender analysis and facilitating women and other stakeholders' meaningful participation in the policy development process.[125]

This call comes at a time when the Liberal government's record of providing resources to advocacy groups and facilitating their access to the state leaves much to be desired. Shortly after securing its first mandate, the Liberal government folded the Women's Program, Secretary of State—which provided core and project funding to women's groups—

into the Status of Women Canada. The Canadian Advisory Council on the Status of Women was eliminated completely.[126] Additionally, advocacy groups, including women's and ethnocultural organizations, have experienced funding cuts. This affects their ability to effectively participate in consultations, generate policy alternatives, or participate in other aspects of policy design. As Judy Rebick, former president of the National Action Committee on the Status of Women (NAC), recently wrote,

> Advocacy groups like NAC, by definition exist to push the government beyond where the government wants to go. If NAC had stayed within the bounds set by government, we wouldn't have won a lot of rights we take for granted today.[127]

Like the Ad Hoc Committee on Gender Analysis, Rebick's comments reinforce the importance of involving independent women's groups within the policy process.

Possibly some community-based involvement might be developed and facilitated by the new Gender Based Analysis Unit established by Citizenship and Immigration Canada. The unit, which is staffed by a manager and one senior analyst, came into operation in 2000. In the words of its manager, Sandra Harder, "its broadest, most encompassing mandate is to build capacity for the ability to incorporate gender-based analysis into the policy, program, and legislative processes of the department." Additionally, the importance of maintaining links and working partnerships with non-governmental groups is emphasized.[128] To some extent the Gender Based Analysis Unit within Citizenship and Immigration Canada is an example of "state feminism"[129] in action. However, it is too early to assess this initiative's effectiveness in bringing a gender-based perspective to policy development and design or in acting as an access point for women's groups to the policy process.

It should be noted that in its press releases regarding Bill C-11, introduced one year after the establishment of the Gender Based Analysis Unit, the government has been careful to emphasize that the Bill does contain provisions that "reinforce the government's commitment to gender equality."[130] The content of the provisions remain unspecified, though certainly the provisions around the reduction of sponsorship duration and the expansion of family class category to include same-sex couples could be seen as examples of this. But, in terms of the other issues women's groups have raised, such as the nature of the points-based selection system and the relations of dependency within sponsorship provisions, the government does not appear to have moved. Indeed, as a women's umbrella group pointed out during the Common's committee hearings,

> Although we recognize that a number of important reforms are being introduced with Bill C-11, we are deeply concerned about the Bill's lack of progress for immigrant and refugee women.[131]

Women's activism around immigration policy changes and specifically Bill C-11, however, did prompt an amendment requiring that a gender-based analysis of the Act's impact be included in annual reports to Parliament.[132]

PROPOSED CITIZENSHIP CHANGES 1999-2001

The Liberal government introduced Bill C-16, "An Act Respecting Canadian Citizenship," in November 1999. Although this Bill received Third Reading in May 2000 it died on the order paper when Jean Chrétien called the November election. As a result, the provisions of the existing Citizenship Act remain in force. It is useful to briefly examine Bill C-16 because it is indicative of the directions that the Liberal government is seeking to pursue. However, it should be noted that as of March 2002, no new Bill has yet been introduced.

While Bill C-16 did outline how people acquire Canadian citizenship, it also contained a number of provisions that would allow the denial or revocation of Canadian citizenship in certain circumstances. Its provisions gave the minister and cabinet the power to deny citizenship in those cases where it is believed that it would not be in the "public interest." The definition of "public interest" remained unspecified. The Act also expanded the list of grounds that would prohibit the granting of citizenship.[133] Many of the measures contained in the proposed Act made accessing formal citizenship tougher.

However, in the public debate around Bill C-16 (and its predecessor Bill C-63), the most controversial provisions related to the residency requirements. Originally, the government proposed that immigrants must be physically present in the country for three years (1,095 days) of a five-year period before being naturalized as Canadian citizens. It also proposed that immigrants take the citizenship test without the help of interpreters. Both measures were the focus of a counter-campaign launched by lawyers, ethnocultural groups, and non-governmental groups, which also made use of the idea of the new global econ-omy. In the debate, many argued that Canada could lose potential busi-ness dollars because investors would go elsewhere if the citizenship test was too difficult. Similarly, residency requirements were attacked on the basis that they did not "recognize the globalization of business" and that, in fact, people could be committed to Canada "by having a business here, employing people … paying taxes, even it you aren't physically pre-sent."[134] To some extent the government noted these concerns, as it sub-sequently proposed changes to the residency requirement to three years in a six-year period and proposed permitting the use of translators for the citizenship test.

The proposed Citizenship Act that died on the order paper and the new Immigration and Refugee Protection Act are designed to meet the perceived needs of Canada in the twenty-first century. They are sug-gestive of the times—they are framed by a particular reading of glob-alization and its consequences for the nation-state by policy-makers. However, gender, class, and race dichotomies present in immigration and citizenship are not explicitly challenged, although they have become much more complex in the twenty-first century. The government seeks to attract highly skilled workers from previously excluded coun-tries; thus, there are some pilot projects for the recruitment of high-tech temporary workers in India, and the majority of the participants in the business class have been from Hong Kong. Yet, despite greater geo-graphical heterogeneity in where immigrants come from, it is the cir-culation of particular kinds of people that are favoured—specifically men from a class-advantaged background. On the one hand, the increas-ing emphasis on attracting highly skilled workers and self-sufficient workers as prospective citizens preserves existing hierarchical patterns present since the 1960s. On the other hand, "highly skilled" is now defined in a different way, because Canada has moved from searching for particular occupations to a selection model that emphasizes trans-ferable skills. It should be noted that Canada is not alone in its pursuit of highly skilled labour; many other countries have embarked on a similar path. As a result, the international dimensions of migration have been impressed on policy-makers. Additionally, in the wake of the events of September 2001, the pursuit of immigrants with "the right stuff" is also framed by security concerns connected to the "war on terrorism"—which, it may be argued, is replacing the security concerns linked to the Cold War era as discussed in Chapter Two.

THE GROWING INTERNATIONALIZATION OF IMMIGRATION POLICY (1993-2001)

Changes in the direction of Canadian immigration policy take place within a policy field that has to some extent always been international-ist in focus. However, the terms of state power and state regulation are being reinscribed and deployed in new ways at the moment. It has been argued that states that have adopted neo-liberalism and pursued conti-nental integration have not necessarily pursued more open immigra-tion policies and freer circulation of people. But what has occurred are regional attempts to "harmonize or at least to co-ordinate migration policies."[135] Take, for example, the North American Free Trade Agreement (NAFTA) which involves Canada, the United States, and Mexico. Despite the fact that Canada and the U.S. are each other's largest trade partner, there are no formal provisions regarding the move-ment of people within NAFTA, other than temporary circulation of par-ticular categories of business persons. Nevertheless, there is some attempt to manage elements of Canada-U.S. border-crossing through initiatives such as the 1995 "Canada-United States Accord on Our Shared Border":

The Accord commits governments to
* promoting international trade;
* facilitating the movement of people;
* providing enhanced protection against drugs, smuggling, and the illegal and irregular movement of people; and
* reducing costs to both governments and people.[136]

An increasingly important aspect of this relationship, whose roots are found in World War II and the Cold War, is the attempt to co-ordi-nate security agencies.[137]

In the wake of the September 2001 attacks in New York and Washington, there have been calls for a North American security perimeter which would see the harmonization of some or all aspects of Canadian and U.S. immigration policies. The concept of a security perimeter is not new; indeed, the American Ambassador to Canada, Paul Celucci, and prominent business groups were already extolling its merits in July 2001.[138] While the exact specifics of a security perimeter are not clear, it is likely to remain on the policy agenda, as Canadians and Americans try to reconcile how to police a border without jeopardiz-ing cross-border movement of goods and investment. A security perime-ter raises a number of sovereignty questions for Canada.

Nations throughout the world, Canada included, are moving to address control and security issues raised by the movement of refugees and people. This issue will remain on the agenda for the foreseeable future, because it is not likely that refugee-generating events, such as wars, are about to disappear. It is in this area that the sharing of security information can lead to a reduction of state sovereignty.

> Coping with refugee movements in the name of national sovereignty entails inevitable diminution of the same sovereignty as a thick and complex web of supranational and international relationships at the political, diplomatic, military, policing, and security levels grows up among host countries to maintain surveillance and control over refugee movements.... [E]xtra-national ties have proliferated with the unification of Europe and the move toward regional integration in North America, and under increasing policy pressure of global refugee and migration movements.[139]

However, Canada has sometimes pursued distinct policies. It is notable that on the issue of gender and refugee status, Canada was the first country to formally make provisions for the admission of refugees facing "gender persecution" (especially women who might face inhuman treatment for transgressing the moral/social norms of their society) through the discretion of the Canadian Immigration and Refugee Board (IRB). The IRB is the body that hears and determines the cases of refugee claimants who arrive in Canada. Guidelines regarding gender persecution claims can be traced to international discussions, involving the European Union as well as the United Nations High Commission for Refugees and international human rights non-governmental organizations.[140] Once Canada had adopted these guidelines, it paved the way for other countries, such as Australia and the United States to articulate for themselves the standards by which gender-related persecution claims might be assessed.[141]

Nonetheless, it should be noted that Sherene Razack's analysis of actual gender-based persecution cases that have gone before the IRB since Canada adopted these guidelines suggests that the standards by which gender persecution is judged are not entirely without problems. Razack finds that "gender persecution," as it is employed in the discourse surrounding refugee cases, is racialized in the sense that Canada, the First World, and white people in general are set up as morally and ethically superior to the Third World and its people. Looking at cases involving survivors of domestic violence, for one example, and women who have transgressed the mores of their birthplace society, for another, Razack argues:

> ... women's claims are most likely to succeed when they present themselves as victims of dysfunctional, exceptionally patriarchal cultures and states. The successful asylum seeker must cast herself as the cultural Other, that is, as someone fleeing from a more primitive culture.[142]

In this way gender-based persecution becomes "visible" through a lens that relies on stereotyping.

In addition to gender-based persecution, there are other areas of refugee policy that have reflected the changing international environment. One major example of this is the idea of "safe third country" in refugee policy. This concept stems from the idea that once an asylum claimant has made a case in one country and, presumably, had a fair hearing, he/she should not be entitled to make a claim in another country. This concept was introduced among the countries of the European Union during the 1980s to "prevent multiple applications for asylum in several states simultaneously or successively."[143] By 1988, Canada was influenced by these developments and introduced "safe third country" provisions to its refugee legislation.[144] Although Canada's use of "safe third country" appears to allow a greater possibility of due process being given to refugee claimants than in the case of countries belonging to the European Union, it is notable that when Sergio Marchi was minister of Citizenship and Immigration he outlined his desire to foster shared responsibility agreements with other [Western] countries on asylum seekers to protect Canada from too many claimants.[145] Moreover, the entire discussion of "safe third country" has proven to be controversial among immigrant and refugee-serving groups who fear that this might lead Canada to send back legitimate refugees to situations of torture and even death.[146] It is for this reason that some analysts have also suggested that the Canadian state retain considerable—even augmented—control and sovereignty when it comes to the refugee field.[147]

In addition to refugee developments which reflect the reciprocal influences between the domestic and international levels, one may also see stiff competition for skilled people—or at least the perception of competition among business-oriented research think tanks. For example, the Fraser Institute has argued that Canada needs to be more aggressive in attracting skilled immigrants who might otherwise go to the U.S. or Australia.[148] Interestingly, it appears that the overall number of skilled (independent) immigrants applying to Australia specifically goes down when there are more applications to the United States, but goes up in Australia when they are also applying to Canada.[149] In trying to explain this, Cobb-Clark and Connolly state:

> This suggests that there is a complementarity between the potential migrant streams facing Canada and Australia or perhaps in the policy decisions made by Canadian and Australian policymakers. Australia modeled its skilled migration program in large part on Canada's program, including the original points test for skilled migrants. Alternatively, it might imply that migrants who were unsuccessful in migrating to the United States then face a choice of migrating either to Canada or Australia.[150]

This leads us to the way in which the Canadian government has increasingly sought to work with other immigrant-receiving states, which relates to the strongly held perception that issues such as people-smuggling, organized crime, and asylum policies require sharing of information and resources because they cannot be addressed by one country alone.[151] As Gerald Dirks notes:

> … the Canadian government values and utilizes its formal and informal links with those global and regional intergovernmental committees, agencies and processes … that already recognize international migration as part of their mandates. Moreover, Canada is offering to share its considerable immigration management expertise with governments such as those in Central Europe which now find themselves having to deal with growing numbers of migrants possibly for the first time.[152]

A pertinent example of information-sharing efforts and the internationalization of policy and policy research is seen in the Metropolis project, involving and spearheaded by Canada. The Metropolis project stems from discussions in 1994 between Canadian Meyer Burstein (of Citizenship and Immigration Canada) and American Demetrios Papademetriou (of the Carnegie Endowment for International Peace), both of whom wanted to create an international forum for policy-makers, academics, and non-governmental organizations in the immigration field. These "stakeholders" were brought together to address how immigration affects cities and how immigrants integrate into urban settings.[153] (The name

"Metropolis" was testimony to the fact that across advanced industrial-ized countries today, immigration is mainly an urban phenomenon.)

In Canada, the research component of Metropolis comprises four centres of research excellence (involving some 15 universities in Vancouver, Edmonton, Toronto, and Montreal) which were created jointly by the Department of Citizenship and Immigration Canada (CIC) and the Social Sciences and Humanities Research Council (SSHRC). SSHRC is the main funding body for research in the social sciences and humanities and has referred to the Metropolis project as its "most sig-nificant program of targeted research support,"[154] because of the com-mitted funding involved (SSHRC and the government are committed to spending $8 million on the project over the six-year-period 1996 to 2002).[155] It is also because the Metropolis model of research aims to bring research findings by academics directly to non-governmental orga-nizations and government policy-makers in an effort to improve immi-gration and settlement policies and practices.[156] The design of the Metropolis project has worried some academics who value their auton-omy and independence from government in pursuing knowledge and research.[157] It is also remains to be seen if and how the research gener-ated through the Metropolis project will impact on government policy discussions and developments. Indeed, the Metropolis project has been granted a second mandate for the years 2002 to 2007.

Nonetheless, the Metropolis project's development abroad attests to its influence. By 2000, there were 21 governments involved in the project: Canada and the U.S., Argentina, Austria, Denmark, France, Germany, Greece, Italy, the Netherlands, Norway, Portugal, Spain, Sweden, Switzerland, the United Kingdom, Israel, South Africa, Hong Kong, Australia, and New Zealand. In addition, the project had attracted international organizations as members, including the Commission of the European Union, UNESCO, the Migration Policy Group, Quartiers en Crise, the International Centre for Migration Policy Development, and the International Organization for Migration.[158]

According to Meyer Burstein, who spearheaded Canada's involve-ment in Metropolis, what unites different countries and international organizations in this effort is a desire for leadership and knowledge, and a "conviction that migration cannot be managed without interna-tional cooperation—cooperation on the policy front and cooperation on the research front."[159] As Burstein states:

> We need international comparative research in order to sort out
> the effectiveness and appropriateness of our domestic policies and

> programs. And we need to exchange information about best prac-
> tices. About the most effective responses to the practical chal-
> lenges that face us in our cities. Collectively, we—the Metropolis
> partners—hold a portfolio of such policy and program solutions....
> And while the strategies employed by one country can rarely be
> transferred, in their entirety, to another, elements of those strate-
> gies can, and should, be traded.[160]

It should be noted that in addition to exchanges between policy-makers in governments and international organizations, this kind of forum might also provide some opportunity for non-governmental organizations working in the immigration sphere to create transnational linkages. Clearly then, Canada has come a distance from the post-war policy articulation of Mackenzie King, who insisted that immigration policy was to be a domestic matter.

CONCLUSION

This chapter has looked at contemporary changes in immigration and citizenship policy. Our examination suggests that policy-makers have invoked a particular reading of globalization in the last decade, one which emphasizes such neo-liberal ideas as global competitiveness, individual self-sufficiency, economic performance, and fiscal restraint. As a result, Canadian immigration policy in particular has emphasized the need to attract highly skilled, well-educated, flexible workers as prospective citizens, to compete in a rapidly changing global economy. This construction of the model citizen tends to favour male applicants from countries with extensive educational and training opportunities, thus serving to reinforce current gender and ethnic/racial exclusions within the policy. At the same time that it has become more difficult to enter Canada and obtain citizenship, the actual social rights associated with citizenship have eroded through a series of administrative and regulatory changes such as the right-of-landing fee. While elements of state sovereignty may be challenged by refugee movements, the Canadian case suggests that, in the main, immigration is one area where the nation-state continues to exercise sovereignty through the selection and control of who gains entry into the country.

In addition, immigration policy is increasingly internationalized. Whereas in the 1940s and 1950s the policy was said to be primarily a matter of domestic concern, today policy-makers perceive it as an area in which Canada both influences and is influenced by developments abroad. Thus, the stress on how contemporary immigration must be situated in the international context and in relation to globalization is qualitatively different than in the past.

Immigration and citizenship reforms are situated in a set of shifting ideas about the contradictory role of the state and the state's relations to its citizens. On the one hand, the state has moved from trying to actively manage some aspects of the economy through immigration policy. For example, Canada is abandoning the practice of matching immigrants to particular labour market niches. On the other, the Canadian state is maintaining and reasserting its control over those categories deemed less desirable, such as women (in the family class) and refugees. With the costs of integration increasingly privatized, the state has more flexibility to cut existing immigrant settlement services.

The emerging "ideal" immigrant/model citizen more often than not will be a highly skilled, well-educated, English- or French-speaking, upper-class male. Viewing people in terms of "skills" therefore has consequences. Ironically, however, while employment is often linked to citizenship, some new immigrants encounter a labour market that does not allocate jobs on the basis of skills and education alone. "Investments" in human capital abroad (in education and training and credentials) might not be recognized. In addition, membership in a particular group may negatively effect employment decisions. This is further taken up in the consideration of employment equity in Chapter 5. The next chapter deals with multiculturalism.

◆ NOTES ◆

1 Paul Hirst and Grahame Thompson, "Globalization and the Future of the Nation State," *Economy and Society* 24.3 (1995): 409.

2 Saskia Sassen, *Globalization and its Discontents* (New York: New Press, 1998) 5.

3 Yasmeen Abu-Laban, "welcome/STAY OUT: The Contradiction of Canadian Integration and Immigration Policies at the Millennium," *Canadian Ethnic Studies* XXX.3 (1998): 200.

4 Maureen Molot and Fen Osler Hampson, *Canada Among Nations* (Don Mills: Oxford University Press, 2000) 65.

5 Barrie McKenna and Campbell Clark, "Fortify the border, Congress tells Bush," *Globe and Mail*, 4 October 2001: A4.

6 Christina Gabriel and Laura Macdonald, "Border Anxieties: Changing Discourses on the Canada-US Border," paper Presented to the Annual Meeting of the International Studies Association, Chicago, Illinois, 21-14 February 2001.

7 "Statement of the Honourable Sergio Marchi" (Ottawa: House of Commons,1 November 1994).

8 Bill C-16 "An Act Respecting Canadian Citizenship" did not pass because Jean Chrétien called the 2000 Federal election. The Liberals have not introduced new legislation. Bill C-11, "Immigration and Refugee Protection Act" received Royal Assent in November 2001.

9 Art Hanger, in Canada, *House of Commons Debates* 133, 013 (2 February 1994) 803; cited by Abu-Laban, "welcome/STAY OUT" 197.

10 Della Kirkham, "The Reform Party of Canada: A Discourse on Race, Ethnicity, and Equality," *Racism and Social Inequality in Canada*, ed. Vic Satzewich (Toronto: Thompson, 1998) 248-55.

11 Kirkham 265.

12 Canada, Citizenship and Immigration Canada (CIC), *Immigration Consultations Report* (Hull: Supply and Services Canada, 1994) 1.

13 Doug Nord, "Strengthening Society II: Immigration Policy," *Canadian Public Policy: Globalization and Political Parties*, ed. Andrew Stritch and Andrew Johnson (Toronto: Copp Clark, 1997) 157.

14 CIC, *Immigration Consultations Report* 16-17.

15 Abu-Laban, "welcome/STAY OUT" 199.

16 CIC, *A Broader Vision: Immigration and Citizenship Plan 1995-2000. Annual Report to Parliament* (Hull: Supply and Services Canada, 1994) xi.

17 Sedef Arat-Koc, "Neo-Liberalism, State Restructuring, and Immigration: Changes in Canadian Policies in the 1990s," *Journal of Canadian Studies* 34.2 (Summer 1999): 36.

18 Stephen McBride, "Policy from What? NeoLiberal and Human Capital Theoretical Foundations of Recent Canadian Labour Market Policy," *Restructuring and Resistance: Canadian Public Policy in an Age of Global Capital*, ed. Mike Burke, Colin Moores and John Shields (Halifax: Fernwood, 2000) 161.

19 See McBride.

20 CIC, *A Broader Vision 1995-2000* 13.

21 CIC, *A Broader Vision 1995-2000* 13.

22 These facets of economic contribution are outlined in CIC, "Canada Changes Immigration Criteria for Skilled Workers," *News Release* 95.20 (17 November 1995): 2.

23 Arat-Koc, "Neo-Liberalism, State Restructuring, and Immigration" 38.

24 CIC, *A Broader Vision 1994-1995* 13-15.

25 Abu-Laban, "welcome/STAY OUT" 199.

26 For a deeper discussion regarding immigrants and foreign credentials see Peter Li, "The Market Worth of Immigrants' Educational Credentials," *Canadian Public Policy* XXVI.1 (March 2001): 23-38.

27 CIC, Strategic Research, Analysis, and Information Branch, Policy Sector, *Facts and Figures. Overview of Immigration* (Ottawa: Minister of Supply and Services, 1994) 22, 36, 50.

28 Arat-Koc, "Neo-Liberalism, State Restructuring, and Immigration" 49.

29 See, for example, 10 issues identified for discussion in public consultations, although it should be noted that issue five did ask "do we need different strategies to integrate three main categories of immigrants (e.g. family class, independent, and refugee)?" CIC, "Facts and Issues."

30 Derrick Thomas, "The Social Welfare Implications of Immigrant Family Sponsorship Default: An Analysis of Data from Census Metropolitan Area of Toronto: Final Report" (Ottawa: Citizenship and Immigration Canada, 1996) 42; cited by Ontario Council of Agencies Serving Immigrants

(OCASI), "Response to the Immigration Legislative Review Advisory Group Report 'Not Just Numbers, A Canadian Framework for Future Immigration,'" 4 March 1998: 7.

31 CIC, *A Broader Vision: Immigration Plan, 1996 Report to Parliament* (Ottawa: Minister of Supply and Services, 1995) 11.

32 Arat-Koc, "Neo-Liberalism, State Restructuring, and Immigration" 44.

33 Andrew Brouwer, "Protection with a Price Tag: The Head Tax for Refugees and Their Families Must Go" (Toronto: Maytree Foundation, 2000) 1. <www.maytree.com/publications_headtax.html>.

34 Arat-Koc, "Neo-Liberalism, State Restructuring, and Immigration" 45.

35 Canadian Council for Refugees (CCR) "Report on Systemic Racism and Discrimination in Canadian Refugee and Immigration Policies," 1 November 2000: 6. <http:www.web.net/~ccr/antiracrep.htm>.

36 CCR, "Report on Systemic Racism and Discrimination" 6.

37 CCR, "Impact of the Right of Landing Fee," February 1997: 2. <http//www.web.net/~ccr/headtax2.htm>.

38 National Action Committee on the Status of Women, cited by CCR, "Impact of the Right of Landing Fee" 1.

39 CCR, "Impact of the Right of Landing Fee" 2.

40 Brouwer 2.

41 Brouwer 3.

42 "Broaden debate on immigration on changes," editorial, *Toronto Star*, 2 March 1998: A16.

43 Nord 160.

44 Immigration Legislative Review Advisory Group, *Not Just Numbers: A Canadian Framework for Future Immigration* (Ottawa: Minister of Public Works and Government Services Canada, 1997). Hereinafter cited as *Not Just Numbers*.

45 *Not Just Numbers* v.

46 CIC, "Speaking Notes for the Honourable Lucienne Robillard, Minister of Citizenship and Immigration for the Launch of the Legislative Review Consultation Process," 27 February 1998: 2.

47 *Not Just Numbers* 6.

48 Calgary Immigrant Aid Society, "Response to *Not Just Numbers*: Canadian Framework for Immigration," 2 February 1998: 2.

49 *Not Just Numbers* 8.

50 *Not Just Numbers* 8.

51 CIC, "Building on a Strong Foundation for the 21st Century: The Legislative Review Process," 2 June 2000 <http://cicnet.ci.gc.ca/English/about/policy/lr/e_lr03.html>.

52 *Not Just Numbers* 126.

53 *Not Just Numbers* 51.

54 *Not Just Numbers* 45.

55 *Not Just Numbers* 8.

56 Alan Simmons, "Racism and Canadian Immigration Policy," Satzewich 109.

57 Metro Toronto Chinese and Southeast Asian Legal Clinic, "Submission to the Minister of Immigration" 4 March 1998: 8.

58 See for example, Ross Howard, "Robillard seeks to cool immigrant policy heat," *Globe and Mail*, 28 February 1998; Bill Mah, "Language no barrier to immigration, minister told" *Edmonton Journal*, 2 March 1998.

59 Anthony H. Richmond, *Global Apartheid: Refugees, Racism, and the New World Order* (Toronto: Oxford University Press, 1994) 136.

60 *Not Just Numbers* 54.

61 *Not Just Numbers* 69.

62 *Not Just Numbers* 76.

63 Stuart Hall and David Held, "Citizens and Citizenship," *New Times*, ed. Stuart Hall and Martin Jacques (London: Verso, 1989) 175.

64 *Not Just Numbers* 39.

65 Ontario Council of Agencies Serving Immigrants (OCASI) "Response to the ILR 'Not Just Numbers' Submission to Honourable Lucienne Robillard, Minister of Citizenship and Immigration," 4 March 1998: 8.

66 *Not Just Numbers* 39-40.

67 Peter Wong, "Response to the Report: Not Just Numbers" 1 February 1998: 4.

68 CIC, *Building on a Strong Foundation for the 21st Century* (Ottawa: Minister of Public Works and Government Services, 1998) 1.

69 Pat Martin (Winnipeg-NDP) <www.parl.gc.ca/36/2/parlbus/cham...debates/102_1200-e.1>.

70 CIC, "Notes for an Address by the Honourable Elinor Caplan, Minister of Citizenship and Immigration to the Standing Committee on Citizenship and Immigration on Bill C-11," Ottawa, 1 March 2001 <www.cic.gc.ca/English/press/speech/c11.html>.

71 Canadian Bar Association, "Submission of the National Citizenship and Immigration Law Section to Senate Standing Committee on Social Affairs, Science and Technology," 2 October 2001: 1-2;

<www.cba.org/News/Archives/ 2001-10-02- submission.asp>.

72 Robert Fife, "Liberals spar over changes to the Immigration Act," *National Post*, 19 March 2001.

73 Canadian Bar Association 5.

74 Maytree Foundation, "Brief to the Standing Committee on Citizenship and Immigration regarding Bill C-11, Immigration and Refugee Protection Act," 26 March 2001: 4 <www.maytree.com>.

75 Canadian Bar Association 5.

76 EGALE, "Brief to the House of Commons Standing Committee on Citizenship and Immigration," 27 March 2001: 4 <www.egale.ca/ documents/c-11 committeebrief. htm>.

77 CIC, "Bill C-11, Explanation of Proposed Regulations," October 2001: 2 <www.cic.gc.ca/English/ about/policy/c11-refs.html>.

78 Canadian Bar Association 6.

79 Maytree Foundation 5-6.

80 CIC, "Bill C-11, Immigration and Refugee Protection Act: Overview, The Reasons for a New Law" <www.cic.gc./ca/English/ about/policy/c11-overview.html>.

81 CIC, "Bill C-11, Immigration and Refugee Protection Act: Overview,"

82 CIC, "Bill C-11, Immigration and Refugee Protection Act: Overview."

83 CIC, "Bill C-11, Immigration and Refugee Protection Act: Overview" 12.

84 CIC, "Bill C-11, Immigration and Refugee Protection Act: Overview" 12.

85 CIC, *Building on a Strong Foundation* 29.

86 See Guy Standing, "Global Feminization through Flexible Labour," *World Development* 17.7 (1989).

87 For a discussion, see Standing Committee on Citizenship and Immigration, *Facilitating the Entry of Temporary Workers to Canada, Fourth Report* (Ottawa: Public Works and Government Services, 1997).

88 CIC, "Backgrounder #2 Making the System Work Better, " News Release, 27 April 2001: 3 <www. cic/gc.ca/English/press/01/ 0101-bg2.html].

89 CIC, *Building on a Strong Foundation* 34-35.

90 CIC, "Bill C-11, Explanation of Proposed Regulations," 18.

91 CIC, "Facts and Figures 1999: Statistical Overview of the Temporary Resident and Refugee Claimant Population" December 2000: 3-4. <www.cic.gc.ca/ English/pub/facts99-temp/ facts-temp-2.html>.

92 See, for example: Sedef Arat-Koc, "NAC's Response to Not Just Numbers," *Canadian Women's Studies* 19:3 (Fall 1999) 19; and National Association of Women and the Law (NAWL), *Gender Analysis of Immigration and Refugee Protection Legislation and Policy* (Ottawa: NAWL, 1999) 10.

93 CIC, News release: "Backgrounder #2" 2-3.

94 NAWL 6.

95 The Ontario Council of Agencies Serving Immigrants (OCASI) made this point in reference to the same provision in earlier legislative proposal. See OCASI, "Brief to House of Commons Standing Committee re: Bill C-31 An Act Respecting Immigration to Canada and the Granting of Refugee Protection to

Persons Who are Displaced, Persecuted or in Danger" August 2000: 4.

96 Colin R. Singer, Canadian Bar
Association, National Citizenship
and Immigration Section,
"Speaking Notes to the National
Congress of Italian Canadians:
'Key Concerns respecting Bill
C-31, Immigration and Refugee
Protection Act,'" 10 June 2000:
2 <www.singer.ca/permres-
new-protection-act.html>.

97 CCR, "Bill C-11 Brief: Summary"
25 March 2001: 1.

98 Tim Harper, "Immigration
Changes would Boost Manley's
Role," *Toronto Star*, 2 October
2001: A6.

99 CIC, "Bill C-11 Immigration and
Refugee Protection Act: What is
New in the Proposed Immigration
and Refugee Protection Act"
March 2001: 6 <www.cic.gc.ca/
English/about/policy/c11-new.
html>.

100 Sharryn J. Aiken, "Comments on
Bill C-11 Related to National
Security and Terrorism. Submission
to House of Commons Standing
Committee on Citizenship and
Immigration," 26 March 2001: 3-4
<www.web.net/~ccr/crsbrief.htm>.

101 Canadian Bar Association, "New
Bill is 'unfair' to immigrants, says
CBA's Immigration Section" 21
February 2001: 1 <http://www.
cba.org/News/News Releases/
01-02021.asp>.

102 CCR, "Bill C-11: New Immigration
Bill," n.p.

103 Michael Greene, Chairman of
Immigration Section, Canadian
Bar Association, cited by Campbell
Clark, "Immigration Bill called
Draconian by Lawyers Group,"
Globe and Mail, 16 March 2001:
A5.

104 CIC, "Bill C-11 Immigration and
Refugee Protection Act.
Overview," 7.

105 CIC, "Bill C-11, Explanation of
Proposed Regulations" October
2001: 16 <www.cic.gc.ca/
English/about/policy/c11-regs.
html>.

106 OCASI "Bill C-31: An Act
Respecting Immigration to
Canada and the Granting of
Refugee Protection to Persons
Who Are Displaced, Persecuted or
In Danger" August 2000: 5.

107 Diane Francis, "Time for a
National Identity Card," *The
Ottawa Citizen*, 25 May 1999: A15.

108 CIC, "What is New in the
Proposed Immigration and
Refugee Protection Act" 5.

109 CIC, "Strengthened Immigration
Measures to Counter Terrorism,"
News Release October 2001: 1
<www.cic.gc.ca/English/press/
01/0119-pre.html>.

110 Tim Harper, "Manley Announces
$280 million to beef up security,"
Toronto Star, 11 October 2001, A3.

111 CIC, News Release "Strengthened
Immigration Measures."

112 Estanislao Oziewicz, "Border Alert
Targets Pilots," *Globe and Mail*, 19
September 2001: A1, A7.

113 Andre Picard, "Most Want PM to
cede sovereignty over border,"
Globe and Mail, 22 September
2001: A1.

114 Kirk Makin, "You'll soon be
watched more," *Globe and Mail*, 19
September 2001: A7.

115 See, in particular, Ronald J.
Daniels, Patrick MacKelm, and
Kent Roach, eds., *The Security of
Freedom: Essays on Canada's Anti-
Terrorism Bill* (Toronto: University
of Toronto Press, 2001).

116 Tonda MacCharles, "Anti-Terror Bill may be Altered" *Toronto Star*, 6 November 2001: A6.

117 Charlie Gillis, "Racial Profiling inevitable: law expert," *National Post*, 10 October 2001 <www.nationalpost.com/search/story.html>.

118 See, for example, CIC, *Immigration Consultations Report*.

119 See, for example, Sedef Arat-Koc, "NAC's Response" 18-23.

120 See, for example, Jennifer Hyndman, "Gender and Canadian Immigration Policy: A Current Snapshot," *Canadian Women's Studies* 19.3 (Fall 1999) 7.

121 Jennifer Curran, "Gender Analysis of Canada's Immigration Legislation," *Jurisfemme* 18.3 (Spring 1999). <www.nawl.ca/v18-no3.htm>.

122 Curran.

123 The Ad Hoc Committee included Disabled Women's Awareness Network (DAWN), FREDA Centre for Research on Violence Against Women and Children, Lesbian and Gay Immigration Task Force (LEGIT), Ottawa Carleton Immigrant Services Organization (OCISO), National Organization of Immigrant and Visible Minority Women of Canada (NOIVMWO), National Association of Women and the Law (NAWL), and West Coast Domestic Workers' Association (WCDWA).

124 NAWL 2.

125 NAWL 3.

126 Jane Jenson and Susan Phillips, "Regime Shift: New Citizenship Practices in Canada," *International Journal of Canadian Studies* 14 (Fall 1996): 120.

127 Judy Rebick, "Liberals Try to Sink NAC," *Herizons* (Winter 1999).

128 Personal Interview Sandra Harder, Gender Based Analysis Unit, CIC, 23 March 2001.

129 For a discussion of state feminism, see Dorothy M. Stetson and Amy Mazur, eds., *Comparative State Feminism* (Newbury Park, CA: Sage, 1995).

130 See, for example, CIC, "Immigration and Refugee Act Introduced," News Release 2001-03.

131 NAWL, NOIVMW, West Coast Domestic Workers Association, West Coast Leaf, La Table feministe francophone de concertation provinciale de l'Ontario, Le Mouvement ontarien des femmes immigrantes fracophones, "Brief on the Proposed Immigration and Refugee Protection Act (Bill C-11)] April 2000: 5 <www.nawl.ca/immigrate_e.html>.

132 CIC, "Amendments to Bill C-11 by the Standing Committee on Citizenship and Immigration" August 2001: 4 <www.cic.gc.ca/English/about/policy/c11-amend.html>.

133 Margaret Young, "Bill C-16: The Citizenship of Canada Act: Legislative History of Bill C-16" <www.parl.gc.ca/36/2/parlbus/chambus/house/bills/summaries/c16-e.1>.

134 Maureen Murray, "Citizen Laws to be made tougher," *Toronto Star*, 8 December 1998: A1.

135 Helene Pellerin, "The Cart Before the Horse? The Coordination of Migration Policies in the Americas and the Neo-Liberal Economic Project of Integration," *Review of International Political Economy* 6:4 (Winter 1999): 469.

136 CIC, *Canada-United States Accord on Our Shared Border* (Ottawa: Minister of Public Works and Government Services, 2000) 3.

137 Reg Whitaker, "Refugees: The Security Dimension," *Citizenship Studies* 2.3 (1998): 430.

138 Tim Harper, "Tightening the Canada-US Border," *Toronto Star,* Monday, October 8, 2001: A1.

139 Whitaker, "Refugees: The Security Dimension," 414.

140 Stephanie Kuttner, "Gender-Based Persecution as a Basis for Refugee Status: The Emergence of an International Norm," *Refuge* 16.4 (October 1997): 18.

141 Kuttner18.

142 Sherene Razack, "Policing the Borders of Nation: The Imperial Gaze in Gender Persecution Cases," *Looking White People in the Eye: Gender, Race, and Culture in Courtrooms and Classrooms* (Toronto: University of Toronto Press, 1999) 92-93.

143 Nazaré Albuquerque Abell, "Safe Country Provisions in Canada and in the European Union: A Critical Assessment," *International Migration Review* 31.3 (Fall 1997): 570.

144 Abell 575.

145 Abell 580-86.

146 Abell 578-80.

147 Tanya Basok, "Refugee Policy: Globalization, Radical Challenge, or State Control?," *Studies in Political Economy* 50 (Summer 1996): 133-66.

148 The Fraser Institute, "The Immigration Dilemma," (1992) 11; cited by Lorne Foster, *Turnstile Immigration* (Toronto: Thompson Education Publishing, 1998).

149 Deborah A. Cobb-Clark and Marie D. Connolly, "The Worldwide Market for Skilled Migrants: Can Australia Compete?," *International Migration Review* 31.3 (Fall 1997): 688-89.

150 Cobb-Clark and Connolly 679.

151 *Not Just Numbers* 116.

152 Gerald E. Dirks, "Factors Underlying Migration and Refugee Issues: Responses and Cooperation among OECD Member States," *Citizenship Studies* 2.3 (1998): 392.

153 Meyer Burstein, "Metropolis: International Directions," *Responding to Diversity in Metropolis: Building an Inclusive Research Agenda,* ed. Baha Abu-Laban and Tracey M. Derwing (Edmonton: Prairie Centre of Excellence for Research on Immigration and Integration, 1997) 18.

154 Norma Vale, "Brave New Partnerships: Learning how to get along with each other in the Metropolis," *University Affairs* (October 1998) 11.

155 Vale 11.

156 Vale 11.

157 Vale 12.

158 Baha Abu-Laban and Hans Vermeulen, "Introduction," *Journal of International Migration and Integration* 1 (Winter 2000): 1.

159 Meyer Burstein, "Metropolis Objectives and Aims of the Conference," *Metropolis: First Conference Milan, 13-15 November 1996,* ed. Marco Lombardi (Milano: Fondazione Cariplo—ISMU, 1997), 12.

160 Burstein 12.

chapter | FOUR
Multiculturalism and Nation-Building

"Multiculturalism ... is one of the greatest competitive advantages we could have. It is the internal globalization of Canada. And it will be key to our succeeding in the global economy. Without diversity of thought, without workers feeling valued for their individuality and uniqueness, firms can spend millions on quality efforts to little or no avail."

—John Cleghorn, President, Royal Bank of Canada[1]

For much of Canada's history, the policies of the Canadian state at their most inclusive recognized a "two nations" vision which gave some recognition to the French and the British as "founding peoples." Most of the time however, there was a policy emphasis on Anglo-conformity—the idea that all groups should assimilate to the language and culture of the dominant British group. Multiculturalism emerged in the 1970s as a uniquely Canadian policy, a new approach to nation-building generated by the Liberal government of Pierre Elliott Trudeau. Multiculturalism policy gave explicit recognition at the federal level to Canadians whose origin was non-French, non-British-, and non-Aboriginal. Thus, the policy served to reconfigure expressions of "Canadian identity" in a way that was inclusive of ethnocultural and racial minorities. Many Quebec academics and politicians were critical of the policy from the outset, viewing it as a weakening of French-Canadians' status as a "founding people" and of Quebec's claim to special recognition.[2] Canada still has a policy of multiculturalism, though in recent years some have come to regard it as antithetical to national unity. The purpose of this chapter is to survey the evolution of multiculturalism policy at the federal level in Canada, as well as perceptions about the policy.

This chapter consists of three parts. First it considers the history of the policy of multiculturalism from its inception in 1971 to 1993, just before the Jean Chrétien Liberal government took power. For much of this period, the policy emphasized the cultural maintenance of diverse ethnic groups through such areas as culture and language. Second, the chapter addresses policy shifts from 1993 to 2001. In this period the business value of multiculturalism was stressed; along with that, there was a focus on enhancing "attachment to Canada." Finally, consideration is given to how multiculturalism has become internationalized in the contemporary period, with other countries looking to Canada as a "model"—a development Canadian policy-makers have actively encouraged.

We also suggest that in the period from 1993 to 2001 the policy of multiculturalism has undergone significant popular criticism, particularly in English-speaking Canada. Along with the argument that Canadian multiculturalism weakens national unity, criticisms have centred around the idea that, while the expression of minority languages and culture are acceptable in the private sphere, the state should have no part in upholding them in the public sphere. In the contemporary multiculturalism debate, the notion of the "private" is used in two main ways. One refers to the household and family, in which case the "public sphere" comprises everything else. "Private" can also refer to "market and business" (as opposed to government and social services); in this context, the "diversity" that multiculturalism represents is valued as something potentially profit-enhancing. Thus, while multiculturalism has faced significant cutbacks at the federal government level, at the same time policy-makers have marshalled a globalization discourse to defend multiculturalism policy. Here, policy-makers maintain that "diversity" benefits Canada's international trade and global competitiveness.

The argument of this chapter is that recent versions of multiculturalism, accentuating business and trade—selling diversity—represent a new vision of nation-building, one that is focussed on the bottom line more than previous articulations of the policy. It is questionable whether or not a multiculturalism of business and trade can adequately deal with the issue of race, class, and gender inequities among Canadians or further advance an agenda based on equity. Another question to consider is whether the notion of "attachment to Canada" is based on a vision of the country with a strong affinity to neo-liberal ideals.

HISTORY: 1971-1993

The antecedents of the 1971 multiculturalism program may actually be traced back to the period of World War II and the immediate post-World War II period.[3] Indeed, in an effort to unite Canadians for the war effort, the Department of National War Services established an Advisory Committee on Cooperation in Citizenship, which in 1942 was charged with five tasks:

1. to maintain contact with Canadian citizens of non-British and non-French origin and to seek to interpret their views to the government and to the Canadian public generally;
2. to cooperate with the Director of the Bureau of Public Information in distributing news to the foreign-language press in Canada and in explaining public policy as it develops;
3. to maintain close relationships with the Canadian Broadcasting Corporation, the National Film Board and other similar services, and the Canadian Council for Education in Citizenship;
4. to encourage cultural activities which may promote mutual understanding and esteem between Canadian citizens of different origin; and
5. to interest itself in situations that appear to be producing misunderstanding, dissatisfaction or discord among groups of Canadians of European origin, non-French and non-British, or between these groups and other Canadian citizens and, if it is thought advisable, to make representations with respect to such situations to the appropriate bodies or authorities.[4]

These developments in the 1940s are notable because they foreshadowed some aspects of multicultural policy, although the formal policy of multiculturalism is really the outgrowth of events of the 1960s and 1970s.

In 1963, in response to a reinvigorated French-Canadian nationalism springing from the Quiet Revolution in Quebec, Liberal Prime Minister Lester Pearson established the Royal Commission on Bilingualism and Biculturalism (the B and B Commission).[5] The Commission, with its emphasis on two languages and two cultures, provoked a counter-response from what has been variously termed the "third force," and the "multicultural movement." Canadians of non-British, non-French, and non-Aboriginal origin (especially second-generation Ukrainians) vociferously objected to the symbolism of the Commission's mandate. In particular, there was a fear among the "third force" that they would be defined as second-class citizens if their contributions were not symbolically valued by the state.[6]

In response to these protests, the B and B Commission released Book IV of its reports, *The Cultural Contribution of other Ethnic Groups*. In 1971, Prime Minister Trudeau tabled the government's response to its recommendations. Interestingly, if all of the recommendations had been followed, a policy of both multiculturalism and multilingualism would have been the result.[7] Instead, Trudeau argued for a policy of multiculturalism within a bilingual framework. The placement of multiculturalism within English and French bilingualism reiterated the 1969 Official Languages Act, which formalized linguistic duality as a characteristic of Canada by ensuring that federal institutions would provide services in both languages. The couching of multiculturalism within a bilingual framework may be seen as an indication of the continued domination of British- and to a lesser extent French-origin groups in Canada.

Multiculturalism did mesh with Trudeau's nation-building vision insofar as there was a stress placed on preserving individual freedom and enhancing national unity.[8] As articulated by Trudeau, the policy of multiculturalism was to involve four main aspects.[9] First, state funding was to be given to ethnocultural groups for cultural maintenance. Second, cultural barriers to full participation in Canadian society were to be removed. Third, there was to be cultural interchange. Finally, there was to be official language training for immigrants to Canada. As Leslie Pal has observed, given wartime and post-war policies in Canada, the main feature of the multiculturalism program that was new was the funding given to support ethnic minority associations.[10] Thus, multiculturalism joined other areas (and groups) which received funding from the Canadian state as part of the post-war, Keynesian-inspired ideas of what it meant to be a citizen in Canada. This funding was given through the Multiculturalism Directorate within the Department of the Secretary of State. From the beginning, and up until 1981, this funding translated into support for folklore activities (e.g., dance troupes or theatre) and to a lesser extent support for "heritage languages" (instruction in languages other than French or English).[11]

The "song and dance" aspect of multiculturalism in the 1970s generated many criticisms from left-leaning academics who viewed the policy as merely symbolic and ineffectual in transforming power relations. As a totality, these criticisms focussed on how the policy gave minimal financial support to minorities to combat racism (at its peak multiculturalism spending amounted to only $27 million a year) and on how the policy obscured both class and gender inequalities within minority communities,[12] because, in stressing ethnicity, it tended to work on and foster the assumption that ethnic groups were internally homogeneous and, thus, that gender, class, or other differences were not relevant.

Yet, at the same time, multiculturalism did serve to fundamentally challenge the symbolic order of the Canadian nation. For most of Canada's history, the policies of the Canadian state tended to fixate on Anglo-conformity (in which subordinate groups were expected to comply with British values) and, to a lesser extent, cultural dualism (where the collective identities of the British and to a lesser extent French were legitimized; this was based on the idea that these were the two "founding peoples" at Confederation).[13] The symbolic importance of multiculturalism in meeting the desire of ethnocultural minorities for official state recognition helps explain why the policy quickly garnered the support of ethnic minority leaders and also the support of other political parties—in particular, the Progressive Conservatives and the New Democrats.

Ultimately, however, the formulation of multiculturalism within a bilingual framework did not meet the needs of all groups in Canada. As noted, many French Quebecers tended to see the policy of multiculturalism as a means of weakening their claims on the state for special status based on being a "founding people." As well, Aboriginal peoples have largely viewed multiculturalism as irrelevant to their claims on the state, which are based on treaty rights. In addition, by the early 1980s it was becoming increasingly clear that the emphasis of the multiculturalism program on folklore was not meeting the needs of many visible minorities who were experiencing racism and systemic discrimination. Indeed, the numbers of visible minorities in Canada had grown as a result of the shift towards countries of the Third World in post-1967 immigration. In response to pressure from the increasingly numerous visible minority groups in Canada, the Multiculturalism Directorate created a race relations unit in 1981.[14]

The new focus on race relations in the multiculturalism program did not end the demands for greater response to inequities resulting from racism. The concept of "race relations" was criticized for its inability to deal with systemic racism in Canada:[15] that racism or discrimination which arises from the rules, organization, and procedures of institutions, rather than individual bias[16] (see Chapter Five). Efforts at combating systematic and other forms of racism stemming from the multiculturalism policy have been said to be hampered by scanty financial resources and a restricted capacity to actually fundamentally affect institutional change.[17] Many projects have been limited to one-time workshops or conferences, rather than being on-going in nature. As well, multiculturalism was seen by some to have empowered "middle-class people of colour to appropriate anti-racist activism from their working-class counterparts, smoothing out its critical edge in the process."[18] Nonetheless, in expanding its parameters to incorporate concerns relating to anti-racism, the policy indirectly helped propel the adoption of employment equity legislation in 1986[19] (the policy of employment equity and its evolution is taken up further in Chapter 5).

The decade of the 1980s was an interesting one for multicultural policy. As racism issues were brought alongside long-standing concerns relating to cultural maintenance, the policy gained some further depth. In 1982, for example, when the Trudeau Liberals moved to patriate the Constitution from Britain and create a Charter of Rights and Freedoms, pressure from minority ethnic groups ensured that the new Charter would recognize multiculturalism.[20] Section 27 of the Charter serves as an interpretive clause which reads that the Charter "shall be interpreted in a manner consistent with the preservation and enhancement of the multicultural heritage of Canadians."

In addition, in 1988, under the Progressive Conservative government of Brian Mulroney, a Multiculturalism Act was passed. This Act served to replace the Trudeau statement of 1971 and gave a firmer legislative basis to multiculturalism, even though many of its provisions allowed considerable discretion for policy-makers. The Act holds that it is the policy of the Canadian government to "recognize and promote the understanding that multiculturalism reflects the cultural and racial diversity of Canadian society and acknowledges the freedom of all members of Canadian society to preserve, enhance, and share their cultural heritage."[21]

As well, in 1989, the Mulroney Conservatives moved to further strengthen multiculturalism by introducing legislation that created a separate Department of Multiculturalism and Citizenship within the federal bureaucracy. When this legislation came into effect in 1991, multiculturalism was still an area of relatively little state spending; however, by placing it in a separate department (rather than as a Directorate within the Department of the Secretary of State), multiculturalism gained additional symbolic stature in the federal bureaucracy.[22]

It was also during the 1980s that multiculturalism first became linked to business interests. Starting with Liberal minister James Fleming in 1981, the federal Liberals began to try to make multiculturalism attractive to business associations and also to strengthen the entrepreneurial segments of ethnocultural minorities.[23] This pattern continued during the governance of Prime Minister Brian Mulroney (1984 to 1993); it is symbolized by the "Multiculturalism Means Business" conference organized by the Progressive Conservatives in Toronto in 1986.[24] At the conference, Brian Mulroney addressed the relevance of multiculturalism in the context of domestic and international trade:

> … our multicultural nature gives us an edge in selling to the world. Canadians who have cultural links to other parts of the globe, who have business contacts elsewhere are of utmost importance to our trade and investment strategy for economic renewal.
>
> We, as a nation, need to grasp the opportunity afforded to us by our multicultural identity, to cement our prosperity with trade and investment links the world over and with a renewed entrepreneurial spirit at home.[25]

Notably, the emphasis on business links and multiculturalism have been even further stressed under the Chrétien Liberals and very clearly tied to a globalization discourse in which multiculturalism is framed as a tool for enhancing Canada's global competitiveness.

Notwithstanding the new emphasis on business and trade, by the end of the decade of the 1980s multiculturalism began to come under heavy criticism from new forces. For the first time, some ethnocultural minorities and popular writers, as well as political parties in English-speaking Canada, began to criticize the policy on new grounds. The new criticism centred on the idea that multiculturalism was divisive and inappropriate. Inherent in the latter argument was the sense that the state should not play a role in the area of culture—that this was a "private" matter to be dealt with in the home and family.

This criticism may be seen to have gained its strength with the inception of the Reform Party in 1987 (the forerunner to the Canadian Alliance). From the beginning the Reform Party criticized both federal immigration policy and the federal policy of bilingualism. In 1989, the Reform Party added multiculturalism to its list of policy critiques, calling for an end to the funding of multiculturalism support, for the preservation of cultural background only as a matter of personal choice, and for the state to promote and encourage minorities to integrate into the national culture.[26]

Reform Party criticisms hinged on its advocacy of individual rights and the formal equality of people and provinces (that is, that every person should have the same rights, and every province should have the same rights). In this formulation, rights given to collectivities other than provinces are rejected, as creating "special treatment."

Attacks on multiculturalism were not confined to the Reform Party. For instance, during the debate over the creation of a separate Department of Multiculturalism in 1989, several Liberal Members of Parliament (all from ethnocultural minority backgrounds) began to criticize multiculturalism. For these MPs, including former Liberal leadership contender John Nunziata, a separate Department of Multiculturalism was a recipe for ghettoization.[27]

More recently, popular writers such as Trinidad-born novelist Neil Bissoondath have also criticized the policy. Bissoondath argues that the policy of multiculturalism—to him only a "song and dance" affair—encourages stereotyping and national divisiveness. Bissoondath has suggested that "multiculturalism, with all its festivals and celebrations, has done—and can do—nothing to foster a factual and clear-minded vision of our neighbours."[28] Bissoondath also holds that culture and ethnicity should be left with individuals and families, "the only sphere where they have any true and lasting value."[29]

Criticism of state involvement in and spending on multiculturalism and of multiculturalism in general did not go unnoticed by the Canadian public, which was consumed, as a result of the constitutional debates of the late 1980s and early 1990s, by issues of national unity and the future of Canada and Quebec. The public mood helps explain why the proposed Charlottetown Constitutional Accord of 1992 did not mention multiculturalism and why the Progressive Conservatives' Pre-election Cabinet in 1993 (as overseen by Prime Minister Kim Campbell) actually disbanded Multiculturalism and Citizenship as a separate department.[30]

THE CONTEMPORARY PERIOD: 1993-2001

When the federal Liberals of Jean Chrétien entered office in 1993, they did so in a context in which multiculturalism was no longer the safe "motherhood and apple pie" electoral issue it had been in the 1970s and 1980s. Like the outgoing Conservatives, the federal Liberals also chose to not reinstate a separate Department of Multiculturalism. In its place, they created the Department of Canadian Heritage, in which several former departments and agencies (the Department of Multiculturalism, the Secretary of State, the Department of Fitness and Amateur Sport, the parks component of Environment Canada, and the cultural broadcasting components of the Department of Communications) were all to be housed. The area of multiculturalism is now overseen by a Secretary of State (a junior minister not represented in Cabinet) who is responsible for both Multiculturalism and for Status of Women. Calling the new mega-department "Canadian Heritage"(rather than multiculturalism) may be read as heavily symbolic. As Michel Dupuy, the first minister of the Department of Canadian Heritage, noted, "the Department of Canadian Heritage is in a sense the flagship of Canadian identity."[31] More specifically, it related to the emphasis the Liberal government began to place on fostering "attachment" to Canada. This became clear in the response of the Chrétien Liberals to the review of the multiculturalism program.

The Multiculturalism Program Review: 1995-1997

In 1995, the federal Liberals moved to evaluate the effectiveness of multiculturalism programs and to plan the direction for future programming. To this end, they commissioned a private company, Brighton Research, to perform an evaluation to review the program, literature, and media coverage related to multiculturalism, as well as to conduct interviews with relevant individuals in government and non-governmental organizations, and to do a statistical analysis of the program's funding patterns.[32]

What has become known as the Brighton Report was released in 1996. The report is emphatic in stressing that many recent critics of multiculturalism (in particular, Neil Bissoondath) "misunderstand and misrepresent Canada's multicultural policy."[33] However, the report's recommendations make it clear that "multiculturalism is unfinished business."[34] In taking the position that the policy was not carved in stone, the Brighton Report made it evident that changes were needed.

Key recommendations emerging from the Brighton Report were that the primary objective of multiculturalism should be "identity, participation, and justice"[35] and that the Department of Canadian Heritage should "eschew initiatives unrelated to identity, participation, and justice because such initiatives appear to many Canadians to weaken the Canadian fabric."[36] In this regard, it was evident that grappling with the argument that multiculturalism weakens Canadian unity was a central motivation behind the report's recommendations.

In response, the federal Liberals announced their redesigned program in 1997-98, premised on three goals:

> IDENTITY: fostering a society that recognizes, respects, and reflects a diversity of cultures such that people of all backgrounds feel a sense of belonging and attachment to Canada.

CIVIC PARTICIPATION: developing, among Canada's diverse people, active citizens with both the opportunity and capacity to participate in shaping the future of their communities and their country.

SOCIAL JUSTICE: building a society that ensures fair and equitable treatment and that respects the dignity of and accommodates people of all origins.[37]

Thus, the current program aims to inculcate an attachment to Canada (as opposed to cultural maintenance) and to create what is referred to as active citizens. In the latter respect, the new multiculturalism program parallels recent neo-liberal discussions around immigration, which have also stressed creating active citizens (see Chapter Three). In the context of these changes active citizenship is implicitly defined by volunteerism. Thus, current proposals for grants are favoured if they can "highlight community initiative, partnership, and self-help,"[38] an indication of how neo-liberal ideals have suffused citizenship discussion.

The second key recommendation made in the Brighton Report related to a sense that the direct funding of ethnocultural organizations was problematic. Making use of the idea of "special interests" (a frequent description in neo-liberal discourse, used for groups such as women and minorities) the Brighton report argued:

> *Notwithstanding the desires of some community members, the funding of ethno-specific organizations should not continue in its present form.* Past funding practices have reinforced the impression that multiculturalism is a "program for special interests," rather than a program for all Canadians. In distinction to what in the past appeared to some people to be "programming for special interests," the *Minister should make clear that all Canadians—rather than sub-groupings of Canadians—are the recipients of the benefits of multiculturalism*[39] [emphasis in original].

In their 1997-98 announcement of the redesigned program, the federal Liberals moved to make funding ethnocultural groups a thing of the past. Noting that they would consider funding "for projects which address the priorities and objects of the Multiculturalism Program," the Liberals advised that the beneficiaries might be "Canadian voluntary and non-profit organizations, educational institutions, non-governmental institutions, individuals, and private sector companies."[40] As Paolo Prosperi notes, a consequence "for ethnocultural organizations who were in the past the beneficiaries of core funding, [is that] those wanting to secure funding from this point forward will likely have to do so on a project-by-project basis."[41] One major criticism of this kind of funding structure is that it makes the activities of ethnocultural associations even more dependent on government.[42] It also adds to an arsenal of strategies pursued by the Liberals since 1993 designed to end funding to advocacy groups (such as women's groups or ethnocultural groups) and to support new models of service delivery. Thus, the delivery of public services traditionally associated with the federal state is moved to provinces, communities, families, or individuals.[43]

Ethnocultural organizations across Canada did not support this change in policy. The Canadian Ethnocultural Council (CEC) is the national coalition of 33 umbrella organizations for ethnocultural minorities (including such groups as the Canadian Jewish Congress, the Chinese Canadian National Council, the Ukrainian Canadian Congress, etc.). The CEC charged that their input was not taken into account in redesigning the program.[44] In particular they complained that the diminishing funding levels (an issue not addressed by the Brighton Report) undermined multiculturalism generally and the 1988 Multiculturalism Act specifically:

> We can only but urge the Government of Canada to revisit the issue of funding, and more specifically the question of appropriate levels of funding which would enable the agencies of government, in partnership with Canada's ethnocultural communities, to carry out the mandate and provisions of the Act and which would give credence to the notion that the Government of Canada is truly committed to the objective of a multicultural society.[45]

Indeed, in this context it should be noted that, as with most areas of cultural spending, multiculturalism has been subjected to funding decreases. Thus, whereas in the early 1990s the budget for multiculturalism was about $27 million annually, by 1996-97 it had gone down to $18.7 million.[46] A program that has always been meagerly supported has, therefore, become even leaner. However, while the federal Liberals may have been accused by ethnocultural groups of being less favourable towards multiculturalism (as measured by funding), the concept of ethnocultural "diversity" has also been touted as an economic boon.

"Diversity" and Globalization

In addition to cutbacks, and following neo-liberal strategies aimed at ending the funding to ethnocultural groups, the federal Liberals have increasingly emphasized multiculturalism as a way to deal with global markets and global competitiveness. Thus the advancement of ethnocultural diversity rests not only on an explicit stress on attachment to Canada, but also on an implicit stress on attachment to markets. As the first Chrétien Liberal Secretary of State for multiculturalism, Sheila Finestone, noted in a speech in 1994:

> Today, for more and more Canadians, multiculturalism means business…. In facing the challenges of globalization, Canada must make the most of its internal globalization—the competitive advantage of a multicultural population.[47]

This perspective was also subsequently taken up by the Secretary of State for Multiculturalism, Hedy Fry, who emphasized the cost-effectiveness of ethnic diversity in terms of corporate business strategies.[48] Fry favourably noted in 1996 that

> [f]ollowing the federal government's leadership in promoting the value of diversity, Canadian businesses are seeing the dollars-and-cents value of managing diversity effectively. Many companies have improved their profitability and competitiveness by linking diversity to corporate strategies, especially in marketing and international business.[49]

In 2000 Prime Minister Jean Chrétien continued the theme by arguing that "in the global economy, maintaining our diversity strengthens our trading links with other countries."[50]

Activities pursued under the rubric of strengthening business ties and marketing included updating the "multiculturalism means business" directory of ethnocultural and professional business contacts; establishing an ethnocultural business community network; funding the Asia Pacific Foundation of Canada to hold round-table sessions on how to better enhance Canada's trade links with the Pacific Rim; researching with the Conference Board of Canada on how valuing diversity in the private sector is of benefit to economic prosperity; and supporting a conference at McMaster University to examine how human resources, diversity, and global competitiveness are best handled.[51]

Such activities have also been highlighted in educational initiatives for young Canadians, which aim to teach the values of diversity, anti-racism, and multiculturalism. In honour of the United Nations' International Day for the Elimination of Racial Discrimination in March 2000, the Multiculturalism Program produced a "Teacher Guide" for secondary school students. One of the units, entitled "Business," suggests activities which in the words of the guide, "explore the impact of multicultural diversity on business practice."[52] To this end, the guide suggests teachers ask students to develop class or individual projects based "on the slogan 'Multiculturalism Means Business.'"[53]

Thus, under the Chrétien Liberals, there has been a much clearer link fostered between business, trade, and multiculturalism/diversity which makes more use of a globalization discourse than existed in the 1980s. This globalization discourse emphasizes the need for competitiveness, cost-effectiveness, and international trade. In this regard, Canada seems to be emulating the strategy of the Australian government, which since the 1980s has been emphasizing multiculturalism in relation to "productive diversity." However, such a strategy raises three questions.[54] Will an emphasis on economics and trade lead to declining attention to anti-racism? Will those minority groups whose home countries do not offer trade opportunities get less attention in policy initiatives? Not least, will immigration policy start to favour immigrants from countries viewed as providing the greatest trade potential? These questions have equivalent resonance for Canada. In addition, the emphasis on international business and trade (areas in which class-advantaged men have traditionally dominated) raises issues about the way in which class and gender issues are handled under the rubric of multiculturalism.

Gender and Multiculturalism

In advance of the United Nations World Conference on Women in Beijing in 1997 Canada, like other member countries of the United Nations, was asked to devise a plan to advance the situation of women. Status of Women Canada responded in 1995 with a plan to implement gender-based analysis throughout all federal departments and agencies. In addressing the area of multiculturalism, this plan called for the federal government to:

1. promote intercultural understanding and acceptance of diversity so all Canadian women, regardless of ethnicity, are valued;

117

2. remove the barriers to full and equitable participation faced by women—including ethnocultural and visible minorities;

3. develop policies, programs, and services which are delivered in recognition of the multicultural character of Canadian society, including issues affecting women;

4. reduce employment barriers within the area of culture (i.e., artistic and performing arts) experienced by first-generation Canadians and ethnocultural and visible minorities, particularly women.[55]

The plan also spelled out the commitment of the federal government to work with other levels of government (provincial, territorial, and municipal) to promote inclusive cultural programs, as well as providing female visible and ethnocultural minorities with technical and financial support to bolster their participation in the artistic and performing arts.[56]

Although there has been no formal response from the multiculturalism program to the federal plan, it is notable that the plan did not deal with some of the criticisms which have been leveled against multiculturalism policy when it comes to gender issues. For instance, Tania Das Gupta has argued that the multiculturalism program itself has worked to reproduce existing power relations in Canada. In terms of women specifically, Das Gupta holds that for many minority and immigrant women, the program's attempts at gender specificity have sometimes amounted only to portraying the "cultures of immigrant women ... [as] inherently conservative, and pathological, not oriented to developing a high level of self-esteem or self-identity and, therefore, of success in participation in social life."[57] This, she suggests, is visible in some policy discussions which have linked the isolation and marginalization experienced by some immigrant women to their place within their ethnocultural community, rather than to systemic structures of racism, sexism, and exclusion in Canada.

While power relations within ethnocultural communities may disadvantage women or other groups, as with power relations within Canadian society, this kind of portrayal of immigrant/minority "culture" and the place of women is problematic. It appears even more problematic when one considers how many of the popular arguments which have emerged against multiculturalism over the 1990s have deployed gender. This is primarily evident in the view that holds that acceptable and unacceptable forms of multiculturalism rest on a split between the public and the private. Thus, for example, one of the things that unite critics such as Neil Bissoondath and the Reform Party/Alliance is that they overtly state that multiculturalism, confined to the private sphere, is acceptable. Yet as Tim Nieguth has observed, it is impossible for the state to be completely neutral when it comes to matters of culture; indeed, many state actions have important cultural implications. Consequently, relegating matters of culture to the so-called private sphere of the home and family does not mean that the state's actions will be culturally neutral. In fact, leaving issues of culture to the resources of groups effectively translates into favouring the dominant (British and French groups) since resources are unevenly distributed.[58] Such an approach also paves the way for popular ethnicized or racialized conceptions of who belongs to the Canadian nation or who is a "Canadian" (e.g., being white and European and Christian) to go unchallenged by the state. Leaving aside the huge problem of whether a multiculturalism unsupported by the state can actually survive and flourish,[59] this emphasis on multiculturalism in the private sphere carries an implicit gendered implication. Since the realm of culture, language, customs, and food (the "private sphere" being referred to) is typically associated with women, there is a construction of women as the bearers and transmitters of culture—a familiar theme in depictions of women, from those involved in nationalist struggles to Third World immigrant women in industrialized countries.[60] Women positioned in this way in the "private sphere" appear to have little place in the realm of the "public" spheres of politics and work.

There are many more direct ways that gender has been deployed in the arguments of those who do not wish to see public recognition of ethnic groups. For instance, the examples that Neil Bissoondath chooses to illustrate his examination of the problem of multiculturalism are weighted to portray immigrant and minority cultures as potentially dangerous to women and girls in a way that "Canadian" culture, untainted by multiculturalism, is not. For example, he suggests that multiculturalism means tolerance for the use of technology for sex-selection (i.e., aborting girl fetuses); the light treatment by the Canadian judicial system of the sodomy of girl children, if the criminal and victim come from "cultures" that value female virginity; and, not least, allowing the practice of female circumcision.[61] Regarding the latter, Bissoondath implores: "[H]ow far in the Canadian context, do we go in accommodation…? Should we, under certain circumstances (a sterile operating room, trained medical personnel), respect the right of certain women to undergo what we see as mutilation?"[62]

For Bissoondath the explicit spectre of multiculturalism in Canada is that it is without limits.[63] Clearly, however, the Canadian Multiculturalism Act must operate within the limits of existing law, as set out in the Constitution of Canada, the Citizenship Act, and the Canadian Human Rights Act, all of which are recognized in its preamble.[64] It is also problematic in that Bissoondath treats minority and Canadian cultures each as essential and homogeneous, rather than as humanly constructed and constantly in flux. Be that as it may, a very intriguing aspect of the examples Bissoondath gives are the way that they implicitly rest on the suggestion that women and girl children lose power with multiculturalism.

In this respect, Bissoondath's discussion of multiculturalism in Canada is not far from how some feminist scholars, such as American philosopher Susan Moller Okin, have viewed the general ideology of multiculturalism (i.e., the ideology premised on giving recognition to cultural groups). Specifically, Okin argues that multiculturalism and feminism are not compatible. She holds that minority women from non-Western cultures are ultimately harmed by the extension of group rights (multiculturalism) because such rights empower minority males to continue oppressive practices against women, especially young women, in the private sphere. The practices Okin has in mind include child marriages, forced marriages, divorce systems biased against women, polygamy, and female circumcision.[65] In response to Okin's essay, other feminist scholars have criticized her representation of non-Western cultures as stereotyped[66] and have raised the issue of how she defines "barbarity," suggesting that "in advocating the abolition of other people's rituals, she fails to see ceremonial acts in her own culture [Western/American] as limiting and abhorrent."[67] Such Western/American rituals and practices Okin ignores include plastic surgery, high heels, and the idea that romantic love is liberating, whereas arranged marriages are not.

Similarly, in the Canadian context, feminist anti-racist scholar Sherene Razack has observed that the kinds of examples used in discussions relating to culture are not innocent. In particular, she suggests that female circumcision has emerged as the "outstanding example of Third World barbarity" by North American scholars.[68] Razack argues that few of these scholars have engaged in a "respectful" First/Third world dialogue and instead have seen Third World women as subjects: "Exotic Other Females in need of their benevolent protection."[69] This portrayal of "Canadian culture" as inherently more "civilized" also treats some women and girl children as passive victims and risks ignoring women's complex struggles within ethnocultural communities or in Canadian society. Clearly, then, with or without a multicultural policy, there are issues pertaining to cultural diversity which require careful dialogue and exchange between women and men within ethnocultural communities and between women and men among communities and the broader Canadian society.

However, in the current situation in Canada, gender has been deployed within the multiculturalism debate in a way that does not always serve to advance respectful dialogue, and this has been inadequately addressed by the multiculturalism program. Moreover, in the current multiculturalism agenda, where there is an emphasis on "attachment to Canada" and a "dollars-and-cents" valuation of multiculturalism, it seems unlikely that gender inequality (or issues relating to class or racism) will be more adequately addressed. Indeed, the current agenda is decidedly silent on gender, despite the fact that most business people and entrepreneurs are male. In this way, this agenda is unlikely to advance greater equality on gender or class terms, and it is not apparent that a more rigorous form of anti-racism will emerge either. Nevertheless, when it comes to multiculturalism, Canadian policy-makers increasingly take the view that Canadian policy is unparalleled.

THE INTERNATIONALIZATION OF MULTICULTURALISM

Today the term multiculturalism is used to refer to a variety of practices and policies and has taken on considerable cross-national variation in meaning (for example, in the United States it has been used to refer largely to educational practices and to efforts by ethnic minorities, women, gays and lesbians, and other groups to foster a more inclusive curriculum in universities and public schools). However, it is notable that the actual term "multiculturalism" was first coined in Canada as a result of the federal policy.[70] The Canadian policy of multiculturalism was also to influence Australia to adopt a multiculturalism policy in 1974.[71]

Notably, at the same time that multiculturalism has come under greater scrutiny and attack within Canada, over the 1990s the area of multiculturalism has increasingly been portrayed, especially by Canadian politicians to a domestic audience, as one in which Canada is a world leader. Thus, for instance, Hedy Fry has argued that Canadian history and values "helped us build the foundation for a society which would eventually pass the Canadian Multiculturalism Act the first of its kind in the world."[72] Prime Minister Jean Chrétien has more broadly argued that "multiculturalism distinguishes Canada, as a country that not only cares equally about all its citizens, but also believes preserving the uniqueness of each holds the promise of a better future for all."[73] It is notable that in lauding the policy, Chrétien ignored the fact that the multiculturalism program (as with many areas of social spending) has faced significant cutbacks.

Moreover, multiculturalism has more frequently been upheld—both by academics and even in the international arena—as an area where Canadians actually have something to share with the world. For instance, internationally renowned Canadian political philosopher Will Kymlicka prefaces his 1998 book on ethnocultural relations in Canada with the observation that his own experiences abroad point to the idea that Canada is viewed as a model by other countries in terms of how ethnic diversity has been managed through multiculturalism and other policies.[74] While Kymlicka notes that Canadians themselves have increasingly lost faith in the efficacy of what is done, he himself feels any rejection of the existing multiculturalism policy is unwarranted. European-focussed scholars have also looked to Canada's multiculturalism and employment equity policies in terms of what countries of Europe can learn from the Canadian experience.[75] In an interesting recent development, the Japanese ambassador to Canada has proclaimed an interest in Canada's experiences dealing with diversity, apparently seeing in them a way of improving the Japanese economy in the context of globalization. Viewing Canadian values on diversity as international values, and aware that Japan's postwar economic strength and productivity are falling, the ambassador mused that "Japan needs to fully integrate itself in the global economy, and to be comfortable working with people from a variety of national and ethnic origins."[76] In addition to this, a report of the UNESCO World Commission on Culture and Development cited Canada's approach to multiculturalism as "a model for other countries."[77]

As a result, Canadian policy-makers have spent time abroad explaining Canada's approach to multiculturalism; for example, the Director of Multiculturalism addressed parliamentarians in the Ivory Coast.[78] Such exchanges of information have also been facilitated by the Metropolis Project, which since its inception has had the partnership of the Department of Canadian Heritage, which houses multiculturalism.[79] (The Metropolis Project, as discussed in Chapter Three, is an international undertaking to exchange policy information in the area of integration and immigration.) In the general area of immigration, policy-makers have looked for mutual international information exchange and learning; the area of multiculturalism, however, has typically been viewed as one in which Canada can instruct and shape a better world. Thus, in 2000, then Minister of Multiculturalism Hedy Fry proclaimed:

> We are now finding that with the increase in ethnic conflict in some parts of the world, our national multiculturalism policy is eliciting international interest. Other countries are seeing the value in multiculturalism as a way of addressing the complex challenges of diversity. Multiculturalism, rooted as it is in integration rather than assimilation, in negotiation as a way to resolve conflict, is increas-

ingly being seen as *a practical tool for advancing peace and human secu-rity around the world* [emphasis added].[80]

While multiculturalism is clearly a domestic policy, by actually stress-ing the relationship between peace, human security, and multicultural-ism, Fry forged a new link with the international political agenda of the Liberal government and specifically with Lloyd Axworthy, former Minister of the Department of Foreign Affairs and International Trade (DFAIT). Between 1997 and 2000, Axworthy pursued an international political agenda stressing human security.[81] Although it remains to be seen whether subsequent ministers will emphasize human security in the same way as he did, particularly in light of unfolding responses to the events of September 11, 2001, it undoubtedly would be difficult to abandon this focus entirely. The concept of human security is premised on the idea that as a result of globalization and the changing nature of international vio-lence in the post-Cold War period, the safety of the individual is now cen-tral to global security and has a prominent place in an agenda for international action.[82] In other words, human security is really about the safety of the individual globally. Thus, in the current period, there is some blurring of the boundaries between the domestic and the interna-tional, even in the area of multiculturalism—a policy which so evidently began as a domestic response to the needs of Canada's ethnically and racially diverse population.

CONCLUSION

In 1971, the Trudeau Liberals announced a policy of multiculturalism within a bilingual framework. In this way, policy-makers engaged in Canadian nation-building in a way that for the first time symbolically rec-ognized the contributions of non-British-, non-French- and non-Aboriginal-origin Canadians. In the nearly 30 years that Canada has had an official policy of multiculturalism, the policy has gone through a number of shifts and evolutions. Beginning as a policy which emphasized folklore and cultural maintenance, it evolved into a policy concerned with anti-racism and, most recently, cultivating business links.

As this chapter has indicated, in its current incarnation federal multi-culturalism policy is heavily shaped by neo-liberal ideas. This is seen in the way that the policy has been characterized by funding cutbacks. Moves such as the dropping of core funding to ethnocultural groups have been encouraged by a new questioning of multiculturalism, which challenges the validity of state spending in the area of culture and cultural maintenance, charging instead that these should be left to private choice and provision. What does this mean in terms of Canadian nation-building? Since the state is never neutral in matters of culture, this emphasis paves the way for a conception of "belonging to the nation" that again favours dominant (British and French) groups.

Canadian policy-makers have also imbued multiculturalism with a globalization discourse that throughout the 1990s has served to draw a link between diversity and business prosperity, international trade links, and Canada's global competitiveness. This has involved redefining the private sphere to focus on business and trade, and emphasizing the export of multiculturalism to these endeavours. This and other aspects of multiculturalism have drawn attention from abroad, leading to an internationalization of the policy in which Canada is a recognized leader. Canada's approach is distinct, and may offer useful lessons elsewhere, especially as the flow of people associated with contemporary globalization means that issues of ethnic and racial diversity are salient in most countries. However, this does not mean that current policy trends in Canada are unproblematic. In the final analysis, a multiculturalism premised on business and trade in an era of globalization—a strategy favoured by the Chrétien Liberals—is limited in dealing with class and gender inequalities among ethnic minorities. In fact, in placing value on the male minority entrepreneur, it may exacerbate such inequalities. It also provides a very narrow rationale for the existence of multiculturalism and diversity because the emphasis is not on national inclusion and belonging, but rather on national and global competitiveness. This appears to be contrary to a multiculturalism based on respect and recognition—the very premise of ethnic minorities' challenge to the Royal Commission on Bilingualism and Biculturalism in the 1960s.

◆ NOTES ◆

1 As cited in Canada, Department of Canadian Heritage, *Annual Report on the Operation of the Canadian Multiculturalism Act, 1993-1994* (Ottawa: Minister of Supply and Services Canada, 1995) 7.

2 Yasmeen Abu-Laban, "The Politics of Race, Ethnicity, and Immigration: The Contested Arena of Multiculturalism," *Canadian Politics*, 3rd ed., ed. James Bickerton and Alain-G. Gagnon (Peterborough: Broadview Press, 1999) 468. For an early critique see in particular Guy Rocher, "Les Ambiguités d'un Canada bilingue et biculturel," *Le Quebec en mutation* (Montréal: Hurtubise HMH, 1973).

3 Canada, Department of Canadian Heritage, *Strategic Evaluation of Multiculturalism Programs Prepared for Corporate Review Branch, Department of Canadian Heritage: Final Report* (Brighton Research, March 1996) 12.

4 Administrative Orders 40-46 (1942), passed under the War Measures Act, R.S.C. 1927, C.206, as cited in Canada, Department of Canadian Heritage, *Strategic Evaluation of Multiculturalism* 15.

5 Yasmeen Abu-Laban, "For Export: Multiculturalism in an Era of Globalization," *Profiles of Canada*, 2nd ed., ed. Kenneth G. Pryke and Walter C. Soderlund (Toronto: Irwin Publishing, 1998) 88.

6 Raymond Breton, "Multiculturalism and Canadian Nation-Building," *The Politics of Gender, Ethnicity, and Language in Canada*, ed. Alan Cairns and Cynthia Williams (Toronto: University of Toronto Press in Cooperation with the Royal Commission on the Economic Union and Development Prospects of Canada, 1986) 44.

7 Evelyn Kallen, *Ethnicity and Human Rights in Canada*, 2nd ed. (Toronto: Oxford University Press, 1995), 172; as cited in Abu-Laban, "For Export: Multiculturalism in an Era of Globalization" 89.

8 Abu-Laban, "The Politics of Race, Ethnicity, and Immigration" 466.

9 Abu-Laban, "The Politics of Race, Ethnicity, and Immigration" 466-67.

10 Leslie Pal, *Interests of State: The Politics of Language, Multiculturalism, and Feminism in Canada*, (Montreal and Kingston: McGill-Queen's University Press, 1993) 115.

11 Abu-Laban, "The Politics of Race, Ethnicity, and Immigration" 467.

12 For a deeper discussion, see Yasmeen Abu-Laban and Daiva Stasiulis, "Ethnic Pluralism Under Siege: Popular and Partisan Opposition to Multiculturalism," *Canadian Public Policy* XVIII.4 (December 1992): 365-86.

13 Abu-Laban, "For Export: Multiculturalism in an Era of Globalization," 88.

14 Daiva K. Stasiulis, "The Symbolic Mosaic Reaffirmed: Multiculturalism Policy," *How Ottawa Spends 1988-89*, ed. Katherine A. Graham (Ottawa: Carleton University Press, 1988) 90.

15 Frances Henry, Carol Tator, Winston Mattis, and Tim Rees, *The Colour of Democracy: Racism in Canadian Society* (Toronto: Harcourt Brace, 2000) 48.

16 Yasmeen Abu-Laban, "Systemic Discrimination," *Routledge Encyclopedia of Feminist Theories*, ed. Lorraine Code (London and New York: Routledge, 2000) 466-67.

17 Daiva K. Stasiulis, "Symbolic Representation and the Numbers Game: Tory Policies on "Race" and Visible Minorities," *How Ottawa Spends: 1991-92*, ed. Frances Abele (Ottawa: Carleton University Press, 1991), 244-250.

18 Tania Das Gupta, "The Politics of Multiculturalism: 'Immigrant Women' and the Canadian State," *Scratching the Surface: Canadian Anti-Racist Feminist Thought*, ed. Enakshi Dua and Angela Robertson (Toronto: Women's Press, 1999) 187.

19 Stasiulis, "The 'Symbolic Mosaic Reaffirmed' Multiculturalism Policy," 91; as cited in Abu-Laban, "The Politics of Race, Ethnicity and Immigration" 470.

20 For a discussion of ethnocultural minorities and constitutional politics, see Yasmeen Abu-Laban and Tim Nieguth, "Reconsidering the Constitution, Ethnic Minorities, and Politics in Canada," *The Canadian Journal of Political Science* 33.3 (September 2000): 465-97.

21 Canadian Multiculturalism Act (as assented to 21 July 1988).

22 Abu-Laban, "The Politics of Race, Ethnicity, and Immigration" 472.

23 Daiva Stasiulis and Yasmeen Abu-Laban, "Ethnic Activism and the Politics of Limited Inclusion in Canada," Bickerton and Gagnon 599.

24 Stasiulis and Abu-Laban, "Ethnic Activism and the Politics of Limited Inclusion in Canada," 588.

25 From the text of a speech by Prime Minister Brian Mulroney to the "Multiculturalism Means Business Conference" (Toronto, 12 April 1986); repr. Canadian Ethnocultural Council, *Ethno Canada* (Spring 1986).

26 Abu-Laban and Stasiulis, "Ethnic Pluralism Under Siege" 372-73.

27 Abu-Laban, "The Politics of Race, Ethnicity and Immigration" 475-76.

28 Neil Bissoondath, *Selling Illusions: The Cult of Multiculturalism in Canada* (Toronto: Penguin Books, 1994) 90.

29 Bissoondath 219.

30 Yasmeen Abu-Laban, "The Politics of Race, Ethnicity, and Immigration" 473.

31 Canada, House of Commons, *Debates* (3 October 1994), 6416.

32 Canada, Department of Canadian Heritage, *Strategic Evaluation of Multiculturalism Programs* 4-5.

33 Canada, Department of Canadian Heritage, *Strategic Evaluation of Multiculturalism Programs* 8.

34 Canada, Department of Canadian Heritage, *Strategic Evaluation of Multiculturalism Programs* 70.

35 Canada, Department of Canadian Heritage, *Strategic Evaluation of Multiculturalism Programs* 71.

36 Canada, Department of Canadian Heritage, *Strategic Evaluation of Multiculturalism Programs* 75.

37 Canada, Department of Canadian Heritage, *1996-1997: 9th Annual Report on the Operation of the Canadian Multiculturalism Act* (Ottawa: Minister of Public Works and Government Services Canada, 1998) 2.

38 Canada, Department of Canadian Heritage, *Multiculturalism: Respect, Equality, Diversity: Program Highlights*, rev. 2nd ed. (July 1998) 2.

39 Canada, Department of Canadian Heritage, *Strategic Evaluation of Multiculturalism Programs* 76.

40 Canada, Department of Canadian Heritage, *1996-1997 9th Annual Report* 3.

41 Paolo Prosperi, "Redefining Citizenship; The Politics of Multiculturalism Reform in Canada," paper prepared for the Annual Canadian Political Science Association meetings, Sherbrooke, Quebec (June 1999) 19.

42 Prosperi 19.

43 See Sandra Back and Susan D. Phillips, "Constructing a New Social Union: Child Care Beyond Infancy?," *How Ottawa Spends: 1997-98*, ed. Gene Swimmer (Ottawa: Carleton University Press, 1997) 235-58.

44 Canadian Ethnocultural Council (CEC), "Multiculturalism, Citizenship, and the Canadian Nation: A Critique of the Proposed Design for Program Renewal," prepared by Bohdan Kordan (Ottawa: CEC, March 1997) 2.

45 CEC, "Multiculturalism, Citizenship and the Canadian Nation" 7.

46 Abu-Laban, "For Export: Multiculturalism in an Era of Globalization," 90.

47 Honourable Sheila Finestone, "Address," *Asian Canadians: Canada's Hidden Advantage, Summary of Roundtable Consultation,* Asia Pacific Foundation of Canada and the Department of Canadian Heritage (November 1994) 76-78.

48 Canada, Department of Canadian Heritage, *Annual Report on the Operation of the Canadian Multiculturalism Act, 1994-1995* (Ottawa: Minister of Supply and Services, 1996), 3.

49 Canada, Department of Canadian Heritage, *Annual Report on the Operation of the Canadian Multiculturalism Act, 1994-1995* 3.

50 Jean Chrétien in Canada, Department of Canadian Heritage, *Annual Report on the Operation of the Canadian Multiculturalism Act 1998-1999* (Ottawa: Minister of Public Works and Government Services, Canada, 2000) iii.

51 Canada, Department of Canadian Heritage, *Annual Report on the Operation of the Canadian Multiculturalism Act, 1993-1994* (Ottawa: Minister of Supply and Services Canada, 1995) 9-15.

52 Canada, Department of Canadian Heritage: Multiculturalism, *Teachers' Guide Secondary Grades: Racism Stop It!* (Ottawa: Minister of Public Works and Services Canada, 1999) 38.

53 Canada, Department of Canadian Heritage: Multiculturalism, *Teachers' Guide* 38.

54 Karim H. Karim, "Australia's Strategy on Productive Diversity," (Hull: Canadian Heritage, Strategic Research and Analysis, September 1995) 11; as cited in Abu-Laban, "For Export: Multiculturalism in an Era of Globalization," 98.

55 Canada, Status of Women Canada, *Setting the Stage for the Next Century: The Federal Plan for Gender Equality* (Ottawa: Status of Women Canada, 1995) 59-60.

56 Canada, Status of Women Canada, *Setting the Stage for the Next Century* 60.

57 Das Gupta 193.

58 See Tim Nieguth, "Privilege or Recognition: The Myth of State Neutrality," *Critical Review of International Social and Political Philosophy* 2.2 (1999): 112-31.

59 See Hermann Kurthen, "The Canadian Experience with Multiculturalism and Employment Equity: Lessons for Europe," *New Community* 23.2 (April 1997): 249-70.

60 See Deniz Kandyoti, "Identity and Its Discontents: Women and the Nation," *Colonial Discourse and*

Postcolonial Theory, eds. Patrick Williams and Laura Chrisman (New York: Columbia University Press, 1994) 376-91.

61 Bissoondath 135-44.

62 Bissoondath 138.

63 Bissoondath 139.

64 Canadian Multiculturalism Act (as assented to 21 July 1988).

65 Susan Moller Okin, "Is Multiculturalism Bad for Women?," *Is Multiculturalism Bad for Women? Susan Moller Okin with Respondents*, eds. Joshua Cohen *et al.* (Princeton, NJ: Princeton University Press, 1999)17.

66 Azizah Y. Al-Hibri, " Is Western Patriarchal Feminism Good for Third World/Minority Women?," Cohen *et. al* 79-84.

67 Sander L. Gilman, " 'Barbaric' Rituals," Cohen *et al.* 57-58.

68 Sherene Razack, *Looking White People in the Eye: Gender, Race, and Culture in Courtrooms and Classrooms* (Toronto: University of Toronto Press, 1998) 97.

69 Razack 97.

70 Christine Inglis, "Multiculturalism: New Policy Responses to Diversity," MOST Policy Papers 4 (Paris: UNESCO, 1996) 16.

71 David Pearson and Patrick Ongley, "Multiculturalism and Biculturalism: The Recent New Zealand Experience in Comparative Perspective," *Journal of Intercultural Studies* 17.1-2 (1996): 12.

72 Hedy Fry, Canada, Department of Canadian Heritage, *Annual Report 1995-1995* vi.

73 Jean Chrétien, Canada, Department of Canadian Heritage, *Annual 1998-1999* iii.

74 See Will Kymlicka, "Introduction," *Finding Our Way: Rethinking Ethnocultural Relations in Canada* (Don Mills: Oxford University Press, 1998).

75 Kurthen 249-70.

76 Katsuisa Uchida, as quoted in Satya Das, "Japan's Budding Renaissance," *The Edmonton Journal*, 31 July 1999: H3.

77 Canada, Department of Canadian Heritage, "Backgrounder: What is Multiculturalism?" n.p. (1996).

78 Erica A.E. Claus, "Implementing Multiculturalism in Canada: Notes for an Address to Parliamentarians of the Republic of Côte d'Ivoire at the National Assembly," Abidjan, Côte d'Ivoire (23 October 1998).

79 There are nine federal departments or agencies which have partnered in the Metropolis Project: Canada Mortgage and Housing Corporation, Human Resources Development Canada, Canadian Heritage, Citizenship and Immigration Canada, Correctional Service Canada, Health Canada, Social Sciences and Humanities Research Council, Statistics Canada, and Status of Women Canada.

80 Canada, Canadian Heritage, *Annual Report 1998-1999* vi.

81 Lloyd Axworthy, "Foreword," *Human Security: Safety for People in a Changing World* Canada, Department of Foreign Affairs and International Trade (April 1999) 1.

82 Canada, Department of Foreign Affairs and International Trade, *Human Security: Safety for People in a Changing World* (April 1999) 1-10.

chapter FIVE

Employment Equity

In an effort to keep up with the changing times, Mattel launched "Working Woman Barbie" in 1999. The new doll is dressed in a grey suit and comes with a briefcase, cell phone, laptop, and a CD-ROM loaded with information on economic literacy. According to a Mattel spokesperson, Working Woman Barbie is designed to do two things: "give girls an idea of what moms are doing when they go off to work; and [it] lets them dream about becoming a working woman."[1] The launch of the doll prompted headlines such as "Barbie puts heels through glass ceiling."[2] Yet the doll, according to one report, "remains Barbie—which is say that she embodies an ideal exceeding what normal gals could achieve, from the top of her sleek blond head to the tips of her impossibly high heels."[3] Apparently diversity is part of that ideal, for, in her 41 years, Barbie has had more than 50 careers. Even Working Women Barbie is not limited— her pencil-grey skirt reverses into a red spangle skirt.

As egregious an exemplar as Barbie may be, women have entered the labour force in greater numbers during the post-war period. The Canadian workforce is growing increasingly more "diverse" in other ways, as well. Analysts point to a number of developments.[4] A significant percentage of the population of Canada's three largest cities— Vancouver, Toronto, Montreal—and their workers are visible minorities. Technological advances have provided means by which people with disabilities may enter the workforce. Youth comprise a significant percentage of Aboriginal communities, and they will be entering the labour market in greater numbers as well. These points, and others, are frequently highlighted in an effort to persuade employers of the necessity to respond to a changing demographic reality[5] not only within workplace organization but also in terms of customer relations and product innovations.

Yet these developments are only part of a more complex story. While women now make up 45 per cent of the Canadian workforce they hold only 6.2 per cent of board of director seats.[6] "Two-thirds of the top 500 Canadian companies have no women directors at all."[7] More importantly, most women workers do not occupy the ranks of prestigious professional occupations but are concentrated in lower status occupations. Many women's work experiences are characterized by low wages and part-time insecure work.[8] Similarly, while the labour force is growing increasingly diverse, due in part to an immigration policy that is emphasizing the need to recruit highly skilled people, there is mounting evidence to suggest that Canada is not adequately harnessing the talents and skills of many of these same immigrants. Statistics Canada reports that, despite the fact that educational skill levels of immigrants had increased in the period from 1986 to 1996, employment levels fell from 81 per cent to 71 per cent for immigrant men and 58 per cent to 51 per cent for immigrant women.[9] Additionally, "immigrants who are visible minorities earn roughly two-thirds the salary earned by white immigrants."[10] Aboriginal people also experience significant degrees of economic marginalization. For example, it was reported in 1995 that, "Aboriginal men make 21 per cent less income than White native-born men, and Aboriginal women make 14 per cent less than White native-born women."[11] The systemic disadvantage of groups and individuals in the labour market has been the focus of much activism by advocacy groups, including those representing people of colour and women. However, policy responses to these concerns have varied.

The focus of this chapter is the evolution of one response to labour market inequality—employment equity—in the period 1993 to 2000. We argue that the fate of this particular policy is intimately tied to shifting conceptions of the welfare state and the growing legitimacy of "market-based," neo-liberal prescriptions. The first section of the chapter illustrates how social justice concerns framed the federal government's initial adoption of employment equity provisions in the 1980s and how the ideological public/private divide found expression in employment equity. In the second section, we examine how Ontario became the only province to adopt stronger legislative provisions than the federal government. We explore the nature of the (negative) response to Ontario's stronger variant of employment equity; notably, as the case of Ontario's experiment with employment equity illustrates, a globalization discourse was wielded by both proponents *and* opponents to the legislated measures. Lastly, we assess the emergence of the "diversity model"—a privatized, voluntary response to diversity in the workplace that is touted by many in the business community as being superior to legislated employment equity measures.

THE ROOTS OF EMPLOYMENT EQUITY

Employment equity is a policy designed to respond to the labour market inequality of women, visible minorities, Aboriginal peoples, and people with disabilities. Employment equity measures seek to identify and eliminate barriers to employment as well as to improve the representation and status of these groups within the labour market.[12] To the extent measures focus on issues of substantive equality, employment equity is concerned with social justice and the social rights attached to a post-war understanding of citizenship.

In the post-war period, the Canadian state assumed new powers and responsibilities. Through the infrastructure of the welfare state, it developed policies and programs to protect citizens from some of the uncertainties generated by a market economy. These uncertainties had become particularly obvious during the Great Depression that preceded World War II. Assessments of post-war citizenship norms have demonstrated how economic and social rights have been defined. For example, Albo and Jenson (1997) have suggested that these norms embodied an idea that there should be some *collective* provision both to protect against life's insecurities—unemployment, sickness—and to respond to life's needs—education, childbearing. "Citizens were not considered to live as isolated individuals facing the risks and costs of everyday life alone. Social solidarity was a 'public good.'"[13] Additionally, there was an understanding that the state would actively intervene and manage national institutions, including the labour market, health care, and education, "to provide at least a minimal level of provision regardless of an individual's economic circumstance."[14] Alongside these new rights of citizenship was recognition that the state should support institutions and advocacy groups that facilitated access of citizens to the state. In this respect there was recognition of the collective rights of citizenship.[15] Employment equity is intimately bound up with these norms of post-war citizenship.

These post-war norms are also underwritten by an ideologically constructed public/private divide. This dichotomy has been characterized as a historically shifting and contested "ideological marker."[16] Feminist scholarship has emphasized that the public/private divide has a number of interrelated meanings. That is, boundaries are frequently drawn between:

- state regulation (government activity) and private economic activity (the market);
- the market (or workplace) in this instance is viewed as "public" in contrast to the "private" sphere of the family; and

131

♦ state regulation and family relations, with the family being viewed as a "haven in a heartless world" that should be protected from the public eye and the scrutiny by state and law.[17]

The public and private dichotomy is not only gendered but also affected by other social relations, including those of race, class, and sexual identity, which influence how the border is constructed (differently for different groups).[18] In part, debates about employment equity are political struggles about where these lines should be drawn. Frequently in these debates the relation between the state and the market comes to the fore. How much, for example, should the state intervene in private market relations, in how individual employers set conditions of work, hire, and promote particular groups of workers?

In the post-war period, "the economic boom that was both a product of and contributor to what has come to be called the welfare state also helped women's groups to demand more regulation of relationships in private and public spheres."[19] But this regulation was often of an uneven nature. To the extent that private sector market relations are seen as beyond the scope of government activity, it has been difficult to promote active government interventions to ensure equity in the labour market. Indeed, it has been suggested that it is "more difficult to introduce regulatory measures that promote women's equality into non-government workplaces as compared with government workplaces."[20] Employment equity measures offer an example. Currently employment equity provisions are in place within the federal public sector and within some provincial bureaucracies, but the only attempt to introduce legislative provisions to cover a large number of private sector workplaces was Ontario's short-lived experiment in the 1990s. The state's attempt to meet or expand social rights becomes constrained in the current moment as a policy discourse emphasizing market values, competitiveness, and individualism becomes more entrenched. Measures such as employment equity are cast as both an infringement on "neutral" market forces and a threat to comparative advantage. For these reasons, employment equity debates are part of a much broader debate about the role of the state in constructing the divide between state activity and the functioning of a capitalist market.

Public/private dichotomies are also intimately bound to familial ideologies; for example, on the premise that women will undertake responsibilities in the private realm of the household.[21] Employment equity debates are more often than not notably silent about the sexual division of labour. Yet, employment equity as an ideal has the potential to destabilize the line between the public realm of the workplace and the private realm of the family. In her comparative study of affirmative action, Carol Lee Bacchi (1996), citing the case of Australia, argues for the need to move beyond an "incorporation model" of affirmative action, which emphasizes measures that focus on training or moving women into non-traditional jobs, because this model "obscures the way in which woman are actively and structurally excluded from non-traditional and other workplaces by some men."[22] She points out that discussions about the need to balance family responsibilities and work life, which are part of affirmative action debates, frequently focus on how women, as opposed to men, will balance these responsibilities.[23] Bacchi highlights the need to develop proposals that would entail a much more profound restructuring of the public/private dichotomy. Such proposals would encourage men to change by taking greater responsibility for domestic and caring labour.[24] Additionally, these measures would underscore the need to address unequal gender relations. This type of restructuring of the public/private division has not been part of employment equity debates in Canada.

While employment equity debates do not pay sufficient explicit attention to the sexual division of labour, familial ideologies are considered. It is suggested that,

> The current backlash against legislative initiatives such as employment and pay equity, while cloaked in the language of restructuring, financial restraint, efficiency, relies partly on an assumption that women's place is in the home and men should be accorded all possible opportunities in the market. Ideological assumptions about women as selfless caregivers, or mothers, of society thus continue to be reproduced in much legal and social policy regulation of work and family.[25]

In Canada, insofar as debates about employment equity have been dominated by questions as to how much the state can intervene in the market, the construction of the public/private divide ignores social relations, including those of gender. Yet, employment equity is precisely designed to address labour market disadvantage based on these social relations.

The Royal Commission on Equality in Employment

The term "employment equity" originates in the 1980s with the Royal Commission on Equality in Employment (the Abella Commission). However, it is important to note that measures that today might also be labeled "employment equity" already had a much longer history in Canada. For example, the 1918 Civil Service Act emphasized merit through "selection and appointment without regard to politics, religion, and influence,"[26] while simultaneously giving hiring priority to male war veterans under the terms of the Veterans' Preference Clause. This clause was in place after both World War I and World War II and has been characterized as "the longest and most powerful affirmative action program ever applied in the federal service, as well as being the least contested."[27] Similarly, in the 1960s the federal government moved to improve the status of francophones within the public service. The Royal Commission on Bilingualism and Biculturalism, established in 1963, supported this initiative. Prime Minister Trudeau, in his 1970 response to the Commission on Bilingualism and Biculturalism report, stated that

> the atmosphere of the public service should represent the linguistic and cultural duality of Canadian society, and ... Canadians whose mother tongue is French should be adequately represented in the public service—both in terms of numbers and in levels of responsibility.[28]

Through the Official Languages Program in 1969, the government sought to enhance the participation, representation, and status of francophones within the public service.

Advocacy groups, including those representing women and visible minorities, were instrumental in raising the issue of employment equity onto the public agenda. Operating under the norms of post-war citizenship, these advocacy groups were recognized by the state as legitimate players in the policy process. As such, the federal government actively funded and supported the representation of group interests—women, ethnic groups, Aboriginal peoples, and francophones—through the Citizenship Branch of the Secretary of State.[29] To some extent, there was recognition that these groups could enhance the policy process. Policy conceived in this way had the potential to be more responsive to the needs of disadvantaged groups whose voices were not always heard. But, as others have pointed out, these forms of representation are also limited insofar as the focus is state representation as opposed to a transformation of unequal relations within the state. Policy outcomes, it is argued, necessarily frequently favour entrenched interests as opposed to advocates of disadvantaged groups.[30] Nevertheless, the representation of women, for example, within the policy machinery of the state and women's mobilization at the grassroots level played a key role in putting employment equity on the public agenda.

To understand how this occurred, events in the 1960s and 1970s need to be examined more closely. In 1967, the federal government established the Royal Commission on the Status of Women (RCSW) in response to women's activism. Its broad mandate was to "inquire into ... the status of women in Canada ... to ensure for women equal opportunities with men in all aspects of Canadian society."[31] After receiving 468 briefs, 1000 letters, and hearing from more than 800 witnesses the commission tabled a report in 1970 with 167 recommendations.[32] One directly challenged the federal government to address as an employer the issue of women's employment inequality in the public service.

> We recommend that, until the sex-typing of occupations is eradicated, the federal Public Service Commission and federal government departments (a) take special steps to increase the number of women appointed to occupations and professions not traditionally female, (b) review and, where necessary, alter their recruitment literature and recruiting programmes to ensure that it is abundantly clear that women are wanted in all occupations and professions, and (c) take special steps to obtain applications from qualified women when appointments for senior levels are being made from outside the service.[33]

These and other recommendations provided a blueprint for government action to address aspects of women's disadvantage in society.[34] While the government did not endorse the entire report, the RCSW itself has been characterized as a "strategic 'marriage' between the interests of women's groups outside the government and the forces inside the government ... that were ready and well situated to push for change."[35]

The recommendations of RCSW did produce a "women's" policy agenda that included a call for increasing the numbers and status of women in the federal public service. In 1972, women met at the Strategy for Change Convention to ensure that the commission's recommendations were addressed by the government. The National Action Committee on the Status of Women (NAC), the largest independent umbrella organization of women's groups today, originated at this meeting. As detailed below, NAC would become a key advocate of employment equity. Similarly, the creation of women's policy machinery within the state created other opportunities to lobby for equity measures.

One of the government's responses to the RCSW was to establish structures designed to "represent" women's interest in the policy-making process. The policy machinery necessary to aid the implementation of the RCSW was put into place through the 1970s under the Liberal government of Pierre Trudeau. In quick succession the government created the Canadian Advisory Council on the Status of Women (CACSW) (1973), a Women's Program within the Department of the Secretary of State (1973), and Status of Women Canada (1971).[36] These bodies helped to further the agenda for affirmative action measures; CACSW, for example, supported the concept of affirmative action as early as 1975. Council members approved a motion endorsing the use of "temporary measures to eliminate the gap between women and men in the labour force."[37]

While women's groups and their organizations raised the issue of employment equity, it was also on the agenda of other advocacy groups. The Canadian Ethnocultural Council, a national umbrella group representing minority groups, which was supported in part by the federal government, "both contributed to and was driven by a broadening discourse on equality rights that rapidly embraced equity employment for visible minorities and other minorities...."[38] In making a demand for equity in the labour market, women and minority groups were demanding a fuller expression of the social rights of citizenship. The focus on the state to legislate equity was guided by a post-war rationale that the state actually could and should intervene to regulate the labour market.

The establishment of Royal Commission on Equality and Employment in 1983 was the federal government's response to equity issues. Judge Rosalie Abella was appointed sole commissioner. The Abella Commission, as it came to be known, was directed to

> ... inquire into the most efficient, effective, and equitable means of promoting employment opportunities, eliminating systemic discrimination, and assisting all individuals to compete for employment opportunities on an equal basis.[39]

In particular, the Abella Commission was mandated to examine the opportunities for employment of women, Native people, disabled persons, and visible minorities in certain Crown corporations and corporations wholly owned by the government of Canada.[40]

The establishment of the Commission represented an implicit recognition that voluntary compliance measures were not proving effective in achieving a more representative workforce. For example, it was reported in 1984 that

> The Affirmative Action Branch of the Canada Employment and Immigration Commission has encouraged and assisted the private sector to develop programs targeted at women, the disabled, aboriginal people, and Blacks in Nova Scotia on a voluntary basis. From 1979 to 1983, 1,130 firms were approached but as of November 1983, only 49 companies throughout the country had signed agreements to establish formal affirmative action programs.[41]

The failure of these voluntary initiatives was linked to employer intransigence.[42]

Additionally, the Abella Commission attempted to address the limited success of existing complaints-based anti-discrimination measures. Throughout the 1960s and 1970s the federal government and the provinces put in place Human Rights Codes. Such codes are designed to protect individuals from discrimination on the basis of race, colour, ethnic background, religion, sex, marital status, and disability. An individual who experiences discrimination can lodge a complaint with a human rights commission and must prove discrimination. This approach is inherently individualistic, and, as a result, complainants are forced to prove harm done in a case-by-case manner. Additionally, the process tends to neglect the fact that there are significant differences in power and resources between the complainants and perpetrator, especially if the latter is an employer.[43] Critics point out that a complaints-driven model is not effective in addressing widespread, systemic discrimination.[44] Employment equity is designed to address the weaknesses of a complaint-driven model.

The Report of the Abella Commission emphasized that "traditionally most firms have regarded the white non-disabled man as the desired worker."[45] The commission called for legislated employment equity to provide employment opportunities for those workers constructed outside the "norm": women, visible minorities, people with disabilities, and Aboriginal people. Abella adopted a very broad definition of equality when she argued:

> Sometimes equality means treating people the same, despite their differences, and sometimes it means treating them as equals by accommodating their differences.

137

> ... We now know that to treat everyone the same way may be
> to offend the notion of equality. Ignoring differences may mean
> ignoring legitimate needs.... Equality means nothing if it does not
> mean that we are of equal worth regardless of differences in gender,
> race, ethnicity or disability....
>
> Ignoring differences and refusing to accommodate them is a
> denial of equal access and opportunity. It is discrimination.[46]

The work of the Abella Commission was complemented by the work of a Parliamentary Special Committee on the Participation of Visible Minorities in Canadian Society. In its report "Equality Now!" (1984), it, too, underscored the inadequacies of voluntary measures and called on the federal government to "promote the hiring of visible minorities in the private sector."[47]

In 1986 the federal Conservative government responded to the findings of the Abella Commission with the introduction of the Employment Equity Act (EEA) and the Federal Contractors Program. These measures marked the "first step" on the part of the government to concretely address systemic discrimination in the workplace.[48] The EEA sought to achieve workplace equality by "ensuring that ability and qualifications are the only criteria for employment opportunities, benefits and achievements."[49] The Act is structured by three principles:

* first, no one shall be denied employment opportunities and benefits for reasons unrelated to ability;
* second, special measures are necessary to improve the employment situation of members of designated groups;
* and third, "reasonable accommodation" requires employers to recognize legitimate differences between groups and take reasonable steps to accommodate those differences.[50]

Three elements were used to implement the spirit of the EEA. First, employment equity provisions would apply to the entire public service. Secondly, the Legislated Employment Equity Program (LEEP) was applied to 370 federally regulated employers, like banks and communications and transportation firms, as well as Crown corporations with more than 100 employees. These employers account for 5.5 per cent of the Canadian labour force.[51] Third was the Federal Contractors Program, which required that firms with more than 100 employees, placing bids on government contracts of $200,000 or more in value, make a commitment to employment equity. Firms meeting this description accounted for

880 employers and 7.5 per cent of the workforce.[52] Thus, the EEA targeted the public sector and workplaces regulated by, or doing business with, the federal government.

Under the provisions of the EEA, employers are required to produce an employment equity plan, which includes goals and a timetable. Additionally, employers are required to submit a progress report to the federal government detailing measures undertaken to improve workforce representation of the four designated groups. The plans must indicate the numbers of workers within each occupational category as well as specifically noting the number of each designated group in occupational categories. Through the employment equity plan, employers must identify workplace policies, practices, and procedures that act as barriers to designated groups and propose measures to address these barriers.[53] Reports are forwarded to the Canadian Human Rights Commission. A $50,000 fine can be imposed on employers for failure to file data.[54]

The Federal Contractors Program requires that employers who wish to bid on government contracts for supply and services provide a certificate indicating a commitment to implement a series of employment equity criteria, thus identifying themselves as a "contractor in compliance." The certificate is the first step in the program. Another step is a compliance review. Firms that fail on-site reviews could be prevented from securing further government contracts.[55]

Additionally, the federal government moved to introduce employment equity across the ranks of the public service in 1986. Among the mandated measures were initiatives to:

- establish an environment that supports the principles of employment equity;
- prepare and analyze statistical data on the work force to identify areas in which persons in designated groups are underrepresented;
- analyze their employment systems to identify systemic barriers facing designated groups;
- develop three-year employment equity plans that include special measures to correct imbalances in the public service work force and contain quantitative and qualitative objectives, activities, schedules, and monitoring mechanisms.[56]

Critics have pointed out that there are a number of flaws inherent in the 1986 EEA and the Contractors Program that weaken their ability to address labour market disadvantage. The National Action Committee on the Status of Women (NAC) has argued that the EEA was lacking in enforcement powers.

> The federal Employment Equity Act only requires the annual reporting of certain employment data. It does not require that employers have employment equity programs and if programs are ineffectual or non-existent, there are no legislated sanctions.[57]

The Abella Commission recommended that an independent mechanism be established to monitor legislative equity.[58] The government rejected this recommendation and instead emphasized public vigilance of employment equity data. There was a belief that "public scrutiny would effectively shame employers into complying with the objectives of the act," thereby rendering a strong enforcement mechanism unnecessary.[59] However, the poor employment performance vis-à-vis representation of the target groups renders this assumption problematic. Indeed, NAC reviewed the employment equity data of three large employers—Bank of Nova Scotia, Canadian Broadcasting Corporation, and Air Canada—over a four-year period. It characterized progress as "glacial" for women in each of the target groups.[60]

In sum, through the EEA and the Federal Contractors Program, the federal government took modest steps to address group disadvantage in the labour market. However, the very nature of these initiatives—limited to certain employers—may have insulated them from a backlash insofar as they were designed and controlled by employers, and employers had only to demonstrate a good-faith effort.

However limited they are, these employment equity initiatives must be seen as part of the state response to equality-based claims of equity groups—women, visible minorities, people with disabilities, and Aboriginal peoples. The response was premised on post-war assumptions: firstly, that the state had an important role to play in supporting social equality of groups and individuals; secondly that the state could and should actively intervene in the labour market to address inequality. These assumptions were already being contested in the 1980s even as the federal government introduced its initiatives.[61] Presently, the hegemony of the understanding of citizenship that emerged with the post-war state continues to wane, although it has not been abandoned completely. As Jane Jenson and Greg Albo write, "there has been fervent struggle over whether the state should even minimally promote social equality or whether everyone must accept 'the discipline of the market,' no matter the social costs."[62] This contest becomes evident when we examine what happened when the province of Ontario moved to introduce tough employment equity provisions which moved beyond those at the federal level in the early 1990s.

EMPLOYMENT EQUITY INITIATIVES 1990-1995

Provincial Experience—Ontario[63]

Employment equity policy and legislation at the federal level and within provincial jurisdictions varies considerably across the country.[64] However, Ontario's experience with employment equity has been uniquely tumultuous. Under a social democratic government, Ontario became the first province to introduce employment equity legislation that also applied to the private sector. Indeed, the leader of the provincial NDP government, Bob Rae, had introduced a private member's bill on equity measures while in opposition. The NDP were committed to employment equity when they came to power in 1990 as the first social democratic government in the province's history. Five years later the NDP went down in defeat. Under the banner of the "common sense revolution" Mike Harris's Progressive Conservatives swept into power and promptly repealed the legislation. Subsequently, in the space of five years Ontario went from being a province with far-reaching legislated, employment equity measures to being a jurisdiction entirely without legislation.

The fate of employment equity in Ontario is important for a number of reasons. Firstly, the debate around employment equity underscores the contradictions between the redistributive concerns of social justice and an ascendant market-oriented neo-liberal approach that celebrates the ideals of efficiency, competitiveness, and individualism. Secondly, in this debate two views of equality are championed, one in which equality equals sameness and the other, somewhat broader view, in which, as Rosalie Abella described it, sometimes equality necessitates the recognition and accommodation of difference. The equality-equals-sameness concept tends to underwrite the image of the model neo-liberal citizen, a self-reliant individual who makes few or no demands on the state.[65] Ultimately, it is this view of equality that prevails in the Ontario case. Finally, Ontario's experiment with employment equity is important for its legacy; it has been suggested that the federal government's overhaul of the Federal Employment Equity Act in 1995, which saw the introduction of amendments to strengthen its provisions, was modelled along the lines of Ontario's failed Act.[66]

Early in its mandate, the NDP government in Ontario moved to pursue wide-ranging legislative employment equity whose scope extended beyond the familiar terrain of the public service into the private sector. The initiative was at the heart of the government's "social equity agenda," which encompassed a number of reforms including collective bargaining reform, broader pay equity (equal pay for work of equal value) provisions, an employee wage protection fund, and daycare reform.[67] All these reforms were located in a rationale that sought to demonstrate that social equity was a necessary complement to economic renewal. This was the means by which the NDP attempted to negotiate the shift between the understanding that underpinned the post-war welfare state and neo-liberal ideals that were infusing many readings of the conditions imposed by processes of globalization.

In 1991, the NDP released its discussion paper on employment equity, called "Working Towards Equality." It epitomized the NDP's vision of equality. Referring to employment equity as a "broad process that means changing the way we think about the workplace," it argued that employment equity "aims to overcome the discrimination which has kept certain groups from being hired or promoted in the same way as other groups."[68] However, the NDP government found that it was unable to convey such ideas to the Ontario public at large. In particular, the meaning of "fairness" in the labour market proved especially controversial within a contracting economy.

"Working Towards Equality" also indicated that that the NDP wanted to develop legislation that would go beyond the federal government initiative. Gay and lesbian advocacy groups made presentations, arguing that they should be included as a designated group; however, the province chose to stick with the federal legislation's designated groups, although it did extend the scope of the proposed Act. Whereas the federal Conservatives' 1986 measures cover only the public service and federally regulated workplaces, the NDP proposal included not only the public sector but the broader public sector[69] and private sector employers. The NDP also announced that its measures would be mandatory. In taking this position the government explicitly challenged private enterprise and the logic of the market. It did so at a time when market ideals were being valorized.

A key justification for employment equity, according to "Working Toward Equality," had to do with economics. Employment equity, according to the NDP, was good for business.

> There is no doubt that businesses and governments are experiencing difficult economic times. Employment equity is critical for

ensuring Ontario's current and future competitiveness. Those employers who make the most effective use of all their human resources are more likely to survive and prosper.[70]

This justification is also used by groups favouring legislative initiatives. Margaret Hageman of the Alliance for Employment Equity stated: "By increasing the human potential within workforces you will increase productivity, generate new ideas, find new markets and become more competitive."[71] This attitude was adopted by some elements of the popular press. One *Toronto Sun* columnist stated:

> Canada's so-called minorities become majorities beyond North America's borders. They are the races, cultures, and nationalities we hope to transform into buyers of Canadian goods and services. Does it not follow that our sales force would be all the stronger if it included men and women with the most thorough knowledge of the cultural nuances abroad?[72]

In their own way, each of these interventions stresses that equity contributes to the bottom line and, as such, is a necessity in a globalizing environment.

The construction of employment equity as a "good business initiative" and the explicit link to "competitiveness" and "sound management procedures," however, tend to displace employment equity from the ambit of social justice that underpinned post-war ideas of social citizenship and the ideals of the Abella Commission. And this strategy is problematic to the extent that dominant readings of globalization are guided by neo-liberalism's guiding premise: the market works in its own best interest. What happens if this logic is applied to employment equity? The private sector response is invariably "if employment equity is good for business it will be taken up voluntarily." Thus, one business lobby group wrote in its brief to the employment equity commissioner:

> The Consortium believes that these concepts and objectives [of employment equity] are best achieved outside of legislation and regulatory controls, as most progressive companies will engage in employment practices that reflect the community that they serve.[73]

In other words there is no need for legislation or the public scrutiny of firms. The invocation of "competitiveness" is similarly problematic. As the private sector deploys it, "competitiveness' is the need to compete in the global economy; hence, it can be turned to strengthen the private sector's very argument against state intervention in the labour market. Such regulation is seen as an "artificial rigidity" that hampers business's ability to compete in the global economy.

Furthermore, Carol Bacchi, in her comparative assessment of affirmative action, has noted that there are consequences of linking equity initiatives to economic imperatives. The link limits demands for making industry socially responsible for its activities. It also tends to leave the reform vulnerable to the vagaries of the economy, to "what the market will bear."[74] Such sentiments found expression during the consultation period prior to the introduction of the NDP's employment equity legislation. The Canadian Manufacturers' Association pushed for voluntary measures, stating in its brief:

> Canada is part of the larger global marketplace and government policy must recognize this. Government must ensure that its policies assist Ontario business to succeed—and to do this *competitiveness* is the *key*. It is to no one's advantage, especially the members of designated groups, to pursue policies that result in Ontario becoming less competitive and a less attractive place to do business...
>
> Ontario is also experiencing one of the worst recessions of the century. The government must ensure that any policy initiatives it implements do not exacerbate the problem. CMA recognizes that it would be inequitable to place the economic burden on those in the designated groups, however it is necessary to ensure that employment equity is pursued in such a way that it enables our economic position to improve.[75]

Similarly, the Canadian Federation of Independent Business rejected the proposals for an independent monitoring body, an Employment Equity Commission, on the basis that there should be no further growth of state bureaucracies.[76]

The Ontario government introduced Bill 79, "An Act to Provide Equity for Aboriginal People, People with Disabilities, Members of Racial Minorities, and Women," in June 1993. It moved beyond federal employment equity provisions in a number of ways. First, the scope of coverage was broader. Bill 79 included the Ontario Public Service (OPS), firms with more than 10 employees in the broader public sector, and those firms in the private sector with more than 50 employees. Second, in unionized workplaces, employers would have to work with unions to develop employment equity plans. Third, under its provisions, any individual in the province could make a complaint against an employer for failing to comply. Fourth, it established a monitoring mechanism in the shape of the Employment Equity Commission. The Commission was empowered to conduct audits and to oversee the compliance process. Disputed cases would be adjudicated by an Employment Equity Tribunal, which had the power to levy fines.[77]

Bill 79 was opposed from the start by employer groups who felt it went too far and was overly interventionist. During the debate on the Bill, the NDP tried to counter this by linking social equity to economic renewal and global competitiveness.

> We literally cannot afford to underutilize the training, skills, talent, and experience of those who work and those who want to work, particularly if we want to gain a competitive edge in a global economy. To do so is not only unjust: it would be economically disastrous.[78]

In the ensuing public debate, the equation of social equity with economic renewal was effectively lost. The message was overwhelmed both by a backlash against equity groups and an opposition rhetoric that emphasized market factors, including potential job losses, necessary job creation, recession, investment priorities, and the business climate. Thus one Tory critic asked during the legislative debate: "Will the administrative costs of employment equity affect the ability of Ontario business to remain competitive?"[79] Throughout the debate the provincial opposition parties, the Conservatives and Liberals, propagated the idea that, however good or viable employment equity measures may be, employers simply could not afford it in a recession. Many opposition MPs and other opponents argued that the legislation itself would cost the province jobs. The argument had resonance with a large majority of Ontario's people who, in the grip of recession, were already feeling insecure about the economy and employment in general and their own jobs in particular.

The other message that found a receptive audience was that employment equity measures were unfair because some groups were demanding "special treatment." The NDP argued that, while each citizen should be equal in worth to another, some people, because of their group membership, experienced systemic discrimination in the workplace. It argued:

> Achieving equity doesn't mean treating everyone in the same way. Employment equity means, rather, we recognize people's different experiences and needs, and adapt our workplace practices accordingly. It might mean, for example, that employers implement flexible working arrangements to accommodate the different people who

> make up the workforce, such as working parents. By using these
> kinds of employment equity measures, we recognize and allow for
> diversity in the workforce.[80]

The NDP government's employment equity initiative therefore embraced a definition of equity that went beyond the moment of hiring. It suggested that employment equity measures might include initiatives that would permit the balancing of work and family responsibilities, flexible working arrangements, and mentoring.[81] The Progressive Conservative Party, however, believed that legislative equity in the labour market was neither desirable or required. For the Conservatives, equality and social justice were based on the absence of discrimination, or equality-equals-sameness; individuals were equal in their role as citizens and should be treated identically by the state. Regarding the under-representation of different groups in the workforce, the Progressive Conservative Party maintained that, although "discrimination is partially responsible for a percentage of the problem ... it cannot be denied that other factors have contributed to the under-representation of groups."[82] One of these factors was the existence of what the Conservatives termed "pre-market conditions," circumstances in which individuals found themselves which might prevent them from competing equally for a job. Thus, during the debate on Bill 79, Conservative labour critic Elizabeth Witmer called upon the government to:

> ... Focus on the pre-market conditions that are presently prevent-
> ing these individuals from successfully competing for employment
> opportunities, such as childcare ... student loans, the English-as-a-
> second language training, and skills upgrading.[83]

Within these remarks is a conception that the public/private dichotomies—in this case market/society, market/family—are natural. This conception is premised on the idea that there are separate public and private spheres and that the former plays no role in the constitution or operation of the latter. This position allows its exponents to downplay the extent to which the sexual division of labour in the home, for example, is connected to women's labour-market disadvantage. It ignores how social reproduction or domestic labour are integral to the workings of the market. In the case of racial minorities, the logic of "pre-market conditions" similarly neglects the ways in which organization practices and patterns can be exclusionary. It is not surprising, therefore, that the Harris Conservatives and other opponents argued that Bill 79 made the private sector responsible for issues beyond its control and which are in fact societal in nature.

There are two implicit outcomes of the deployment of this type of logic. First, individual members of designated groups are constructed as being responsible for their labour market disadvantage. Members of designated groups, by implication, lack the right skills, training, organization, etc., necessary to enter the labour market as equals. If these individuals experience forms of disadvantage then it is due to their own inherent characteristics. Second, and related to this, is the point Bacchi makes in her work, that the disaggregation of social groups into competing individuals places the focus on barriers to individual achievement. That there might be unequal power relations between and among groups is neglected.[84] This is especially true in the backlash—fanned by the opposition—against equity groups.

The emergence of employment equity on the legislative agenda as a measure to confront group disadvantage speaks to the success of equity advocacy groups, including women's organizations and ethnocultural groups, in raising the awareness of systemic discrimination in the workplace. The debate around the employment equity bill inverted this partial recognition; opposition forces to the NDP's employment equity legislation tended to construct designated groups (women, racial minorities, Aboriginal people and people with disabilities) as "advantaged" and white men were discursively constructed as "disadvantaged." For example, the Conservative labour critic Elizabeth Witmer argued that the proposed legislation,

> ... was not based on fairness and equal opportunity, nor was it
> devoted to ending discrimination in the workplace, but rather that
> it meant reverse discrimination and that for a growing number of
> jobs white males need not apply, or even if they do they will not
> be considered.[85]

Equity groups were attacked for demanding "special treatment" and for not wanting to compete by the rules of the game, and charges of reverse discrimination were leveled. Umbrella groups and the government were put on the defensive.

The proposed legislation was also attacked on the grounds that it was an assault on the principles of merit and fairness;[86] by this reasoning "disadvantage" became related to "undeserving" and "incompetent." Repeatedly the public was told—by some employer groups, by opposition parties, and by some members of the press—that employment equity would force employers to hire unqualified people. The backlash against employment equity grew more vocal,[87] and by the time Bill 79 was passed in 1994 the initiative—a measure designed to counteract disadvantage—came to be seen as a "handout."[88]

The public debate surrounding Bill 79 went far beyond the legislation itself. On one hand, as one assessment pointed out, the debate raised awareness of the issues that in effect "laid the basis for, and also reflected the existence of, a politicized constituency determined to defend the principles on which employment equity is based." On the other hand, the debate produced "a profound backlash against employment equity in any form."[89] Indeed, attacks on employment equity were central to the Harris Conservatives' "Common Sense Revolution" and Lynn Macleod's Liberal election campaigns.[90] One of the first acts of the newly elected Conservative government was to enact Bill 8, "An Act to Repeal Job Quotas and to Restore Merit-Based Employment Practices." The ideological underpinnings of the Harris government and its clear rejection of employment equity and the concept of systemic discrimination were captured in the title of this Act[91] which stressed "quotas" and "merit." In adopting this wording, the Harris government further perpetuated the notion that the NDP legislation mandated that members of the designated groups would be selected on criteria other than the standard of merit; a numeral quota was being adhered to.[92]

The demise of employment equity legislation in Ontario is a marked example of an explicit withdrawal of the (provincial) state from the labour market regulation. Moreover, the adoption of Bill 8 signaled a rejection of Abella's broad definition of employment-equity-related equality in favour of a narrower conception of it—equality-as-sameness. The Harris government's subsequent actions in the field, discussed in the next section, signal that state intervention has become subordinate to market aspirations.

Federal Experiences with Equity—Bill C-64

Jean Chrétien's Liberal government was elected in 1993. From its first mandate it pursued a strong neo-liberal agenda. However, the degree to which neo-liberal ideas have found expression varies considerably across policy areas and jurisdictions. Employment equity offers a case in point. Just as the Province of Ontario was debating the pros and cons of employment equity the federal government was moving to amend the Federal Employment Equity Act. The federal Liberal government had made a pre-election commitment to strengthen employment equity provisions;[93]

it was also increasingly evident that EEA had produced less-than-significant results.[94] The CACSW reported, for example:

> The data from employers covered by the *Employment Equity Act* during the first four reporting years (1987-1990) indicate [...] *limited progress* in representation, occupational profiles, salary profiles, and opportunities for change of all women, and more specifically women of other designated groups.[95]

Under the terms of the 1986 EEA the government was mandated to conduct a review after five years. In May 1992, the government established a Special Committee on the Review of EEA. A number of groups made presentations to the Special Committee on the Employment Equity Act to proposed ways in which the Act should be amended.[96] The Canadian Advisory Council on the Status of Women was not alone when it recommended that the scope of the EEA should be widened, that there should be mandatory goals and timetables, and that there should be an improvement in enforcement measures.[97]

The Special Committee report "A Matter of Fairness" made 31 recommendations to revise EEA. Following from this the Liberal government introduced Bill c-64, "An Act Respecting Employment Equity." Among its key provisions were the extension of coverage to all employees in the federal public service, agencies and commissions, and the strengthening of the powers of the Canadian Human Rights Commission to allow it to undertake audits of employers. In addition, the Canadian Human Rights Tribunal would act as an enforcement body when required.[98]

These provisions were in many ways similar to Ontario's ill-fated Bill 79,[99] yet they did not produce the same type of vitriolic debate. However, Bill c-64 was not without critics. It was vigorously opposed by Reform MPS in Parliament who were more numerous following the 1993 election. Reform members, echoing the Harris Conservatives, spoke to issues of merit and fairness and raised the spectre of quotas. They also argued that the scope of the Bill should be limited to the federal public sector only (a *de facto* call for the repeal of the existing EEA).[100] The Liberal response to these attacks was to reiterate a vision of Canada that was more inclusive.

> Our Canada would be one that builds on our traditional core values of equality, justice and fair shares of the opportunities that build better lives and a better country. It would recognize, as the red book did,

> that we exist in this society together not apart.... Employment
> equity is a basic part of making our vision real.[101]

Additionally, the Liberal government was careful while outlining how stronger employment equity measures could more effectively address systemic discrimination to distance itself from Ontario's legislative provisions. But Liberal MPs also used economic rationales to defend C-64. Sheila Finestone, Secretary of State (Multiculturalism) (Status of Women), for example stated that

> Fairer access, meritorious advancement and equality of opportunity
> are key for all corporations that want to compete in the global mar-
> ketplace. Our Canadian people often reflect and know the cultures
> of the new global markets. Why not use diversity as a valued com-
> petitive edge to our mutual benefit? Global business is multicultural,
> multilingual and multiracial.[102]

Despite the debate within the House of Commons, proposed revisions to the Federal Employment Equity Act never captured the public agenda in the same way as debates about equity infused public opinion in Ontario. The federal government successfully passed Bill C-64 in 1995. (It has been speculated that Bill C-64 passed without significant public outcry because the country was too preoccupied with the 1995 Quebec Referendum.[103] This may be too superficial a reading.)

Janet Lum and A. Paul Williams suggest that the passage of the Act would seem to be at odds with key neo-liberal claims but offer an interesting and useful set of linkages to it. Firstly, they argue, advocacy groups such as NAC, the Women's Educational and Action Fund, and the Canadian Ethnocultural Council continued to press the government for change.[104] Now, it should be noted that these groups were operating in an environment in which they were more often than not castigated as "special interests," for the 1990s saw an ideological attack on both social solidarity and collective political action.[105] The Liberal government also was moving to reduce support for these groups by cutting funding and eliminating points of access within the state. In short order the government disbanded CACSW and folded the Women's Bureau into Status of Women Canada. These actions epitomize neo-liberal politics of "aggressive exclusion," which seek to narrow the social citizenship rights of subordinate groups, such as women.[106]

Nevertheless, the 1986 Employment Equity Act, though weak, did create a "focal point" around which groups could mobilize, in Lum's and

Williams's view. Their efforts were supported by court decisions upholding a more equitable work environment. Additionally, say Lum and
Williams, partisan concerns underwrote the Liberal government's actions:

> At an estimated cost of 1.5 million, the 1995 legislation was a rel-
> atively inexpensive but politically powerful means of establishing fed-
> eral Liberal government popular credentials vis-à-vis rightist federal
> political contenders like the Reform Party and provincial parties like
> the Progressive Conservatives in Ontario and Alberta.[107]

This last reason may be the most compelling. The new federal employment equity legislation was very limited in its scope, covering only 8 per
cent of the workforce. It applied only to federal Crown corporations with
100 or more employees and federal departments and agencies along with
public sector "separate employers" of 100 or more employees, such as
the RCMP.[108] Indeed, the very limited nature of these initiatives may
have insulated them from a backlash insofar as they were designed and
controlled by employers, and employers had only to demonstrate a good
faith effort. In large part, the federal government was the chief employer
involved. For this reason the EEA and Federal Contractors Program have
been characterized as successful in "persuading the corporate climate to
embrace the employment equity mission but also in avoiding resistance
and backlash."[109]

Additionally, as Bakan and Kobayashi assert, recent federal governments
have been unequivocal in their public support of employment equity. In
contrast, the fate of the initiative in Ontario was linked, they argue, to a
"deliberate ideological campaign to dismantle employment equity" that
generated a backlash.[110] Consequently, at one and the same time, apparently robust employment equity legislation remains in place at the federal level but is in tatters within the Province of Ontario. And indeed, in
terms of the former jurisdiction, it has been suggested that there has been
an increase in employment equity-related activity at the federal level following the adoption of the new Act.[111] Meanwhile, in Ontario, the
provincial government has dismantled all employment equity infrastructure within the public service and legislated employers to do the same.[112]

The 1995 federal employment equity provisions demonstrate that the
imposition of neo-liberal prescriptions takes place within the terms of existing policy arrangements. As suggested above, employment equity was very
much shaped by post-war norms and values. The espousal of neo-liberal
ideas, as the federal experience with employment equity suggests, does
not signal the jettisoning of previous commitments and policy arrange-

ments. As suggested above, the 1986 Employment Equity legislation produced a legacy that withstood some of the attacks upon it. The limited scope of the EEA ensures that many of these attacks were less vitriolic than they might have been.

MANAGING DIVERSITY

In Ontario private sector employers have moved to the fore in developing models to address workplace diversity. The degree to which these models address labour market disadvantage remains in question. Recent private-sector efforts have been actively encouraged and fostered by the Progressive Conservative government. The Harris Conservatives introduced a non-legislative, voluntaristic "Equal Opportunity Plan" to replace legislative equity. According to then-Minister of Citizenship, Culture and Recreation, Marilyn Mushinski, the Equal Opportunity Plan was "merit-based, inclusive, voluntary and built on partnership. It is based on co-operation, not coercion."[113] In a subsequent interview, Mushinski argued that previous administrations had created a "culture of dependency" and the new Equal Opportunity Plan not only "restores some common sense to the workplace" but focusses on "what can we do to make you more self-sufficient."[114]

To this stated end the provincial government unveiled its official "Gateway to Diversity Web Page" in 1998. It defined Equal Opportunity as:

> ... the Government of Ontario's approach to building workplaces where merit is the basis of employment practices. Its goal is to help organizations be more effective and competitive....
>
> Employment Equity and affirmative action refer to approaches that focus on particular groups and require specific types of policies and actions. Equal Opportunity is broader, recognizing the importance and contribution of every single member of the workforce.[115]

In short, the government of Ontario removed itself from legislative equity options in favour of encouraging employers to develop firm specific "diversity" measures. The Harris government's "Equal Opportunity" framework, in its rejection of state regulation, epitomizes a neo-liberal agenda— the repudiation of the big stick of legislation. Within the plan the focus is on the individual because there is no conception of systemic group disadvantage.[116] Additionally, the market (in effect, the bottom line) was to guide the implementation of diversity—hence, the pre-eminent role accorded to business groups and employers. According to the government, Ontario's new Equal Opportunity Plan "recognizes that the province's diverse population offers business a substantial advantage for building competitive strength."[117] In many ways this message is not far from the key message that the previous NDP government used to extol its legislated employment equity plan. In both cases the province's diverse population is constructed as a resource. But the Harris government's "diversity" model clearly articulated its departure from legislated options. Additionally, where the NDP had attempted to link employment equity to social justice, the clear message from the Harris government was that Equal Opportunity should be adopted because it contributed to business advantage—the bottom line.

A recent joint publication "Business Results Through Diversity: A Guidebook"[118] epitomizes the new government-business stakeholder partnership. At a cost of $15, the resource manual presents step-by-step information on how to assess your workplace for diversity and develop an action plan for implementation. It stresses that "diversity is *not*: quotas; a legislative program with bureaucratic requirements; employment equity or affirmative action; special privileges; window-dressing."[119] This approach, as the government's "Gateway to Diversity Web Page" informs you, "calls for the recognition of the contributions that individuals can make as individuals, not just members of legislatively designated groups." It is important to emphasize that the Harris government is not denying the existence of discrimination, but it subscribes to a view that holds that acts of discrimination happen to individuals, not groups. Consequently, the appropriate course of action against perceived discrimination is through the Ontario Human Rights tribunals. In adopting the business case for diversity, the Harris government embraces a trend that was already well-established in many workplace organizations, "managing diversity."

Managing Diversity

Now common in management or human resources literature, the term "managing diversity" was developed in the early 1980s[120] by R. Roosevelt Thomas, a diversity consultant to Fortune 500 companies. This management model suggests that changes in the demographics of the labour market and client base require new organizational responses;[121] in it, people (a firm's workforce) are constructed as a dimension of comparative advantage in a globalizing economy. In 1990, Thomas outlined the business case for diversity in the *Harvard Business Review*:

> A lot of executives are not sure why they should want to learn to manage diversity. Legal compliance seems like a good reason. So does community relations. Many executives believe they have a social and moral responsibility to employ minorities and women. Others want to placate an internal group or pacify an outside organization. None of these are bad reasons, but none of them are business reasons, and given the nature and scope of today's competitive challenges, I believe only business reasons will supply the necessary long term motivation.... Learning to manage diversity will make you more competitive.[122]

Within Canada, advocates of the model include academics at business schools, such as the University of Western Ontario's Ivey Business School; independent think-tanks, such as the Conference Board of Canada; and business leaders. For example, the former president of National Grocers Company, which controls Loblaws, stated emphatically:

> People are the driving force for excellence. Any competitor can get our products, our technology or pricing, but no one can get our people. Our people are key to our competitive edge.[123]

Additionally, within a managing diversity model there is an emphasis on securing new markets internally, through reaching previously untapped customer bases. For example, the president of the Canadian Imperial Bank of Commerce, extolling the virtues of diversity told his audience:

> Even at the retail level, diversity may be more relevant to you than you think. If you're involved in the oil and gas sector think of the service stations that distribute your products. How many are operated by women? How many car dealerships employ women salespeople?
>
> And yet women represent over 50% of the Canadian population. Women buy gasoline. Women purchase cars ... they have more earning power than ever before. Does your industry reflect this reality? Has it moved to accommodate it? There is an opportunity here for companies with a diversity strategy.[124]

Having more women in an organization's workforce becomes a means to reach a new market. This logic is also applied to ethnic minorities. The Canadian Advertising Foundation reported that the visible minority market is worth $78 million.[125] Figures like this have prompted people to argue for better customer service. One quiz designed to test whether a company's sales force can meet the needs of ethnocultural customers asked questions such as: "Are your salespeople familiar with the shopping habits, communications, styles, and negotiation tactics of their ethnocultural customers? Are your managers knowledgeable enough about the ethnic market to make appropriate changes in the design of products or services?"[126]

The diversity model also holds out the promise that new markets can be tapped abroad and that diverse workplaces are one way to do it. China, the Pacific Rim, and India are all seen as new, emerging global markets. It is argued that "differences in language, culture, and business practices are keeping us from exploiting these emerging markets."[127] For these reasons, Tim Reid, President of the Canadian Chamber of Commerce, told a Vancouver audience in 1998 that Canada's cultural diversity, which he referred to as the "Canadian advantage," was one means by which Canadian companies could expand into new markets. He said, "those who learn to navigate the contrasts and capitalize on our diversity that are our powerhouses—no matter whether they are big or small."[128]

Arguments like this have prompted many large firms to look at diversity as a business strategy. Indeed one survey, taken two weeks after the NDP defeat in Ontario, reported that more than half of 221 firms stated they would continue with their own equity initiatives regardless of the repeal of employment equity legislation.[129] The Trinity Group, founded in 1997, is a consortium of Canadian companies that have made a commitment to corporate diversity. Among the 15 members are blue-ribbon firms such as IBM, ScotiaBank, Dupont, National Grocers, and Nortel.[130] Initiatives such as the Trinity Group seem to suggest that the private sector has overtaken the public sector in terms of equity strategies. Some assessments have suggest that legislated equity measures at the provincial and federal level had the effect of raising awareness in the private sector of the need for equity initiatives.[131] The NDP government's attempt at linking social equity to economic renewal certainly may have contributed to a change in corporate attitudes.

Advocates of the "managing diversity" model suggest that is it an effective response that moves beyond the perceived limitations of legislated employment equity.[132] Agocs and Burr have examined this claim and find it wanting. They argue that there are significant and important differences between the two approaches. It is important to stress that they are not dismissing the "managing diversity" model outright. In fact, they underscore how diversity training has the potential to subvert stereotypes and can contribute to the ability to communicate with people of different backgrounds and cultures.[133] But they also emphasize the need to distinguish between employment equity and diversity.

155

The diversity model, despite its benefits, is problematic. It leaves employers in control—employers will drive the choice of appropriate equity models and targets.[134] Its voluntary nature has been characterized as a "market commodity and its blessing will never be enjoyed across the board."[135] Many of the firms that adopt diversity models appear to already be "best practice" corporate employers. Thus, many members within the Trinity Group are likely top corporations that may have some sense of ethical and social responsibility already. DuPont Canada, a Trinity Group member, is listed as one of the 35 best companies to work for.[136] National Grocers, another member, was a strong supporter of the NDP proposals, and its own literature makes reference to issues of systemic discrimination and the need to focus on "recruitment, and selection, career mobility and opportunities."[137] Given the changing nature of the economy it is unlikely that the majority of people who are most in need of labour market equity will be working for "best practice" corporate employers. As one study emphasized:

> Equity policies have far less salience in smaller scale firms which, in a period of downsizing and retreat into core business and subcontracting, represent an ever-increasing part of total volume of employment. Such firms often lack the human resources capacity to address legal requirements.... Hence it might not be very realistic to expect them to follow the example set by larger corporations.[138]

Consequently, it is unlikely that smaller firms with neither the resources nor the resolution will pursue this option. As a privatized strategy, the diversity model may help some individuals within a particular workplace but it does not address broader issues of group disadvantage.

Also problematic is the way that the diversity model views all difference as equally important (what advocates of the model describe as its "inclusionary" nature). With difference levelled out this way, real differences in power and access to resources between groups—in short, inequality—gets ignored.[139] The diversity model acknowledges neither the privilege and power that some groups have enjoyed, nor the very real effects racial and gender inequality have on the groups that experience them. It is also argued that the diversity model neglects the larger dynamics—employment practices and systemic barriers—within an organization that produce and reproduce systemic disadvantage.[140]

Consequently, despite the claims that the diversity model offers a more refined variant of employment equity, or even supercedes it, the strategy itself appears to be limited. Unlike employment equity, there are no claims regarding its ability to bring about social change. Its attractiveness is very much tied up with the degree to which its rationale is congruent to prevailing neo-liberal norms. The diversity model offers a privatized, voluntaristic, employer-driven strategy directed at all individuals. It is intimately connected with the market and the bottom line insofar as it is concerned with harnessing the skills and talents of people for comparative advantage in reaching new clients and customers.

EMPLOYMENT EQUITY AND INTERNATIONAL POLICY DEVELOPMENTS

Employment equity is a policy very much directed at a national labour market. However, both its place on the policy agenda in the 1970s and 1980s and the emergence of the diversity model in the 1990s were connected to policy developments at the international level. Canada's international commitments helped to shape a policy environment that engendered an initiative directed at labour market inequality: Canada was a signatory to international labour agreements, and the United Nations 1975 Year of Women also helped to forge a commitment to women's labour market inequality in Canada.

In Canada, employment equity was influenced by the U.S. experience of affirmative action, which emphasized contract compliance and numerical representation through targeted hiring. The Abella Report was very much concerned not to repeat some of the problems attendant on affirmative action; though it also focussed on numbers, it sought to move beyond numbers as well. To distinguish Canada's variant of similar policies, Abella coined the term "employment equity."

> The Canadian response to inequality has sought to avoid the controversy and stigma attached to affirmative action, but more important, it is a much broader strategy designed to not only improve numerical representation through hiring, but to provide fair employment systems and a supportive organizational culture for women, racial minorities, aboriginal peoples and persons with disabilities.[141]

Both advocates and proponents of employment equity found experiences in other jurisdictions to further their positions. During the debate on revisions to the federal employment equity legislation, Liberal MPs pointed favourably towards equity initiatives in the Netherlands and

Australia. Conversely, those that attacked legislative measures drew particularly on policy developments in the United States, suggesting that

> ... a decade of experience with employment equity quotas and targets in the U.S., Canada and Europe have demonstrated that the province's employment equity legislation was killed by a simple reality. Quota's do not work. Quota-system equity is fundamentally limited concept.[142]

CONCLUSION

This chapter has traced the fate of employment equity initiatives at the federal level and within the province of Ontario. Employment equity emerged on the policy agenda as a measure to address socio-economic inequality. Its emergence was directly linked to social group activism and the Canadian state's recognition of the legitimacy of group concerns. One of the assumptions that underwrote the post-war state was that social justice and equity were legitimate goals. Additionally, there was an understanding that the state should and would actively intervene in the labour market.

The fate of employment equity, as the case in Ontario illustrates, demonstrate how these assumptions have shifted. In part, employment equity has been subverted by the emergence of new neo-liberal norms associated with a discourse of globalization. These norms emphasize minimal state action in the economy and privilege the market; they offer narrower understandings of equality, which effectively reject group-based claims. Women, racial minorities, people with disabilities and Aboriginal people have been subject to the consequences of this shift. Where once their demands were seen as matters of social justice and equality, these demands—at least in the case of Ontario—are now more often constructed as "special treatment."

The emerging voluntary "equal opportunities" plans and "managing diversity" models in firms tend to focus on how diversity can help to secure the bottom line. In this case, diversity is viewed as favorable in relation to competitiveness both at home and abroad. These market-orientated constructions of diversity effectively displace issues of systemic discrimination.

◆ NOTES ◆

1 Lisa McKendall, Director of Marketing Communication in Mattel's El Segundo, CA office cited in "Home/ Work: Toys that Teach" in *home/work* editorial, <wysiwyg://73/http://sanjose.citysearch.com/E/V/SJOCA/0024/77/53/CS1.html>

2 Teresa Gubbins, "Barbie puts heels though glass ceiling," *Dallas Morning News*, 12 December 1999, <http://seattletimes.nsource.com/news/lifestyles/html98/barb.19991212.html>

3 Gubbins.

4 Victor Hayes, "Beyond Employment Equity: The Business Case for Diversity," *The Ivey Business Journal* (September/ October 1999): 48. See also, Laura Talbot-Allan, "Viewpoint: Measuring the Impact of Diversity," *CMA Magazine* (June 1996): 3.

5 Hayes 48.

6 Heather Mallick, "Women Don't Matter," *The Globe and Mail Report on Business Magazine*, February 2000: 36.

7 Mallick 36.

8 See for example, Canadian Labour Congress, *Women's Work: A Report* (Ottawa: CLC, 1997).

9 Mark Mackinnon, "Give Us Your Highly Educated," *The Globe and Mail*, 24 May 1999: B1.

10 Mackinnon B3.

11 Pendakur and Pendakur (1995), cited by James Frideres, "Altered States: Federal Policy and Aboriginal Peoples," *Race and Ethnic Relations in Canada*, ed. Peter Li (Toronto: Oxford University Press, 1999) 137-38.

12 Mark Charlton and Paul Barker, "Is Employment Equity Fair and Necessary," *Contemporary Political Issues*, 3rd ed., ed. Mark Charlton and Paul Barker (Toronto: Nelson, 1998) 518.

13 Gregory Albo and Jane Jenson, "Remapping Canada: The State in the Era of Globalization," *Understanding Canada: Building on the New Canadian Political Economy*, ed. Wallace Clement (Montreal: McGill-Queens University Press, 1997) 233.

14 Albo and Jenson 233.

15 Jane Jenson and Susan Phillips, "Regime Shift: New Citizenship Practices in Canada," *International Journal of Canadian Studies* 14 (Fall 1996).

16 Susan B. Boyd, "Challenging the Public/Private Divide: An Overview," *Challenging the Public Private Divide: Feminism, Law and Public Policy*, ed. Susan Boyd (Toronto: University of Toronto Press, 1997) 4.

17 Boyd "Challenging the Public/Private Divide" 8-9.

18 Barbara Arneil, *Politics & Feminism* (Oxford: Blackwell Publishers, 1999) 64-76.

19 Pat Armstrong, "Restructuring Public and Private: Women's Paid and Unpaid Work," Boyd 39.

20 Boyd, "Challenging the Public/Private Divide" 8.

21 Boyd, "Challenging the Public/Private Divide" 17.

22 Carol Lee Bacchi, *The Politics of Affirmative Action* (London: Sage, 1996) 84.

23 Bacchi 84.

24 European Parliament, 1993: 18, cited by Bacchi 84.

25 Boyd, "Challenging the Public/Private Divide" 17.

26 Kenneth Kernaghan and David Siegel, *Public Administration in Canada*, 4th ed. (Nelson: Toronto, 1999) 557.

27 Nicole Morgan, *The Equality Game: Women in the Federal Public Service, 1908-1987* (CACSW: Ottawa, 1988) 6.

28 House of Commons, Debates, 23 June 1970, 8487, cited by Kernaghan and Siegel 585.

29 Leslie Pal, *Interests of the State: The Politics of Language, Multiculturalism and Feminism in Canada* (Montreal: McGill-Queens University Press, 1993).

30 Sue Findlay, "Democratizing the Local State: Issues for Feminist Practice and the Representation of Women," *A Different Kind of State? Popular Power and Democratic Administration*, ed. Gregory Albo, David Langille, and Leo Panitch (Toronto: Oxford University Press, 1993) 162.

31 RCSW, *Report of the Royal Commission on the Status of Women* (Ottawa: Information Canada, 1970) ix.

32 RCSW ix-x.

33 RCSW 400.

34 An assessment of the RCSW is beyond the scope of this paper. For an overview see, for example Monique Begin, "The Royal Commission on the Status of Women in Canada," *Challenging Times: The Women's Movement in Canada and the US*, ed. Monique Begin and David Flaherty (Montreal: McGill-Queens University Press, 1992). See also contributions in *Women and the Canadian State*, ed. Caroline Andrew and Sanda Rodgers (Montreal: McGill-Queens University Press, 1997).

35 Maureen O'Neil and Sharon Sutherland, "The Machinery of Women's Policy: Implementing the Royal Commission on the Status of Women," Andrew and Rodgers 198.

36 O'Neil and Sutherland 208-09.

37 CACSW Recommendation: "Affirmative Action," June 1975, cited by Anne Molgat, *Expanding Our Horizons: The Work of CACSW And Its Context* (Ottawa: CACSW, 1993) 78.

38 Pal 209.

39 Canada, Royal Commission on Equality in Employment (RCEE), *Equality in Employment: Report of the Royal Commission on Equality in Employment* (Ottawa: Minister of Supply and Services, 1984).

40 RCEE ii.

41 Canada, House of Commons, Report of the Special Committee on Visible Minorities in Canadian Society, *Equality Now!* (Ottawa: Queen's Printer of Canada, 1984) 35. Hereafter referred to as *Equality Now!*

42 Marjorie Griffin Cohen, "Paid Work," *Canadian Women's Issues Volume II*, ed. Ruth Roach Pierson and Marjorie Griffin Cohen (Toronto: James Lorimer, 1995) 102.

43 Tania Das Gupta, *Racism and Paid Work* (Toronto: Garamond Press, 1996) 95.

44 Frances Henry, Carol Tator, Winston Mattis, and Tim Rees, *The Colour of Democracy: Racism in Canadian Society*, 2nd ed. (Toronto: Harcourt Canada, 2000) 343.

45 RCEE 19.

46 RCEE 3.

47 *Equality Now!* 35.

48 Pat McDermott, "Employment Equity and Pay Equity," *Canadian Women's Studies* 12.3 (1992): 25.

49 Brenda Cardillo "Defining and Measuring Employment Equity," *Perspectives* (Ottawa: Statistics Canada, Cat. No. 75-001E) 43.

50 Cardillo 43.

51 Julia S. O'Connor, "Employment Equality Strategies and Their Representation in the Political Process in Canada, 1970-1994," *Women and Political Representation in Canada*, ed. Caroline Andrew and Manon Tremblay (Ottawa: University of Ottawa, 1998) 94.

52 O'Connor 94.

53 Carole Ann Reed, "Contradictions and Assumptions: A Report On Employment Equity in Canada," *Resources for Feminist Research* 24.3-4 (Fall 1995/Winter 1996).

54 O'Connor 95.

55 Elaine Campbell, *Canada, Excluding Ontario: Current Issue Paper 146* (Toronto: Legislative Research Service, 1993) 3.

56 Canada 1994: 6, cited by Abigail Bakan and Audrey Kobayashi, *Employment Equity Policy in Canada: An Interprovincial Comparison* (Ottawa: Status of Women Canada, 2000) 15.

57 National Action Committee on the Status of Women (NAC), "Justice Works: Response of NAC to 'Working Towards Equality' Ontario's Discussion Paper on Employment Equity Legislation" (February 1992) 1.

58 Abella 195-202

59 Janet Lum, "The Federal Employment Equity Act: Goals vs Implementation," *Canadian Public Administration* 38.1 (Spring 1995): 48.

60 NAC 2.

61 See for example, Jenson and Phillips, or Janine Brodie, *Politics on the Margins* (Halifax: Fernwood, 1994).

62 Albo and Jenson 216.

63 Portions of this section are taken directly from Christina Gabriel, "Recasting Citizenship: The Politics of Multiculturalism Policy in Canada" diss., York University, 1997.

64 See Bakan and Kobayshi.

65 Brodie 57.

66 Folke Glastra, Petra Schedler, and Erik Kats, "Employment Equity Policies in Canada and the Netherlands," *Policy and Politics* 26.2 (April 1998): 168.

67 Richard Mackie, "Rae to push 'equity agenda,'" *Globe and Mail*, 30 December 1990, A1.

68 Ontario, Office of the Employment Equity Commissioner, Ministry of Citizenship, *Working Towards Equality: The Discussion Paper on Employment Equity Legislation* (Toronto: Queen's Printer for Ontario, 1991) 61-62. Hereafter referred to as *Working Towards Equality*.

69 The broader public sector was defined as including "hospitals, school boards, colleges and universities, municipalities, crown corporations, public authorities such as housing authorities and conservation authorities, as well as organizations providing human services which are wholly or partially funded by the provincial government." *Working Towards Equality* 54.

70 *Working Towards Equality* 3.

71 Bruce DeMara, "Getting ready for 'Job Equity,'" *Toronto Star*, 25 August 1994.

72 Robert Payne, "Jobs equity can pay off abroad," *Toronto Sun*, 19 September 1993.

73 Business Consortium on Employment Equity ii.

74 Baachi 83.

75 Canadian Manufacturers Association 1992:2.

76 Canadian Federation of Independent Business, "Employment Equity with Equanimity: A Small Business Perspective," *Submission to the Ontario Employment Equity Commission* (12 February 1992) 5.

77 Bill 79, "An Act to Provide for Employment Equity for Aboriginal People, People with Disabilities, Members of Racial Minorities and Women," 25 June 1992.

78 Legislative Assembly of Ontario Debates, Third Session, 35th Parliament, 16 June 1993. Hereafter referred to as Third Session.

79 Third Session, 16 June 1993.

80 Third Session, 9 December 1993.

81 *Working Towards Equality* 36.

82 Third Session, 13 July 1993.

83 Third Session, 13 July 1993.

84 Bacchi 22.

85 Third Session, 9 December 1993.

86 Martin Mittelstaedt, "Business splits on equity bill," *Globe and Mail*, 18 August 1993, B1.

87 See for example, Avvy Go, "Equity formula isn't strong enough," *Toronto Star*, 25 June 1993; Martin Mittelstaedt, "Opposing views heard about equity law," *Globe and Mail*, 17 August 1993.

88 For a discussion of "reverse discrimination" and the construction of affirmative action measures as "handouts," see Bacchi 20-25.

89 Bakan and Kobayashi 28.

90 Editorial, "Sloganeering on employment equity," *Toronto Star*, 14 May 1995: F2.

91 Bakan and Kobayashi 28. Also, Frances Henry and Carol Tator, "State Policy and Practices as Racialized Discourse: Multi-culturalism. The Charter and Employment Equity," Li 104-05.

92 Henry and Tator 104-05.

93 Bakan and Kobayashi 20

94 Sean Fine, "Equity laws first report card," *Globe and Mail*, 30 December 1992.

95 Canadian Advisory Council on the Status of Women (CACSW), "Re-evaluating Employment Equity: A Brief for the Special House of Commons Committee on the Review of the Employment Equity Act" (Ottawa: CACSW, 1992) 5.

96 For a selection of these briefs see "Reviewing the Federal Employment Equity Act," *Canadian Women's Studies* 12.3 (Spring 1992): 28-33.

97 CACSW 41.

98 O'Connor 95.

99 Glastra, Scheder and Kats 168

100 Canada, House of Commons, *Debates*, 3 October 1995.

101 Canada, House of Commons, *Debates*, 3 October 1995: 15173.

102 Canada, House of Commons, *Debates*, 16 October 1995: 15416.

103 Sandra Martin, *The Politics of Equity* (Toronto: Atkinson, Charitable Foundation, 1995) 6.

104 Janet Lum and A. Paul Williams, "Out of Synch with a 'Shrinking State'? Making Sense of Employment Equity Act (1995)," *Restructuring and Resistance: Canadian Public Policy in an Age of Global Capitalism*, ed. Mike Burke et al. (Halifax: Fernwood, 2000) 198.

105 See Jenson and Phillips 111-35.

106 Mike Burke, Colin Moores and John Shields, "Critical Perspectives on Canadian Public Policy," Burke et al. 13.

107 Lum and Williams 198.

108 Lum and Williams 198.

109 Reed 48.

110 Bakan and Kobayashi 45.

111 Bakan and Kobayashi 21.

112 Bill 8 required that all data gathered in relation to employment equity such as workforce surveys be destroyed.

113 Ontario Ministry of Citizenship, Culture and Recreation, News Release, "Government Provides Framework for Equal Opportunity Plan in Ontario," 4 December 1995.

114 Marilyn Mushinski, cited by Martin 20.

115 Canadian Alliance of Manufacturers and Exporters, "Appendix C— Questions and Answers about Equal Opportunity and Diversity," *Business Results Through Diversity Handbook* (Toronto: Queen's Printer for Ontario, 1997) 79.

116 Bakan and Kobayashi 30-31.

117 Alliance of Manufacturers and Exporters Canada 10.

118 Alliance of Manufacturers and Exporters Canada.

119 Alliance of Manufacturers and Exporters Canada 11.

120 Carol Agocs and Catherine Burr, "Employment equity, affirmative action and managing diversity: assessing the differences," *International Journal of Manpower* 17.4/5 (1996): 36.

121 Erin Kelly and Frank Dobbin, "How Affirmative Action Became Diversity Management," *American Behavioural Scientist* 41.7 (April 1998): 973.

122 R. Roosevelt Thomas (1990/1994:3), cited by Kelly and Dobin 973.

123 Cited in Hayes 48.

124 Speech, Holger Kluge, President, Personal and Commercial Bank, CIBC, "Reflections on Workplace Diversity," *Canadian Speeches: Issues of the Day* (March 1997) 56.

125 Cited in Harish Jain and Anil Verma, "Managing workforce diversity for competitiveness: The Canadian experience," *International Journal of Manpower* 17, 4/5 (1996): 27.

126 Bobby Siu, "How Diversity Management Can Fill Out Your Bottom Line" <http://www. equalopportunity.on.ca/enggraf/ resource/botline.html>

127 Martin 26.

128 Speech, Tim Reid, President, Canadian Chamber of Commerce, "Cultural diversity: the Canadian Advantage in Asia Pacific Trade," *Canadian Speeches: Issues of the Day* (January/February 1998): 34-35.

129 Martin 21.

130 Hayes 45.

131 Glastra, Schedler, and Kats 168.

132 Trevor Wilson, *Diversity at Work: The Business Case for Equity* (1997), cited by Hayes 45.

133 Agocs and Burr 39.

134 Bacchi 51-52.

135 Glastra, Schedler and Kats 173.

136 Andrea Gordon, "Thirty-five Best Companies to Work For," *Report on Business* February 2000.

137 <www.equalopportunity.on.ca/ enggraf/business/grocers.html>

138 Glastra, Schedler and Kats 172; see also Bacchi 53.

139 Glastra, Schedler and Kats 172.

140 Agocs and Burr 38.

141 Agocs and Burr 35.

142 Hayes 44.

chapter SIX

Selling (Out) Diversity in an Age of Globalization

In this chapter we summarize our major findings on the historical and contemporary evolution of immigration, multiculturalism, and employment equity policies in Canada and outline the implications of our findings. Finally and certainly not least, we turn our attention away from the empirical facts ("what is") and instead consider the grand normative question of "what ought to be." Specifically, we advocate the need for a new discourse on globalization that does not assume that there are global economic "imperatives," which necessitate neo-liberal policy rationales. A new framework and perspective on globalization might allow Canadians (and Canadian policy-makers) the room to really think about what kind of political community Canadians want in the future. A new perspective on globalization might allow the space to consider alternatives to neo-liberalism and political agendas that might really foster substantive equality for diverse groups in Canada and even globally.

SUMMARY OF FINDINGS

Globalization has become one of the most frequently invoked ideas of our time. We suggested that a useful understanding of contemporary globalization processes would see these processes as not necessarily new, but nonetheless distinct. As such, there is an intensification of economic, political, and cultural processes that transcend, but do not necessarily completely supercede, the state or its sovereignty. In terms of Canadian public policy specifically, we argued that instead of only engaging in abstract scholarly debates, it was useful to examine if and how state actors make use of a discourse of globalization and the extent to which policy ideas and rationales were "imported" to Canada or "exported" from Canada.

In terms of understanding contemporary public policy in Canada, our findings suggest that internationalization might go in different directions (both to and from Canada) depending on the policy. We demonstrated that recent policy changes and debates in the interrelated policy domains of immigration, multiculturalism, and employment equity have been underpinned by a particular reading of globalization that stresses measures informed by neo-liberal ideals. Together, each of these policy areas was (and is) implicated in the funding, framing, and managing of Canadian ethnocultural and racial relations, as well as other forms of diversity—including those relating to class and gender. In the contemporary moment, the policies of immigration, employment equity, and multiculturalism are all being rewritten in new directions. Each new policy script epitomizes how "diversity" has been constructed—albeit in a number of shifting ways—in a manner that is often congruent with various neo-liberal ideals.

These neo-liberal ideals include the valuing of a smaller welfare state, whereby governments do less, and individuals, families, and volunteers undertake to do more in the area of social services. Neo-liberal ideals also stress the commodification of social goods (e.g., health care, education, and welfare services). In this process, Canadians are treated less as "citizens" and more as "individuals," "clients," or "customers." Not least, neo-liberal ideals emphasize and privilege the "free" market, economic efficiency, and unfettered competition. Thus, neo-liberal ideals carry a new understanding of what is "public" and what is "private," and many services that were considered public with the Keynesian welfare state are under threat of being wholly or partially privatized.

Over the contemporary period under examination (1993 to 2001) neo-liberal values have been stressed by state actors, and in the process the demands of groups that were viewed as disadvantaged during the rapid expansion of the welfare state during the 1960s and 1970s have been subject to a radical shift. Thus groups such as women, racial and ethnic minorities, Aboriginal people, people with disabilities, and the poor have increasingly been represented as "special interests" and different from so-called "ordinary Canadians."[1] In this context, the demands of these groups for social justice and equality have sometimes even been transformed in popular and partisan debates into a threat to the cohesion and unity of the Canadian polity.

In the case of ethnic and racial minorities, their concerns for equality *via* the policies of immigration, multiculturalism, and employment equity have been repositioned by state actors as valuable to the Canadian polity insofar as these demands conform to a discourse on globalization that stresses neo-liberal ideals. However, the stress on attracting immigrants with skills and other human capital characteristics, or on the idea that workforce diversity or societal diversity can enhance national and global competitiveness and foster trade links abroad is not without consequences, as this book has detailed. Like neo-liberal repositionings of what is "public" and what is "private," such developments may threaten the possibility of those marginalized by virtue of their gender, race/ethnicity, and class for achieving greater substantive equality.

Immigration

The state has always played a key role in the selection of immigrants—that is, prospective citizens. The Canadian case demonstrates that this selection has always been premised on the perceived needs of the Canadian economy. The current period is marked by contradictory tendencies. Policy directions suggest Canada is opening its doors to individuals with human capital, those people who are highly skilled, well-educated, and perceived as self-sufficient. Simultaneously, state power is being used to enact tougher border control through the adoption of stricter selection criteria for those deemed less desirable, especially members of the family class and refugees, erroneously constructed as "dependent" non-contributors. This dichotomy is very much premised on the need to attract immigrants/prospective citizens with the "right stuff" who will enhance Canada's competitive position in a global economy, but it has a differential impact on women and the poor. As a whole, the area of immigration reveals a powerful way in which the nation-state continues to exercise power in the contemporary era of globalization, which is certainly not "shrinking" as a result of neo-liberalism. Recent policy moves, such as the Metropolis project, suggest that Canadian policy-makers are eager both to share its own experiences and learn from the experiences of other countries (especially the wealthy countries belonging to the Organization for Economic Cooperation and Development/OECD).

Multiculturalism

We suggest that supposed economic imperatives also inform recent directions in Canadian multiculturalism policy. Where immigration policy may be seen as the source of Canada's increasing ethnocultural and racial diversity, multiculturalism policy addresses the value of this diversity for the Canadian nation. Thus, the emergence of multiculturalism policy in the 1970s signaled an important reconfiguring of Canada's symbolic order to include recognition of those groups that were not French, not British, and not Aboriginal in origin. The rearticulation of Canadian identity marked some departure from the implicit and explicit privileging of Anglo-conformity that framed Canadian national identity and nation-building historically. This rearticulation also provided the basis for subsequent—although limited—policy initiatives that attempted to address systemic racism. However, starting in the 1990s, these fragile initiatives have been challenged by a new debate (particularly in Canada outside Quebec) which has brought forward the idea that the state has no business in the area of culture and cultural maintenance, which should be left to the "private" sphere of the home and family. At a policy level, multiculturalism has been challenged by a new emphasis on diversity as a competitive lever. Under the initial call in 1986 that "multiculturalism means business" the policy focus since the 1990s especially emphasized the economic exploitation of Canada's racial and ethnic diversity to capture markets at home and abroad, at the probable expense of gender equality and other equality initiatives. Multiculturalism has also been increasingly positioned as an area where Canada can "export" policy ideas to other countries.

Employment Equity

Our assessment of legislated employment equity programs at the federal level and in Ontario leads to some similar findings. Employment equity emerged as a social justice measure designed to address substantive inequality in the labour market. The federal government has pursued employment equity within the federally regulated sector with a record of limited success. The more ambitious experiment of the NDP government in Ontario sank under the weight of its own contradictions, partisan attack, employer opposition to government intervention in the "private sphere," and a virulent backlash against disadvantaged groups. What has come to the fore, in Ontario especially, are "managing diversity" measures often mistakenly presented as "employment equity." Such "managing diversity" measures construct diversity of any kind—gender, race, disability, age, or sexuality—as a means to enhance the bottom line. The managing diversity model has been a particular idea "imported" from recent American developments. Thus, a workforce is constructed in terms of comparative advantage, as a bridge to new markets (both at home and globally) and as a source of product innovation. This market-orientated emphasis effectively sidelines issues of systemic discrimination and inequality that employment equity was intended to address.

THE IMPLICATIONS OF THE RESEARCH FINDINGS

We would suggest that the trends in the policy areas of immigration, multiculturalism, and employment equity—trends which we call "selling diversity"—are premised on a particular reading of globalization by Canadian policy-makers. In no case has this meant that all the earlier incarnations and emphases in policies have been abandoned. This may be related to the continued importance of Canadian historical traditions and the kinds of connections that developed between state institutions and subordinate groups in Canada during the post-war period when Keynesian-inspired ideas created a rationale for the state to fund the activities of such groups as women and minorities. Not least there are international pressures and ideas that effect the Canadian state, like the salience of international human rights and the United Nations protocol regarding the protection of refugees. Nonetheless, the understanding of globalization taken by Canadian policy-makers has profound implications for the future of the role of the state, substantive equality, identity, and diversity in Canada.

The economic advantage to be gleaned from "selling diversity" seems to underwrite many of the recent policy changes within immigration, multiculturalism, and employment equity. Thus, immigration changes are predicated on easing the entry of high-skilled workers and investors who can "contribute" to the Canadian economy. Similarly, multiculturalism and employment equity have been presented as areas in which to maximize comparative advantage in order to secure markets. This logic is premised on the assumption that a strategic alliance between economic competitiveness and equity commitment can peacefully co-exist with the equity commitments enshrined in the post-war incarnation of each policy. Whereas in the past competitiveness and equity may have been viewed as antithetical, the rationale behind selling diversity is that it is possible and desirable to have the best of both worlds. The implication of this is that there would be a new relationship between states, citizens, and markets. Increasingly, market ideals and private sector initiatives are constructed as the driving forces of change and dynamism. Presumably, such initiatives have the potential to provide equal opportunity to all individuals within a framework of formal equal rights. Within this refashioning, the state is to play a very different role compared to that of the post-war redistributive Keynesian welfare state.

The recent invocation of the "marketing and selling of diversity," we suggest, represents a distancing from the post-war ideal that was captured to some extent in Prime Minister Pierre Trudeau's vision of a "just society." This vision was articulated in the following manner:

> … Now Canada seems to me a land blessed by the gods to pursue a policy of the greatest equality of opportunity. A young country, a rich country, a country with two languages, a pluralist country with its ethnicities and its religions, an immense country with varied geographic regions, a federalist country. Canada had, besides, a political tradition that was neither completely libertarian nor completely state dominated, but was based, rather, on the collaboration necessary between government and the private sector and on direct action of the State to protect the weak against the strong, the needy against the wealthy.[2]

The "just society" emphasized a pan-Canadian identity and a national set of institutions. It was a vision of the political community marked by the post-war ideals of social solidarity and collective values. Consequently, through the 1960s and 1970s the state consolidated a number of welfare provisions and labour market regulations, and equally importantly recognized the collective needs and demands of groups such as women, francophones, linguistic minorities, and ethnocultural minority groups. Thus, for example, through the Secretary of State, many advocacy organizations representing these groups received state funding. In the 1970s the state also established structures of representation within the bureaucracy, such as Status of Women Canada and a Multiculturalism Directorate. Other para-public bodies such as the Canadian Advisory Council on the Status of Women (CSCSW) also played a role in generating research and policy advice on behalf of women.

Through these measures, the state recognized the collective needs and demands of groups, including women, linguistic minorities, and multicultural groups. This recognition contributed to a broader policy agenda that was underwritten by ideals of fairness, solidarity, equity, and social justice. These found expression to some extent in immigration reform and the removal of overt criteria relating to race/ethnicity from the criteria for entry and through the attempt to balance, somewhat, humanitarian considerations with the points system (refugees, the family class). The emergence of multiculturalism and its subsequent legislative basis also signaled a commitment to these ideals. Legislated employment equity at the federal level is perhaps the most concrete expression of equity concerns. The recent emergence of the "marketing and selling of diversity" within these three areas marks a clear retreat from the post-war ideal of a "just society." This emergence comes alongside increasing inequality and polarization as well as a virulent backlash against marginalized groups who are often cast as the architects of their own misfortune.

In different ways each of these policy areas also plays a role in structuring the symbolic aspects of Canadian national identity. Canadians and Canadian policy-makers often take pride in the UN Human Development Index that places Canada as the best (or nearly best) country in which to live. Canadians often emphasize that we are a nation of immigrants and laud Canada's "multicultural" and "tolerant" face. Canadian social programs are held up as evidence of our more caring and compassionate nature, especially in comparison to the United States. This is the public persona that Canadian officials also like to present to the world community.

Paradoxically, this image may prove more difficult to sustain at the current moment, when the discursive construction of "diversity" portrays the ideal/model citizens as self-sufficient, self-reliant individuals. In the process, equity-seeking groups—women, people of colour, people with disabilities—have been cast as "special interests" whose demands are outside the norm of the "ideal citizen." Thus, state funding that was designed to improve representation and access to decision-making bodies is now often depicted as a "handout." Struggles for equality and inclusion within the Canadian nation are portrayed as divisive. As well, attempts to address labour market inequality have been attacked as "reverse discrimination." The very social programs that addressed issues of equality and inclusion and infused the content of the Canadian nation and Canadian identity are being eroded. Increasingly neo-liberal visions articulated through a particular reading of globalization dominate the public agenda and these are at odds with the promise of a "just society."

Under the guise of responding to a globalizing economy, state actors have emphasized neo-liberal values to guide new policy directions in immigration, multiculturalism, and employment equity. Central to these new directions is a re-conceptualization of the role of the state, for it coincides with various redrawings of the boundaries between "the public" and "the private." Increasingly, there has been a shift from a strong interventionist state that actively attempts to manage the economy and is focused on redistributive concerns and equity, to a decentralized, less interventionist state that tends to prioritize market-driven prescriptions and emphasize cost savings. Within this shift, the policy infrastructure of immigration, employment equity, and multiculturalism has not been completely torn down, but neither has it been consolidated or strengthened. New policy directions have weakened the value of equality that was found in some measure within each policy area during the 1980s.

Additionally, responses in these policy areas to the perceived exigencies of a global economy are almost solely couched in terms of economic processes (and supposed economic imperatives) associated with globalization. In this respect the purported needs of the economy are prioritized. Thus, there have been initiatives to secure border-free economies through the removal of trade barriers; to attract and foster a flexible, highly skilled workforce; and to encourage freer, more open markets through de-regulation and privatization. Yet, as noted in the introduction to this book, globalization also involves other crucial dimensions, including global cultural flows of people, images, and ideas. Policymakers, in the three areas of immigration, multiculturalism, and employment equity, appear to have paid little attention to global cultural flows or their implications. Consequently, as the nation becomes more demographically diverse there is relatively less discussion of measures required to ensure belonging to Canadian society or the articulations of more inclusive variants of Canadian identity. Clearly, the populations in Canada's three major cities (Montreal, Toronto, and Vancouver) in the twenty-first century will be profoundly different than in twentieth century, but existing measures to ensure the full integration of immigrants and minorities are being scaled back, and new initiatives to meaningfully accomplish this do not appear to be on the agenda.

A key implication of our assessment of the three policy areas is that people with certain characteristics and attributes are particularly valued. Increasingly, immigration policy is emphasizing the human capital strengths of independent applicants. People who are highly skilled, well-educated, have job experience, and can speak one of the official languages are sought. As a country Canada has embarked on a project of trying to attract wealthy investors and entrepreneurs who will create jobs. Similarly, within multiculturalism policy the emphasis is placed on minority ethnic business leaders who have the potential to act as bridges to new markets. These class-advantaged people embody the very spirit of neo-liberalism—they are independent, self-reliant, active, and entrepreneurial. Within the "managing diversity model" workers of a firm or sector or even the entire workforce itself is constructed as a lever of global competition. Within these varying constructions of "diversity" there is a growing emphasis on the economic or potential economic contribution of individuals as the sum worth of a person. We suggest that constructing people as trade-enhancing commodities is a particularly superficial and narrow reading of diversity.

This is why the conceptualization of "diversity" within each policy area warrants further interrogation. In terms of immigration new directions emphasize diversity only within certain bounds. To the extent that new directions celebrate human capital characteristics and prize entrepreneurial and business activity there is a celebration of class advantage. Along with relations of class going unchallenged, there is silence on the consequences for other groups (such as women). As we noted, current immigration changes render most women, the poor, and other marginalized groups as not "desirable." They are not particularly valued as potential citizens. Additionally, multiculturalism policy, initially constructed as a reordering of Canada's symbolic identity to address increasing diversity, has become increasingly implicated in consumer culture. "Diversity" here is little more than something that can be consumed (products of "ethnic culture") or a feature to be capitalized upon and marketed. The diversity within the "managing diversity" model that has supplanted employment equity in important ways suggests that all individual differences are important and that firms and sectors that fail to acknowledge this will not be able to compete effectively in a global market. This reading of diversity is also narrow insofar as it fails to problematize structural inequalities that exist between groups of people. In each of the policy areas—immigration, multiculturalism, and employment equity—the focus on economic rationalism has rendered a profoundly narrow vision of diversity, which is basically a selling-out of an agenda based on pursuing substantive equality for those marginalized by race/ethnicity, gender, and class.

THE CANADIAN POLITICAL COMMUNITY IN THE TWENTY-FIRST CENTURY

In many ways our analysis suggests that the Canadian polity—at least as it was presented and discussed by policy-makers since the 1990s—defines the ideal citizen as someone who is economically productive and can contribute to Canada's national and global competitiveness. In this context, a narrow notion of "diversity" may be acceptable only to the extent that it does not conflict with the values underpinning the twenty-first century "ideal citizen." Yet, in reality, diversity in Canada is extremely broad. Canadian men and women live in a society that is increasing multicultural, multiethnic, multi-religious, and multi-racial.

In the final analysis, our critique of "selling diversity" raises the very question of what we, as Canadians, actually want to value. Should economic productiveness be the basic measurement of membership in the Canadian polity? Should entrepreneurship be imperative to our definition of national belonging? Should economic efficiency be the rationale behind measures aimed at increasing the numeric representation of historically under-represented groups in the Canadian labour market and promoting social justice? Indeed, there are potentially a host of ways in which membership, belonging, and social justice may be approached, which look at indicators of worth other than the standard economic measures associated with productivity. These might include things like care-giving to children or the elderly; sense of family, community, or global responsibility; respect for the environment; respect for a wide range of cultures and languages; the desire to create a more egalitarian society and world by engaging in social action; or simply a shared sense of destiny. Answering the questions of how membership, belonging, and social justice should be approached in Canada requires entering the realm of the normative—the realm of what ought to be.

As noted, all three public policy areas—immigration, multiculturalism, and employment equity—have been, since the 1990s, the subjects of partisan media and popular debate and attack. Yet in these debates the increasing emphasis on "selling diversity" and "productivity," influenced by neo-liberal ideals, has seldom been noted. As well, the implications of these directions that we have outlined have seldom been noted; namely, that the commitment to enhance gender equality, ethnic and racial equality, and class equality has been watered down in the last decade. As a result, there has really not been a full and complete consideration given to the normative questions concerning how we may better define membership, national belonging, and social justice in the Canadian polity.

However, by explicitly considering both the direction charted in policy areas related to diversity over the last decade and normative questions about the future of the Canadian polity, Canadians would be given an opportunity to engage in deeper thinking and rethinking about the kind of community they want to live in.

These sorts of normative questions also require thinking through whether or not there are alternatives to the direction public policy initiatives have taken in Canada over the course of the 1990s. We believe that there are indeed options which Canadian policy-makers and Canadian citizens have in the twenty-first century.

In many ways, the reading of globalization given by Canadian policy-makers rests on the idea that there is no other alternative to neo-liberalism. If there is no other alternative, then the stress on the free market, the individual, and competitiveness is seemingly inevitable. It is true that a return to the "welfare state model" prevalent in the 1960s and 1970s may not realistically happen. Indeed, through the 1980s and 1990s politicians across the political spectrum in Western industrialized countries, including Canada, faulted this model for the creation of public deficits. While it may be argued that the ideas of Keynes (especially those relating to saving during better economic periods) were never really followed by policy-makers, there are other alternatives to neo-liberal values even within a capitalist system.

For example, there is so-called "progressive competitiveness" whereby the economy is restructured, but measures are taken to make sure that there are provisions for adjustment, such as training allowances, job placement assistance, or income security.[3] Such ideas do have a practical example, if we consider developments in Great Britain under Labour Prime Minister Tony Blair, who has advocated a "Third Way" between the Keynesian welfare state and neo-liberalism. Blair's agenda has been influential with other current social democratic governments in Europe (e.g., Germany).

The Third Way has its detractors. It has been criticized by those on the left for not going far enough in challenging neo-liberal values and creating equality,[4] and those on the right for being too tied to state intervention and thus being a kind of "ill-disguised Second Way."[5] We view the discussion surrounding the Third Way as important primarily because it signals the possibility of options that do not simply rest on the ideals of neo-liberalism—and so opens up political space.

However, we do not find the Third Way an entirely satisfactory response in that aspects of it are still rooted in a sense of inevitability. This is exemplified in the thinking of the leading intellectual figure behind Tony

Blair's Third Way, British sociologist Anthony Giddens. In a recent article Giddens suggests that globalization is a dominant influence that requires inevitable political responses. Hence,

> All center-left governments of Europe have given up their traditional hostility to markets while, at the same time, embracing the idea that there must be new regulations on international currency flows and global companies. All the social democratic leaders of Europe have a similar interest in forging a new model of responsible capitalism because they know there is no alternative to a global market economy.[6]

This kind of discussion around globalization borders on some of the criticisms we have had of Canadian policy-makers insofar as it treats globalization as producing a certain inevitable logic that should lead to certain inevitable policies. In the British context, Hay and Watson have criticized the work of Giddens as insensitive to the diverse and uneven impacts globalization processes may have on different states and for narrowing a sense of political options for a host of actors, including policy-makers. As they put it:

> While such a conception remains relatively unchallenged, the greatest threat to democratic political choice is not the 'harsh economic reality' of globalisation as much as the convenient alibi it appears to provide in the view of many centre-left thinkers. If politicians continue to internalise the radical globalisation orthodoxy, there may well be no alternative to processes of economic convergence which increasingly bypass national democratic structures. However, if they choose to resist such a position, then the parameters of the possible are both less economically restrictive and less democratically debilitating. The choice is stark; its consequences could scarcely be more significant.[7]

Our understanding of the case of Canada would lead us to a similar position as that articulated by Hay and Watson.

The reading of globalization advanced by Canadian policy-makers, which rests on neo-liberalism, comes with possible alternatives, which might place more emphasis on issues of equity. In the current period, Canadians still have an opportunity to conceive of ways of achieving greater equality between men and women, between ethnic and racial groups, and between classes. At the federal level, the Chrétien Liberals began the process of "post deficit" budgeting in 2000. This leaves open the possibility of more money being directed into areas of social spending than was the case in the 1990s. It remains an open question whether the groups maligned and scapegoated as "special interests" and subjected to severe cutbacks in recent years (e.g., groups representing women or minorities) will have the strength to mobilize and successfully lobby for an alternative agenda. However, this budgetary development at least raises the possibility that understandings based on the emphasis on the "free market" so prevalent through the 1990s may be challenged.

Moreover, there are alternative readings of globalization that might be given to the contemporary order, for it is not only economic processes, global competitiveness, and a corporate agenda that could be considered. For example, Richard Falk has talked about the possibility of a "globalization from below." Thus, whereas "globalization from above" revolves around the political elites of core states and the agents of transnational capital, a "globalization from below," is driven by transnational social forces concerned variously with the future of the environment, improving human rights, and ending patriarchy, poverty, and oppression.[8] The emergence of a Hemispheric Social Alliance to address free trade issues in the Americas offers a case in point. Among its many activities during the April 2001 Quebec meetings on the Free Trade Areas of the Americas was an alternative "People's Summit." The Summit's workshops, discussions, and panels offered alternatives to neo-liberal strategies and provided a forum for the development of "people-centred alternatives."[9] These are premised on the idea that governments are responsible to the concerns of their populations and do not have to cede all control to corporations or be driven by a corporate agenda.

In addition to providing a different reading of globalization, the discussion of Richard Falk on globalization from below directly raises the possibility of a new form of citizenship—namely, a global citizenship. The idea of global citizenship (like that of global civil society) is highly debated and contested.[10] The notion of global citizenship "encompasses rights and obligations and/or forms of political participation and belonging which are de-territorialized and take on transnational and/or global forms."[11] In a world where there continues to be gross economic inequality between states, and where states continue to guard their borders from would-be immigrants (particularly Western states *vis à vis* migrants coming from the South), it is difficult to imagine a truly global citizenship easily emerging.[12] Nonetheless, a discourse on globalization from below and on global citizenship offers a very different reading of globalization, and thus offers a form (or even forms) of possible political engagement.

In fact, resistance to the neo-liberal reading of globalization has been a rallying point in transnational mobilization, as demonstrated by the wave of popular protests dubbed "anti-capitalist" or "anti-globalization" that accompanied the World Trade Organization meeting in Seattle in 1999, the meeting of the World Bank and the International Monetary Fund in Prague in 2000, and the summit for a proposed Free Trade Agreement of the Americas in Quebec City in 2001. Moreover, the fact that, as a result of popular protests, OECD countries (which include Canada) abandoned the proposed Multilateral Agreement on Investment in 1998 also highlights that nothing is inevitable when it comes to the neo-liberal reading of globalization.[13]

A reading of globalization that replaces neo-liberalism with a stress on transnational solidarity in struggles for equality opens the door to different kinds of concerns. For example, proponents of cosmopolitanism suggest that democratization in an era of globalization requires a greater transfer of power from the state to regional (e.g., continental) and especially global levels.[14] Instead of a corporate agenda driving the neo-liberal understanding of globalization, this understanding of globalization is driven by ways of improving the rights and sense of connectedness between peoples across the globe.

Such an understanding of globalization may be used to view Canadian citizenship in a different light as well. Cultural diversity, and ways to understand cultural diversity (e.g., through immigration, international travel, and new communications technologies like the World Wide Web) could become something that increases understanding between peoples of the world as a good in its own right, rather than as a mere means to achieve greater trade links and national prosperity as measured in Gross National Product or Gross Domestic Product indicators.

In addition, forms of globalization which impact culture—including the movement of people, the movement of ideas, the movement of images, and the movement of information—allow Canadians to engage in the wider world in ways that may be very different from that of the not-so-distant past. As a result, the possibility of being linked to peoples and struggles in other parts of the world can add a new dimension to the sense of citizenship rights, belonging, identity, and social justice than has been previously marshaled in the name of equality. Such possibilities give new life-force to the potential of respect for a wide range of diversity (ethnic, cultural, gender, and so on) in an era of globalization, and illuminate the fact that "selling diversity" is but one approach to chart in the twenty-first century.

◆ NOTES ◆

1 See Jane Jenson and Susan Phillips, "Regime Shift: New Citizenship Practices in Canada," *International Journal of Canadian Studies* 14 (Autumn 1996): 111-35.

2 "The values of a just society," *Towards a Just Society, The Trudeau Years* (Markham: Viking, 1990), 358-59; cited in Claude Couture, *Paddling With the Current: Pierre Trudeau, Etienne Parent, Liberalism and Nationalism in Canada* (Edmonton: University of Alberta Press, 1996) 89-90.

3 For a discussion of progressive competitiveness, see Stephen McBride, "Policy from What?," *Restructuring and Resistance*, ed. Mike Burke, Colin Mooers, John Sheilds (Halifax: Fernwood, 2000) 162-65. Also, on socialist economic policy, see Gregory Albo, "A World Market of Opportunities? Capitalist Obstacles and Left Economic Policy," *Socialist Register*, ed. Leo Panitch (London: Merlin, 1997).

4 John Westergaard, "Where Does the Third Way Lead?," *New Political Economy* 4.3 (November 1999): 429-36. *Academic Search Elite*, University of Alberta Library System, 10 April 10, 2001: 3.

5 Robert Higgs, "The So-Called Third Way," *Independent Review* 4.4 (Spring 2000): 625-30. *Academic Search Elite*, University of Alberta Library System, 10 April 2001: 5.

6 Anthony Giddens, "Still a Third Way for Europe," *New Perspectives Quarterly* 17.1 (Winter 2000): 50-52. *Academic Search Elite*, University of Alberta Library System, April 10, 2001: 2.

7 Colin Hay and Matthew Watson, "Globalization: 'Sceptical' Notes on the 1999 Reith Lecture," *Political Quarterly* 70.4 (Oct-Dec 1999): 418-25. *Academic Search Elite*, University of Alberta Library System, April 10, 2001: 7.

8 Richard Falk, "The Making of Global Citizenship," *Global Visions: Beyond the New World Order,* ed. Jeremy Brecher, John Brown Childs, and Jill Cutler (Montreal: Black Rose Books, 1993) 39-40.

9 See: Action Alert: "Join Thousands protesting the proposed FTAA, April 20-21" <www.corpwatch.org/action/2001/007.html> and "Building a Hemispheric Social Alliance to Confront Free Trade" <www.igc.org/trac/feature/humanrts/resistance/hemispheric.html>

10 Yasmeen Abu-Laban, "Reconstructing an Inclusive Citizenship for a New Millennium: Globalization, Migration, and Difference," *International Politics* 37.4 (December 2000): 517-19.

11 Abu-Laban, "Reconstructing an Inclusive Citizenship" 517.

12 Abu-Laban, "Reconstructing an Inclusive Citizenship" 518-22.

13 Yasmeen Abu-Laban, "The Future and the Legacy: The Impact of Globalization on the Canadian Settler-State," *Journal of Canadian Studies* 35.4 (Winter 2000-2001): 262-76.

14 David Held, "Democracy and Globalization," *Re-imagining Political Community: Studies in Cosmopolitan Democracy*, ed. Daniele Archibugi, David Held, and Martin Kohler (Stanford: Stanford University Press, 1998) 180.

SELECTED BIBLIOGRAPHY

Abell, Nazaré Albuquerque. "Safe Country Provisions in Canada and in the European Union: A Critical Assessment." *International Migration Review* 31.3 (Fall 1997).

Abu-Laban, Baha, and Hans Vermeulen. "Introduction." *Journal of International Migration and Integration* 1 (Winter 2000).

Abu-Laban, Baha, and Tracey M. Derwing (eds.). *Responding to Diversity in Metropolis: Building an Inclusive Research Agenda.* Edmonton: Prairie Centre of Excellence for Research on Immigration and Integration, 1997.

Abu-Laban, Yasmeen. "For Export: Multiculturalism in an Era of Globalization." *Profiles of Canada.* 2nd ed. Ed. Kenneth G. Pryke and Walter C. Soderlund. Toronto: Irwin Publishing, 1998.

——. "The Future and the Legacy: Globalization and the Canadian Settler-State." *Journal of Canadian Studies* 35.4 (Winter 2000-2001): 262-76.

——. "Keeping 'em Out: Gender, Race, and Class Biases in Canadian Immigration Policy." *Painting the Maple: Essays on Race, Gender, and the Construction of Canada.* Ed. Veronica Strong-Boag. Vancouver: University of British Columbia Press, 1998.

——. "The Politics of Race, Ethnicity and Immigration." Bickerton and Gagnon. 468-72.

——. "Reconstructing an Inclusive Citizenship for a New Millennium: Globalization, Migration, and Difference." *International Politics* 37.4 (December 2000).

——. "Systemic Discrimination." *Routledge Encyclopedia of Feminist Theories.* Ed. Lorraine Code. London and New York: Routledge, 2000.

——. "welcome/STAY OUT: The Contradiction of Canadian Integration and Immigration Policies at the Millennium." *Canadian Ethnic Studies* XXX.3 (1998).

Abu-Laban, Yasmeen, and Daiva K. Stasiulis. "Ethnic Pluralism Under Siege: Popular and Partisan Opposition to Multiculturalism" *Canadian Public Policy* XVIII.4 (December 1992): 365-86.

Abu-Laban, Yasmeen, and Tim Nieguth. "Reconsidering the Constitution, Ethnic Minorities, and Politics in Canada." *The Canadian Journal of Political Science* 33.3 (September 2000): 465-97.

Action Alert. "Building a Hemispheric Social Alliance to Confront Free Trade" <www.igc.org/trac/ feature/humanrts/resistance/ hemispheric.html>

———. "Join Thousands protesting the proposed FTAA, April 20-21" <www.corpwatch.org/action/ 2001/007.html>

Agnew, Vijay. *Resisting Discrimination.* Toronto: University of Toronto Press, 1996.

Agocs, Carol, and Catherine Burr. "Employment equity, affirmative action and managing diversity: assessing the differences." *International Journal of Manpower* 17.4/5 (1996).

Albo, Gregory. "A World Market of Opportunities? Capitalist Obstacles and Left Economic Policy." *Socialist Register.* Ed. Leo Panitch. London: Merlin, 1997.

Albo, Gregory, and Jane Jenson. "Remapping Canada: The State in the Era of Globalization." Clement.

Al-Hibri, Azizah Y. " Is Western Patriarchal Feminism Good for Third World/Minority Women?" Cohen *et al.*

Andrew, Caroline, and Sanda Rodgers (eds.). *Women and the Canadian State.* Montreal: McGill-Queens University Press, 1997.

Andrew, Caroline, and Manon Tremblay (eds.). *Women and Political Representation in Canada.* Ottawa: University of Ottawa Press, 1998.

Appadurai, Arjun. "Disjuncture and Difference in the Global Cultural Economy." *Global Culture: Nationalism, Globalization and Modernity.* Ed. Mike Featherstone. London: Sage, 1990

Arat-Koc, Sedef. "From 'Mothers of the Nation' to Migrant Workers." *Not One of the Family, Foreign Domestic Workers in Canada.* Ed. Abigail Bakan and Daiva Stasiulis. Toronto: University of Toronto Press, 1997.

———. "NAC's Response to *Not Just Numbers.*" *Canadian Women's Studies* 19:3 (Fall 1999).

———. "Neo-Liberalism, State Restructuring, and Immigration: Changes in Canadian Policies in the 1990s." *Journal of Canadian Studies* 34.2 (Summer 1999).

Armstrong, Pat. "Restructuring Public and Private: Women's Paid and Unpaid Work." Boyd.

Armstrong, Pat, *et al. Exposing Privatization: Women and Health Care Reform in Canada.* Toronto: Garamond, 2002.

Arneil, Barbara. *Politics & Feminism.* Oxford: Blackwell Publishers, 1999.

Ashford, Douglas E. *The Emergence of the Welfare States.* Oxford: Basil Blackwell, 1986.

Bacchi, Carol Lee. *The Politics of Affirmative Action.* London: Sage, 1996.

Back, Sandra, and Susan D. Phillips. "Constructing a New Social Union: Child Care Beyond Infancy?" *How Ottawa Spends: 1997-98.* Ed. Gene Swimmer. Ottawa: Carleton University Press, 1997. 235-58.

Badets, Jane. "Canada's Immigrant Population." *Social Trends.* Ed. Craig McKie and Keith Thompson. Toronto: Minister of Supply and Services Canada and Thompson Educational Publishing, 1990.

Bakan, Abby, and Audrey Kobayashi. *Employment Equity Policy in Canada: An Interprovincial Comparison.* Ottawa: Status of Women Canada, 1999.

Bakker, Isabella. *Rethinking Restructuring*. Toronto: University of Toronto Press, 1996.

Bakker, Isabella, and Katherine Scott. "From the Postwar to the Post-Liberal Keynesian Welfare." Clement 286–310.

Basok, Tanya. "Refugee Policy: Globalization, Radical Challenge, or State Control?" *Studies in Political Economy* 50 (Summer 1996): 133–66.

Begin, Monique. "The Royal Commission on the Status of Women in Canada." *Challenging Times: The Women's Movement in Canada and the U.S.* Ed. Monique Begin and David Flaherty. Montreal: McGill-Queens University Press, 1992.

Bickerton, James, and Alain Gagnon (eds.). *Canadian Politics*. 3rd ed. Peterborough: Broadview Press, 1999.

Bissoondath, Neil. *Selling Illusions: The Cult of Multiculturalism in Canada*. Toronto: Penguin Books, 1994.

Boyd, Monica. "Migration Policy, Female Dependency, and Family Membership: Canada and Germany." Evans and Wekerle.

——. "Migration Regulations and Sex Selective Outcomes in Developed Countries." *International Migration Policies and the Status of Female Migrants*. Proceeding of the UN Expert Group Meeting on International Migration Policies and the Status of Female Migrants. New York: United Nations, 1995.

Boyd, Susan (ed.). *Challenging the Public/Private Divide: Feminism, Law, and Public Policy*. Toronto: University of Toronto, 1997.

Breton, Raymond. "Multiculturalism and Canadian Nation-Building." *The Politics of Gender, Ethnicity, and Language in Canada*. Ed. Alan Cairns and Cynthia Williams. Toronto: University of Toronto Press in Cooperation with the Royal Commission on the Economic Union and Development Prospects of Canada, 1986.

Briskin, Linda, and Mona Eliasson (eds.). *Women's Organizing and Public Policy in Canada and Sweden*. Montreal: McGill-Queens University Press, 1999.

Brodie, Janine. *Politics on the Margins: Restructuring and the Canadian Women's Movement*. Halifax: Fernwood, 1995.

—— (ed.). *Critical Concepts: An Introduction to Canadian Politics*. Scarborough: Prentice Hall, 1999.

—— (ed.). *Women and Canadian Public Policy*. Toronto: Harcourt Brace and Jovanovich, 1996.

Brodie, Janine, and Christina Gabriel. "Canadian Immigration Policy and the Emergence of the Neo-Liberal State," *Journal of Contemporary International Issues* 1.11. <www.yorku.ca/research/cii/journal/issues/vol1no1/article_3.html>

Brouwer, Andrew. "Protection with a Price Tag: The Head Tax for Refugees and Their Families Must Go." Toronto: Maytree Foundation, 2000. <www.maytree.com/publications_headtax.html>.

Bullock, Susan. *Women and Work*. London: Zed Books, 1994.

Burke, Mike, et al. (eds.). *Restructuring and Resistance: Canadian Public Policy in an Age of Global Capitalism*. Halifax: Fernwood, 2000.

Burstein, Meyer. "Metropolis Objectives and Aims of the Conference." *Metropolis: First Conference Milan, 13-15 November 1996.* Ed. Marco Lombardi. Milano: Fondazione Cariplo—ISMU, 1997.

Burt, Sandra. "Looking Backward and Thinking Ahead: Toward a Gendered Analysis of Canadian Politics." *Canadian Politics in the 21st Century.* Ed. Michael Whittington and Glen Williams. Scarborough: Nelson Canada, 2000.

——. "The Several Worlds of Policy Analysis: Traditional Approaches and Feminist Critiques." *Changing Methods: Feminist Transforming Practice.* Ed. Sandra Burt and Lorraine Code. Peterborough: Broadview Press, 1995.

Cameron, David, and Janice Gross Stein. "Globalization, Culture and Society: The State as Place Amidst Shifting Spaces." *Canadian Public Policy* 26 (August 2000).

Campbell, Elaine. *Canada, Excluding Ontario: Current Issue Paper 146.* Toronto: Legislative Research Service, 1993.

Canada. Citizenship and Immigration Canada (CIC). *Building on a Strong Foundation for the 21st Century.* Ottawa: Minister of Public Works and Government Services, 1998.

——. "Building on a Strong Foundation for the 21st Century: The Legislative Review Process." 2 June 2000. <http://cicnet.ci.gc.ca/English/about/policy/lr/e_lr03.html >.

——. *Canada-United States Accord on Our Shared Border.* Ottawa: Minister of Public Works and Government Services, 2000.

——. *Facts and Figures. Overview of Immigration.* Ottawa: Minister of Supply and Services, 1994.

——. *Immigration Consultations Report.* Hull: Supply and Services Canada, 1994.

——. Immigration Legislative Review Advisory Group. *Not Just Numbers: A Canadian Framework for Future Immigration.* Ottawa: Minister of Public Works and Government Services Canada, 1997.

——. Department of Canadian Heritage. *1996-1997: 9th Annual Report on the Operation of the Canadian Multiculturalism Act.* Ottawa: Minister of Public Works and Government Services Canada, 1998.

——. *Annual Report on the Operation of the Canadian Multiculturalism Act, 1993-1994.* Ottawa: Minister of Supply and Services Canada, 1995.

——. *Annual Report on the Operation of the Canadian Multiculturalism Act, 1994-1995.* Ottawa: Minister of Supply and Services, 1996.

——. *Annual Report on the Operation of the Canadian Multiculturalism Act 1998-1999.* Ottawa: Minister of Public Works and Government Services, Canada, 2000.

——. *Multiculturalism: Respect, Equality, Diversity: Program Highlights.* Rev. 2nd ed. July 1998.

——. *Strategic Evaluation of Multiculturalism Programs Prepared for Corporate Review Branch, Department of Canadian Heritage: Final Report.* Brighton Research, March 1996.

——. *Teachers' Guide Secondary Grades: Racism Stop It!* Ottawa: Minister of Public Works and Services Canada, 1999.

——. Department of Foreign Affairs and International Trade. *Human Security: Safety for People in a Changing World.* April 1999.

——. House of Commons. Report of the Special Committee on Visible Minorities in Canadian Society. *Equality Now!* Ottawa: Queen's Printer of Canada, 1984.

——. Manpower and Immigration. *A Report of the Canadian Immigration and Population Study, Volume Two: The Immigration Program.* Ottawa: Information Canada, 1974.

Canada. Manpower and Immigration. *White Paper on Immigration.* Ottawa: Queen's Printer, 1966.

——. Royal Commission on Equality in Employment (RCEE). *Equality in Employment: Report of the Royal Commission on Equality in Employment.* Ottawa: Minister of Supply and Services, 1984.

——. Royal Commission on the Status of Women. *Report of the Royal Commission on the Status of Women.* Ottawa: Information Canada, 1970.

——. Standing Committee on Citizenship and Immigration. *Facilitating the Entry of Temporary Workers to Canada, Fourth Report.* Ottawa: Public Works and Government Services, 1997.

——. Statistics Canada. *1996 Census: Ethnic Origin, Visible Minorities.* <http://www.statcan.ca/Daily/English/980217/d980217.htm>

——. Statistics Canada. *1996 Census: Immigration and Citizenship.* <http://www.statcan.ca/english/census96/nove4/naliss.htm>.

——. Status of Women Canada. *Gender Based Analysis: A Guide for Policy Making.* Ottawa: Ministry of Supply and Services, 1996.

——. Status of Women Canada. *Setting the Stage for the Next Century: The Federal Plan for Gender Equality.* Ottawa: Ministry of Supply and Services, 1995.

Canadian Alliance of Manufacturers and Exporters. "Appendix C— Questions and Answers about Equal Opportunity and Diversity." *Business Results Through Diversity Handbook.* Toronto: Queen's Printer for Ontario, 1997.

Canadian Bar Association. "Submission of the National Citizenship and Immigration Law Section to Senate Standing Committee on Social Affairs, Science and Technology." 2 October 2001. <www.cba.org/News/Archives/2001-10-02- submission.asp>.

Canadian Council For Refugees (CCR). *Canadian NGO Report on Women and Children Migrants* (February 2000). <www.webnet/%7Eccr/womench.htm>.

——. "Impact of the Right of Landing Fee." February 1997. <http//www.web.net/~ccr/headtax2.htm>.

——. "Report on Systemic Racism and Discrimination in Canadian Refugee and Immigration Policies." 1 November 2000. <http:www.web.net/~ccr/antiracrep.htm>.

Canadian Ethnocultural Council (CEC), "Multiculturalism, Citizenship, and the Canadian Nation: A Critique of the Proposed Design for Program Renewal." Prepared by Bohdan Kordan. Ottawa: CEC, March 1997.

Canadian Federation of Independent Business. "Employment Equity with Equanimity: A Small Business Perspective." *Submission to the Ontario Employment Equity Commission,* 12 February 1992.

Canadian Labour Congress. *Women's Work: A Report*. Ottawa: CLC, 1997.

Cardillo, Brenda. "Defining and Measuring Employment Equity." *Perspectives*. Ottawa: Statistics Canada, Cat. No. 75-001E.

Carty, P. Kenneth, and W. Peter Ward (eds.). *National Politics and Community in Canada*. Vancouver: University of British Columbia Press, 1986.

Charlton, Mark, and Paul Barker. "Is Employment Equity Fair and Necessary." *Contemporary Political Issues*. 3rd ed. Ed. Mark Charlton and Paul Barker. Toronto: Nelson, 1998.

Chilcote, Ronald H. *Theories of Comparative Politics*. 2nd ed. Boulder: Westview Press, 1994.

Clement, Wallace (ed.). *Understanding Canada: Building on the New Canadian Political Economy*. Kingston: McGill-Queens University Press, 1997.

Cobb-Clark, Deborah A., and Marie D. Connolly. "The Worldwide Market for Skilled Migrants: Can Australia Compete?" *International Migration* Review 31.3 (Fall 1997).

Cohen, Marjorie Griffin. "From the Welfare State to Vampire Capitalism." *Women and the Canadian Welfare State*. Ed. Patricia M. Evans and Gerda R. Wekerle. Toronto: University of Toronto Press, 1997.

——. "Paid Work." *Canadian Women's Issues Volume II*. Ed. Ruth Roach Pierson and Marjorie Griffin Cohen. Toronto: James Lorimer, 1995.

Cohen, Marjorie Griffin, *et al.* eds. *Is Multiculturalism Bad for Women? Susan Moller Okin with Respondents*. Princeton, NJ: Princeton University Press, 1999.

Couture, Claude. *Paddling With the Current: Pierre Trudeau, Etienne Parent, Liberalism and Nationalism in Canada*. Edmonton: University of Alberta Press, 1996.

Crane, David. *The Canadian Dictionary of Business and Economics*. Toronto: Stoddart, 1993.

Curran, Jennifer. "Gender Analysis of Canada's Immigration Legislation." *Jurisfemme* 18.3 (Spring 1999). <www.nawl.ca/v18-no3.htm>.

Daniels, Ronald J., Patrick MacKelm, and Kent Roach (eds.). *The Security of Freedom: Essays on Canada's Anti-Terrorism Bill*. Toronto: University of Toronto Press, 2001.

Dirks, Gerald E. "Factors Underlying Migration and Refugee Issues: Responses and Cooperation among OECD Member States." *Citizenship Studies* 2.3 (1998).

Doern, G. Bruce, Leslie Pal, and Brian Tomlin (eds.). *Border Crossings: The Internationalization of Canadian Public Policy*. Toronto: Oxford University Press, 1996.

Dua, Ena, and Angela Robertson (eds.). *Scratching the Surface: Canadian Anti-Racist Feminist Thought*. Toronto: Women's Press, 1999.

Eichler, Magrit. *Nonsexist Research Methods: A Practical Guide*. Boston: Unwin Hyman, 1988.

Equality for Gays And Lesbians Everywhere. "Brief to the House of Commons Standing Committee on Citizenship and Immigration." 27 March 2001. <www.egale.ca/documents/c-11 committeebrief.htm>.

Evans, Patricia M., and Gerda R. Wekerle (eds.). *Women and the Canadian Welfare State*. Toronto: University of Toronto Press, 1997.

Falk, Richard. "The Making of Global Citizenship." *Global Visions: Beyond the New World Order.* Ed. Jeremy Brecher, John Brown Childs, and Jill Cutler. Montreal: Black Rose Books, 1993.

Findlay, Sue. "Democratizing the Local State: Issues for Feminist Practice and the Representation of Women." *A Different Kind of State? Popular Power and Democratic Administration.* Ed. Gregory Albo, David Langille, and Leo Panitch. Toronto: Oxford University Press, 1993.

Foster, Lorne. *Turnstile Immigration: Multiculturalism, Social Order, and Social Justice in Canada.* Toronto: Thompson Educational Press, 1998.

Frideres, James. "Altered States: Federal Policy and Aboriginal Peoples." Li.

Gabriel, Christina. "Recasting Citizenship: The Politics of Multiculturalism Policy in Canada." Diss. Toronto, York University, 1997.

——. "Restructuring at the Margins: Women of Colour and the Changing Economy." Dua and Robertson.

Gabriel, Christina, and Laura Macdonald. "Border Anxieties: Changing Discourses on the Canada–US Border." Paper Presented to the Annual Meeting of the International Studies Association, Chicago, Illinois, 21–14 February 2001.

Gerth, H.H., and C. Wright Mills (eds. and trans.). *Max Weber: Essays in Sociology.* New York: Oxford University Press, 1958.

Giddens, Anthony. "Still a Third Way for Europe." *New Perspectives Quarterly* 17.1 (Winter 2000).

Gilman, Sander L. " 'Barbaric' Rituals," Cohen *et al.*

Glastra, Folke, Petra Schedler, and Erik Kats. "Employment Equity Policies in Canada and the Netherlands." *Policy and Politics* 26.2 (April 1998).

Gosine, Andil. "Presenting Adrienne Clarkson: Gender, Nation and a New Governor-General." *Canadian Women's Studies* 20.2 (Summer 2000): 6–10.

Gupta, Tania Das. "Families of Native People, Immigrants, and People of Colour." *Canadian Families Diversity, Conflict, and Change.* Ed. Nancy Mandel. Toronto: Harcourt Press, 1995.

——. "The Politics of Multiculturalism: 'Immigrant Women' and the Canadian State." Dua and Robertson.

——. *Racism and Paid Work.* Toronto: Garamond Press, 1996.

Hall, Stuart, and Martin Jacques (eds.). *New Times: The Changing Face of Politics in the 1990s.* London: Verso, 1990.

Hall, Stuart, David Held, Don Hubert, and Kenneth Thompson (eds.). *Modernity: An Introduction to Modern Societies.* Cambridge: Polity Press, 1995.

Harrison, Trevor. "Class, Citizenship and Global Migration: The Case of the Canadian Business Immigration Program, 1978–1992." *Canadian Public Policy* XXII.1 (1996).

Hawkesworth, Mary. "Policy Studies Within a Feminist Frame." *Policy Sciences* 27 (1994).

Hawkins, Freda. *Canada and Immigration: Public Policy and Public Concern.* 2nd ed. Montreal: McGill-Queen's University Press, 1988.

Hay, Colin, and Matthew Watson. "Globalisation: 'Sceptical' Notes on the 1999 Reith Lectures." *Political Quarterly* 70.4 (Oct.-Dec. 1999).

Hayes, Victor. "Beyond Employment Equity: The Business Case for Diversity." *The Ivey Business Journal* (September/October 1999).

Held, David. "The Decline of the Nation State." Hall and Jacques.

——. "Democracy and Globalization." *Re-imagining Political Community: Studies in Cosmopolitan Democracy*. Ed. Daniele Archibugi, David Held, and Martin Kohler. Stanford: Stanford University Press, 1998.

Held, David, *et al. Global Transformations: Politics, Economics, and Culture*. Stanford: Stanford University Press, 1999.

Henry, Frances, and Carol Tator. "State Policy and Practices as Racialized Discourse: Multiculturalism. The Charter and Employment Equity." Li.

Henry, Frances, Carol Tator, Winston Mattis, and Tim Rees (eds.). *The Colour of Democracy, Racism in Canadian Society*. 2nd ed. Toronto: Harcourt Brace, 2000.

Higgs, Robert. "The So-Called Third Way." *Independent Review* 4.4 (Spring 2000): 625-30.

Hirst, Paul, and Grahame Thompson. "Globalization and the Future of the Nation State." *Economy and Society* 24.3 (1995).

Holton, Robert, and M. Lanphier. "Public Opinion, Immigration and Refugees." *Immigration and Refugee Policy Australia and Canada Compared*. Ed. Howard Adelman, *et al.* Toronto: University of Toronto Press, 1994.

Hyndman, Jennifer. "Gender and Canadian Immigration Policy: A Current Snapshot." *Canadian Women's Studies* 19.3 (Fall 1999).

——. "Globalization, Immigration and the Gender Implications of *Not Just Numbers* in Canada." *Refuge* 18.1 (February 1999).

Inglis, Christine. "Multiculturalism: New Policy Responses to Diversity." MOST Policy Papers 4. Paris: UNESCO, 1996.

Jain, Harish, and Anil Verma. "Managing workforce diversity for competitiveness: The Canadian experience." *International Journal of Manpower* 17, 4/5 (1996).

Jakubowski, Lisa Marie. *Immigration and the Legalization of Racism*. Halifax: Fernwood, 1997.

Jary, David, and Julia Jary, *The Harper Collins Dictionary of Sociology*. New York: Harper Collins, 1991.

Jenson, Jane. "Fated to Live in Interesting Times: Canada's Changing Citizenship Regimes." *Canadian Journal of Political Science* 30.4 (December 1997).

——. "The Talents of Women, the Skills of Men." *The Transformation of Work: Skills, Flexibility and the Labour Process*. Ed. S. Wood. London: Routledge, 1989.

——. "Understanding Politics: Concepts of Identity in Political Science." Bickerton and Gagnon.

Jenson, Jane, and Susan Phillips. "Regime Shift: New Citizenship Practices in Canada." *International Journal of Canadian Studies* 14 (Autumn): 111-35.

Kallen, Evelyn. *Ethnicity and Human Rights in Canada*. 2nd ed. Toronto: Oxford University Press, 1995.

Kandyoti, Deniz. "Identity and Its Discontents: Women and the Nation." *Colonial Discourse and Postcolonial Theory*. Eds. Patrick Williams and Laura Chrisman. New York: Columbia University Press, 1994. 376-91.

Kaplan, William (ed.). *Belonging: The Meaning and Future of Canadian Citizenship*. Kingston: McGill-Queens University Press, 1993.

Karim, Karim H. "Australia's Strategy on Productive Diversity." Hull: Canadian Heritage, Strategic Research and Analysis, September 1995.

Kelly, Erin, and Frank Dobbin. "How Affirmative Action Became Diversity Management." *American Behavioural Scientist* 41.7 (April 1998).

Kernaghan, Kenneth, and David Siegel. *Public Administration in Canada*. 4th ed. Nelson: Toronto, 1999.

Kirkham, Della. "The Reform Party of Canada: A Discourse on Race, Ethnicity, and Equality." Satzewich 248-55.

Knowles, Valerie. *Strangers at Our Gates*. Toronto: Dundurn Press, 1997.

Kurthen, Hermann. "The Canadian Experience with Multiculturalism and Employment Equity: Lessons for Europe." *New Community* 23.2 (April 1997): 249-70.

Kuttner, Stephanie. "Gender-Based Persecution as a Basis for Refugee Status: The Emergence of an International Norm." *Refuge* 16.4 (October 1997).

Kymlicka, Will. *Finding Our Way: Rethinking Ethnocultural Relations in Canada*. Don Mills: Oxford University Press, 1998.

Landes, Joan (ed.). *Feminism, The Public, and The Private*. Oxford: Oxford University Press, 1998.

Laxer, Gordon. "Introduction." *The Canadian Review of Sociology and Anthropology* 32.3 Special Issue: Globalization (August 1995).

Li, Peter. "The Market Worth of Immigrants' Educational Credentials." *Canadian Public Policy* XXVI.1 (March 2001): 23-38.

—— (ed.). *Race and Ethnic Relations in Canada*. Toronto: Oxford University Press, 1999.

Lister, Ruth. *Citizenship: Feminist Perspectives*. London: MacMillan Press, 1997.

Lum, Janet. "The Federal Employment Equity Act: Goals vs Implementation." *Canadian Public Administration* 38.1 (Spring 1995).

Lum, Janet, and A. Paul Williams. "Out of Synch with a 'Shrinking State'? Making Sense of Employment Equity Act (1995)." Burke et al.

Luxton, Meg (ed.). *Feminism and Families: Critical Policies and Changing Practices*. Halifax: Fernwood, 1997.

Macklin, Audrey. "Foreign Domestic Workers: Surrogate Housewife or Mail Order Servant?," *McGill Law Journal*, 37:3 (1992).

Marshall, T.H. "Citizenship and Social Class." *Citizenship and Class*. Ed. T.H. Marshall and Tom Bottomore. London: Pluto Press, 1991.

Martin, Paul Sr. "Citizenship and the People's World." Kaplan.

Martin, Sandra. *The Politics of Equity*. Toronto: Atkinson, Charitable Foundation, 1995.

Maytree Foundation. "Brief to the Standing Committee on Citizenship and Immigration regarding Bill C-11, Immigration and Refugee Protection Act." 26 March 2001 <www.maytree.com>.

McBride, Stephen. "Policy from What? NeoLiberal and Human Capital Theoretical Foundations of Recent Canadian Labour Market Policy." Burke *et al.*

McBride, Stephen, and John Shields. *Dismantling a Nation: Canada and the New World Order.* Halifax: Fernwood, 1993.

McDermott, Pat. "Employment Equity and Pay Equity." *Canadian Women's Studies* 12.3 (1992).

McGrew, Anthony. "A Global Society?" Hall *et al.*

Molgat, Anne. *Expanding Our Horizons: The Work of CACSW And Its Context.* Ottawa: CACSW, 1993.

Molot, Maureen, and Fen Osler Hampson. *Canada Among Nations.* Don Mills: Oxford University Press, 2000.

Morgan, Nicole. *The Equality Game: Women in the Federal Public Service, 1908-1987.* CACSW: Ottawa, 1988.

Murray, Robin. "Benetton Britain: The New Economic Order." Hall and Jacques.

National Association of Women and the Law (NAWL). *Gender Analysis of Immigration and Refugee Protection Legislation and Policy.* Ottawa: NAWL, 1999.

Neysmith, Sheila M. *Restructuring Caring Labour.* Toronto: Oxford, 2000.

Nieguth, Tim. "Privilege or Recognition: The Myth of State Neutrality." *Critical Review of International Social and Political Philosophy* 2.2 (1999): 112-31.

Nord, Doug. "Strengthening Society II: Immigration Policy." *Canadian Public Policy: Globalization and Political Parties.* Ed. Andrew Stritch and Andrew Johnson. Toronto: Copp Clark, 1997.

O'Connor, Julia S. "Employment Equality Strategies and Their Representation in the Political Process in Canada, 1970-1994." Andrew and Rodgers.

O'Neil, Maureen, and Sharon Sutherland. "The Machinery of Women's Policy: Implementing the Royal Commission on the Status of Women." Andrew and Rodgers. Okin, Susan Moller. "Is Multiculturalism Bad for Women?" Cohen, *et al.*

Ontario. Office of the Employment Equity Commissioner, Ministry of Citizenship. *Working Towards Equality: The Discussion Paper on Employment Equity Legislation.* Toronto: Queen's Printer for Ontario, 1991.

Overbeek, Henk. "Towards a New International Migration Regime: Globalization, Migration, and the Internationalization of the State." *Migration and European Integration: The Dynamics of Inclusion and Exclusion.* Ed. Robert Miles and Dietrich Thränhardt. London: Pinter, 1995.

Pal, Leslie. *Beyond Policy Analysis.* Scarborough: Nelson, 1997.

—. *Interests of State: The Politics of Language, Multiculturalism, and Feminism in Canada*. Montreal and Kingston: McGill-Queen's University Press, 1993.

Palmer, Douglas L. "Determinants of Canadian Attitudes toward Immigration: More than Just Racism?" *Canadian Journal of Behavioural Science* 28.3 (July 1996): 180–92.

Pearson, David, and Patrick Ongley. "Multiculturalism and Biculturalism: The Recent New Zealand Experience in Comparative Perspective." *Journal of Intercultural Studies* 17.1–2 (1996).

Pellerin, Hélène. "The Cart Before the Horse? The Coordination of Migration Policies in the Americas and the Neo-Liberal Economic Project of Integration." *Review of International Political Economy* 6:4 (Winter 1999).

—. "Global Restructuring in the World Economy and Migration: The Globalization of Migration Dynamics." *International Journal* XLVIII (Spring 1993).

Phillips, Anne (ed.). *Feminism and Politics*. Oxford: Oxford University Press, 1998.

Phillips, Susan. "Discourse, Identity and Voice: Feminist Contributions to Policy Studies." *Policy Studies in Canada*. Ed., Laurent Dobuzinskis, Michael Howlett, and David Laycock. Toronto: University of Toronto Press, 1996.

Prosperi, Paolo. "Redefining Citizenship; The Politics of Multiculturalism Reform in Canada." Paper prepared for the Annual Canadian Political Science Association meetings, Sherbrooke, Quebec, June 1999.

Rawlyk, G.A. "Canada's Immigration Policy: 1945–1962." *Dalhousie Review* 42.3 (1962).

Razack, Sherene. *Looking White People in the Eye: Gender, Race, and Culture in Courtrooms and Classrooms*. Toronto: University of Toronto Press, 1999.

Rebick, Judy. "Liberals Try to Sink NAC." *Herizons* (Winter 1999).

Reed, Carole Ann. "Contradictions and Assumptions: A Report On Employment Equity in Canada." *Resources for Feminist Research* 24.3-4 (Fall 1995/Winter 1996).

Richmond, Anthony. *Global Apartheid*. Toronto: Oxford University Press, 1994.

Rocher, Guy. "Les Ambiguités d'un Canada bilingue et biculturel." *Le Quebec en mutation*. Montréal: Hurtubise HMH, 1973.

Roniger, Luis. "Public Life and Globalization as Cultural Vision." *The Canadian Review of Sociology and Anthropology* 32.3 (August 1995).

Sassen, Saskia. *Globalization and its Discontents*. New York: New Press, 1998.

Satzewich, Vic (ed.). *Racism and Social Inequality in Canada*. Toronto: Thompson, 1998.

Sears, Alan. "The 'Lean' State and Capitalist Restructuring: Towards a Theoretical Account." *Studies in Political Economy* 59 (Summer 1999): 91–114.

Shepard, R. Bruce. "Plain Racism: The Reaction Against Oklahoma Black Immigration to the Canadian Plains." *Racism in Canada*. Ed. Ormand McKague. Saskatchewan: Fifth House Publishing, 1991.

Ship, Susan. "Problematizing Ethnicity and 'Race' Feminist Scholarship on Women and Politics." Andrew and Tremblay.

Simmons, Alan. "Racism and Immigration Policy." Satzewich.

Simms, Glenda. "Racism as a Barrier to Canadian Citizenship." Kaplan.

Singer, Colin R. "Speaking Notes to the National Congress of Italian Canadians: 'Key Concerns respecting Bill C-31, Immigration and Refugee Protection Act.'" 10 June 2000 <www.singer.ca/permres-new-protection-act.html>.

Siu, Bobby Siu. "How Diversity Management Can Fill Out Your Bottom Line." <http://www.equalopportunity.on.ca/enggraf/resource/botline.html>

Skogstad, Grace. "Globalization and Public Policy: Situating Canadian Analysis." *Canadian Journal of Political Science* 34.4 (December 2000): 805-28.

Standing, Guy. "Global Feminization through Flexible Labour." *World Development* 17.7 (1989).

Stasiulis, Daiva K. "The Symbolic Mosaic Reaffirmed: Multiculturalism Policy." *How Ottawa Spends 1988-89*. Ed. Katherine A. Graham. Ottawa: Carleton University Press, 1988.

———. "Symbolic Representation: And the Numbers Game: Tory Policies on 'Race.'" *How Ottawa Spends 1991-1992*. Ed. Frances Abele. Ottawa: Carleton University Press, 1991.

Stasiulis, Daiva, and Radha Jhappan. "The Fractious Politics of a Settler Society: Canada." *Unsettling Settler Societies: Articulations of Gender, Race, Ethnicity, and Class*. Eds. Daiva Stasiulis and Nira Yuval-Davis. London: Sage, 1995.

Stasiulis, Daiva, and Yasmeen Abu-Laban. "Unequal Relations and the Struggle for Equality: Race and Ethnicity in Canadian Politics." *Canadian Politics in the 21st Century*. Ed. Glen Williams. Scarborough: Nelson Thomson Learning, 2000.

Stetson, Dorothy M. and Amy Mazur (eds.). *Comparative State Feminism*. Newbury Park, CA: Sage, 1995.

Stone, Diane. "State of the Art: Learning Lessons and Transferring Policy Across Time, Space and Disciplines." *Politics* 19.1 (1999).

Talbot-Allan, Laura. "Viewpoint: Measuring the Impact of Diversity." *CMA Magazine* (June 1996).

Thomas, Derrick. "The Social Welfare Implications of Immigrant Family Sponsorship Default: An Analysis of Data from Census Metropolitan Area of Toronto: Final Report." Ottawa: Citizenship and Immigration Canada, 1996.

Thompson, Grahame. "The Evolution of the Managed Economy in Europe." *Economy and Society* 21,2 (1992): 129-151.

Trimble, Linda. "The Politics of Gender." Brodie.

UN Secretariat. "The International Migration of Women: An Overview." Department for Economic and Social Information and Policy Analysis Population Division. *International Migration Policies and the Status of Female Migrants*, Proceeding of the UN Expert Group Meeting on International Migration Policies and the Status of Female Migrants. New York: UN, 1995.

Vale, Norma. "Brave New Partnerships: Learning how to get along with each other in the Metropolis." *University Affairs* (October 1998).

Valverde, Mariana. *The Age of Light, Soap, and Water.* Toronto: McClelland and Stewart 1991.

Veuglers, John. "State-Society Relations in the Making of Canadian Immigration Policy During the Mulroney Era." *Canadian Review of Sociology and Anthropology,* 37.1 (February 2000): 95-111.

Vickers, Jill. *Reinventing Political Science.* Halifax: Fernwood, 1997.

Vipond, Mary. "Nationalism and Nativism: The Native Sons of Canada in the 1920s." *Canadian Review of Studies in Nationalism* 9 (Spring 1982).

Westergaard, John. "Where Does the Third Way Lead?" *New Political Economy* 4.3 (November 1999): 429-36.

Whitaker, Reg. *Canadian Immigration Policy.* Ottawa: Canadian Historical Association, 1991.

——. *Double Standard: The Secret History of Immigration.* Toronto: Lester and Orpen Dennys, 1987.

——. "Refugees: The Security Dimension." *Citizenship Studies* 2.3 (1998).

Williams, Fiona. *Social Policy: A Critical Introduction.* Cambridge: Polity Press, 1986.

Williams, Glen (ed.). *Canadian Politics in the 21st Century.* Scarborough: Nelson Thomson Learning, 2000.

INDEX

Abella, Judge Rosalie, 136, 141, 148
Abella Commission, 134, 136–38, 140,
   143, 157
Aboriginal people
   backlash, 147
   economic marginalization, 130
   employment equity, 11, 131,
      136–37, 140
   federal funding, 134
   franchise, 42
   special interests, 158, 166
   youth, 129
"An Act Respecting Canadian
   Citizenship," 63, 89
"An Act Respecting Employment
   Equity," 149
Ad Hoc Committee on Gender
   Analysis, 87–88
Advisory Committee on Cooperation
   in Citizenship, 107
advocacy groups, 22
   backlash, 147
   employment equity, 136
   ethno-cultural, 53
   funding, 87, 115, 134, 170
   labour market, 130
   state support, 131
affirmative action, 134, 136, 144,
   152–53
   Australia, 133
   U.S. experience, 157
Albo, Greg, 140
Alliance for Employment Equity, 143
"An Act to Repeal Job Quotas and to
   Restore Merit-Based Employment
   Practices," 148
androcentrism, 24
Anti-Terrorism Plan, 85

Asia Pacific Foundation of Canada,
   116
Axworthy, Lloyd, 123

B and B Commission, 107–8, 124, 134
Bacchi, Carol Lee, 133, 144, 147
best immigrants. *See under* model
   immigrants/citizens
"best practice" corporate employers,
   156
bilingualism, 108–9
   Reform Party criticism, 111
Bill 8, 148
Bill 79, 144, 146, 148
   opposition to, 145
Bill C-11, 63, 75–79
   control measures, 84
Bill C-16, 63, 75, 89
Bill C-31, 75, 84
Bill C-64, 149–50
Bissoondath, Neil, 112–13, 118–20
Blair, Tony, 175–76
borders and border control. *See under*
   state sovereignty
Brighton Report, 113–15
*A Broader Vision: Immigration and
   Citizenship Plan, 1995-2000*, 55
*Building on a Strong Foundation for the
   21st Century*, 87
Burstein, Meyer, 94–95
Burt, Sandra, 24
business class, 90
   investors, 49, 66, 169, 172
"Business Results Through Diversity:
   A Guidebook," 153

Calgary Immigrant Aid, 70
Campbell, Kim, 112

Canada
  competitive advantage, 62, 72
  domestic and external policies, 20,
    22–23
  export of policy ideas, 22–23
  as model of multiculturalism, 30,
    106, 122
Canadian Advisory Council on the
    Status of Women, 88, 136,
    149–50, 170
Canadian Alliance. *See* Reform Party
Canadian Bar Association, 76, 83
Canadian Citizenship Act, 43
  review, 44
Canadian Council of Refugees, 48–49,
    52, 68–69, 83, 86
Canadian Ethnocultural Council, 115,
    136, 150
Canadian Federation of Independent
    Business, 144
Canadian Human Rights Act, 119
Canadian Human Rights Commission,
    138–39, 149
Canadian Human Rights Tribunal, 149
Canadian Immigration and Refugee
    Board, 92
Canadian Jewish Congress, 115
Canadian Manufacturers' Association,
    144
Canadian Multiculturalism Act, 119,
    121
Canadian Pacific Railway, 38
Canadian Security and Intelligence
    Service (CSIS), 85
Caplan, Elinor, 76, 83
Celucci, Paul, 91
Charlottetown Constitutional Accord,
    112
Charter of Rights and Freedoms, 110
China, 155
Chinese Canadian National Council,
    115
Chinese Immigration Act, 38
Chinese labourers, 38
Chrétien, Jean, 11, 14–15, 29, 47, 62,
    75, 89, 106, 116, 148
  on multiculturalism, 121
Chrétien government. *See* Liberal gov-
    ernment
citizenship, 20, 69–70. *See also* immigra-
    tion
  active, 114
  changes, 96

criteria, 73
franchise, 42–43
global, 177
legislation, 75
neo-liberal assumptions, 21
politics of, 41, 63
reforms, 61, 97
residency requirements, 89–90
rights and duties, 44, 131, 178
selection, 48, 54
sexual orientation and, 53
social, 143
social rights of, 45, 68, 73–74
substantive, 29, 51
as taxpayers, 74
test, 90
Citizenship Act, 30, 75, 89–90, 119
Citizenship and Immigration Canada,
    65–66, 80
Citizenship Branch of the Secretary of
    State, 134
Civil Service Act (1918), 134
Clarkson, Adrienne, 14
  media coverage of appointment, 15
class, 13, 15, 27, 29, 68, 109, 117, 166,
    173
  biases, 81
  class-advantaged people, 90, 173
  class-based hierarchies, 49, 63
Coll, Bridget, 53
collective action, 13, 21, 150
commodification
  of minorities, 30
  of people, 65, 69, 173
  of social goods, 166
Common Sense Revolution, 141, 148,
    152
Communism, 40, 54
competitiveness, 12, 21, 81, 141
  and equity, 143, 169
  global, 20, 61, 96, 111, 116, 124,
    167, 173–74
  international, 70
  and international trade, 117
  progressive, 175
  unfettered, 166
Conference Board of Canada, 116, 154
*The Cultural Contribution of other Ethnic
    Groups,* 108
culture
  of dependency, 152
  diversity, 178
  dualism, 109

maintenance, 110
as private, 111–12, 119, 124, 168

Das Gupta, Tania, 118
Davis, Susan, 69
democracy, 17, 70
Department of Canadian Heritage,
112–13, 122
Department of Citizenship and
Immigration Canada (CIC), 65-66,
80, 95
Department of Multiculturalism and
Citizenship, 110, 112
Department of National War Services,
107
deportation, 40, 52, 85
Dirks, Gerald, 94
discrimination, 11, 48, 137, 146, 153
systemic, 109, 158, 169
diversity model. See managing diversity
domestic violence, 52, 82, 92
domestic work, 53, 66, 74
domestic worker program, 54
Dupuy, Michel, 113

economic imperatives, 61–62, 165, 168,
172
education, 48, 65, 68
formal, 50–51
language, 52, 68, 71, 74, 108
training allowances, 175
vocational training, 50
efficiency, 12, 20–21, 141, 166
employment equity
backlash and opposition, 145,
147–48, 151, 168, 171, 174
Crown corporations, 136
federal level, 132, 148, 158, 168, 171
gender relations, 133
as good business initiative, 143
managing diversity and, 155–56, 169,
173
multiculturalism, 110
Ontario, 141–42, 144, 146, 151, 153,
158, 168
private sector, 140–42
reverse discrimination, 147, 171
and social justice, 30, 131, 153, 168
"special interests," 166
targeted hiring, 157
technological advances and, 129
United States, 158
Veteran's Preference Clause, 134

voluntary initiatives, 130, 137–38,
144
weakened, 172
women's mobilization and, 135
Employment Equity Act, 138–41,
148–52
Employment Equity Commission
(Ontario), 144–45
Employment Equity Tribunal
(Ontario), 145
entrepreneurship, 49, 124, 172–74
Equal Opportunity Plan, 152–53
equality, 12, 21, 29, 70, 146, 166–67,
171–72, 174
Abella's definition, 137, 148
equal opportunities, 158
ethnic and racial, 142
inequality, 15, 27, 156
men and women, 176
in non-government workplaces, 132
as sameness, 141, 148
substantive, 131, 169, 173
Equality for Gays and Lesbians
Everywhere (EGALE), 77
"Equality Now!", 138
ethnocultural groups, 119, 147, 170
European Court of Justice, 22
European Union, 92–93, 95

fairness, 147, 149, 171
Falk, Richard, 177
familism, 52–53
family class. See under immigration
Federal Contractors Program, 138-40,
151
Federal Plan for Gender Equality, 27
female circumcision, 119–20
feminists and feminism, 24, 243. See also
gender; women
policy framework, 24
policy studies, 27
scholarship, 22, 25, 28, 131
Finestone, Sheila, 116, 150
Fleming, James, 110
Foreign Domestic Movement Program
(FDM), 53
Fourth United Nations World
Conference of Women, 26
Francis, Diane, 84
francophones, 170
federal funding, 134
Fraser Institute, 93
fraud control, 84

free trade issues, 177
freedom, 17, 70
Fry, Hedy, 116, 121–22

G7, 23
"Gateway to Diversity Web Page,"
    152–53
gay and lesbian advocacy groups, 142
gender, 13–15, 23, 29, 90, 109. *See also*
    feminists and feminism; women
    equality, 28, 88, 121, 142, 168, 173
    immigration and, 50, 66
    immigration policy, 49, 67–68, 73,
        81, 90, 96
    managing diversity and, 169
    neo-liberalism and, 63, 166–67
    persecution, 92
    and refugee status, 92
    relations, 24, 50, 133
    roles, 25, 47
gender analysis, 24–28, 70, 86–87
    multiculturalism, 117
    of social diversity and public policy,
        12
*Gender-Based Analysis: A Guide for Policy
    Making*, 27
Gender Based Analysis Unit (Citizenship
    and Immigration Canada), 88
Giddens, Anthony, 176
globalization, 12, 54, 63, 75, 90, 96–97,
    142–43, 166, 169, 171
    alternative readings, 177
    and disadvantaged groups, 19
    discourse, 19–23, 29, 61, 106, 111,
        117, 124, 130, 158, 165
    economic, 62, 69, 78, 81, 122
    economic imperatives, 62, 165, 172
    global economy, 72, 144, 172
    inevitabillity, 21, 175–76
    information technology, 17
    protests, 178
    security and, 123
    state sovereignty and, 16, 18, 61, 70
    technological and cultural implica-
        tions, 17
government-business stakeholder part-
    nership, 153

Hageman, Margaret, 143
Hanger, Art, 63
Harder, Sandra, 88
Harris Conservatives, 141, 146, 148–49,
    152–53

Harrison, Trevor, 49
Hay, Colin, 19, 176
head tax. *See* right-of-landing fees
Hemispheric Social Alliance, 177
Hong Kong, 48–49, 90
human capital, 65, 72, 78, 80, 167, 172
    investments in, 97
Human Rights codes, 137

ideal citizen. *See* model immigrants/cit-
    izens
identity, 41, 61, 169, 178
    Canadian, 63, 105, 113, 168, 171–72
    cultural, 18
    politics of, 13–14
    and voice, 27
identity cards, 76, 84–85
identity politics, 14, 16
immigration, 41, 174, 178. *See also* citi-
    zenship
    agricultural workers, 39
    Bill c-11, 63, 75–84, 88–89
    business class, 90
    bypassing regulations, 73
    changes, 62, 64–65, 80, 96, 173
    cost recovery, 61, 67–68
    country of origin, 14–15, 63
    as domestic policy, 40, 55, 96
    domestic worker program, 54
    economic criteria, 54, 65, 69, 167
    European, Southern and Eastern, 39
    family class, 44, 47, 50–53, 62,
        66–67, 69, 71, 79, 81, 88, 97, 167,
        171
    family reunification, 77
    gender-based analysis, 86
    gender division, 67
    gendered nature, 39
    and globalization, 54, 70, 166, 172
    harmonizing of Canadian and U.S.
        policy, 62, 91
    inadmissibility grounds, 83
    independent class, 44, 48, 66, 69, 72,
        78, 81, 172–73
    integration, 65, 67, 71, 73, 97, 122,
        172
    internationalization, 96
    and labour market, 37–38, 66, 130
    and nation-building, 42
    neo-liberal discussion, 114
    opening the door, 42, 76, 79, 82
    points system, 43–44, 46–51, 54–55,
        65, 72–73, 78–79, 81, 88, 171

popular opposition, 47
quotas, 149, 153, 157–58
reform, 61, 77, 97, 171
Reform Party criticism, 64, 111
security controls, 41, 54, 79, 82–83, 91–92
selection criteria, 65–67, 78–80, 82, 167
settlement process, 67, 74
social justice and, 45
temporary worker programs, 80-81
trade potential, 117
trends, 169
unemployment and, 40, 47
Immigration Act, 47, 69, 76
Immigration and Refugee Protection Act, 90
proposals for, 30
Immigration Canada, 53
India, 155
information technology, 17, 81
International Centre for Migration Policy Development, 95
international human rights, 169
International Olympic Committee (IOC), 11
International Organization for Migration, 95
internationalization, 23, 61, 166
immigration, 91, 94, 97
multiculturalism, 124
of public policy, 22
investors. See business class
Ivey Business School, 154

Japan, 122
Jenson, Jane, 140
just society, 170–71

Keynes, John Maynard, 20, 175
Keynesian-inspired ideas. See welfare state
King, William Lyon Mackenzie, 40, 55, 96
Kunic, Roslyn, 69
Kymlicka, Will, 122

labour market, 42–43, 50, 55, 65–66, 72, 78
fairness, 142
global, 80
government interventions, 132
immigration policy and, 37–38, 130

inequality, 130–31
regulation, 24, 30, 170
women, 129
landing fees. See right-of-landing fees
language requirements, 71–72, 172
language training, 52, 68, 71, 74, 108
Legislated Employment Equity Program (LEEP), 138
Liberal government, 29, 74
citizenship policy, 75
control measures, 83–84
employment equity, 148, 150–51
globalization, 78
immigration, 47, 62–64, 67, 70, 77
landing fee, 69
multiculturalism, 111–13, 117, 124
post deficit budgeting, 176–77
Live-in Caregiver Program (LCP), 54
live-in caregivers, 81
love bug virus, 17
Lum, Janet, 150–51

Macdonald, John A., 38
managing diversity, 30, 153–58, 168–69, 171, 173
Marchi, Sergio, 55, 62, 64, 93
market economy, 12, 16, 30, 45, 131, 140, 142, 148, 169–70
free market, 21, 166, 175, 177
markets
deregulation, 172
emerging global markets, 155
ethnic market, 155
foreign markets, 66
visible minority market, 154
Marshall, T.H., 44–45
Martin, Paul, Sr., 43
"A Matter of Fairness," 149
Maytree Foundation, 77–78
McCarthyism, 86
Macleod, Lynn, 148
Medicare, 45
merit, 134, 147, 149, 152
Metropolis, 94–96, 122, 167
migrant trafficking, 79
Migration Policy Group, 95
model immigrant/citizen. See under citizenship
model immigrants/citizens, 29–30, 38, 42, 65, 96–97, 171, 174
best immigrants, 62
immigrants with the right stuff, 90, 167

model neo-liberal citizen, 141
Morrisey, Christine, 53
Mulroney, Brian, 11, 46, 110–11
Mulroney Conservative government,
    49, 110
multicultural groups. *See* ethnocultural
    groups
    government funding, 45, 114–16,
        134
multiculturalism, 28–29
    antecedents, 107
    in bilingual framework, 123
    business and, 106, 110–11, 116–17,
        123–24
    Canada as model of, 124
    criticism, 106, 111–12
    dollar and cents valuation, 121
    and feminism, 120
    folklore, 109, 123
    funding, 108, 114
    gender issues, 117–19
    and national unity, 106, 108, 112
    new policy directions, 171–72
    popular attacks, 30, 174
    and race relations, 109
    review, 113
    trends, 169
Multiculturalism Act, 110, 115
Multiculturalism Directorate, 108–9,
    170
"Multiculturalism Means Business,"
    110, 116–17, 168
Multilateral Agreement on Investment,
    178
Mushinski, Marilyn, 152

NAFTA, 24, 91
nation-building, 30, 38, 42, 106, 108,
    123–24, 168
    French Canadian nationalism, 107
nation-states, 21, 41, 79, 90
    effect of globalization, 12
    power, 167
National Action Committee on the
    Status of Women, 68, 88, 135–36,
    139–40, 150
National Association of Women and
    the Law, 82, 87
Native people. *See* Aboriginal people
NDP (Ontario), 141–42, 144–47, 153,
    156
    defeat in Ontario, 155
neo-liberalism

alternatives to, 175–77
    definition, 21-22
    resistance to, 178
Nieguth, Tim, 118
North American Free Trade
    Agreement, 24, 91
North American security perimeter, 62,
    91–92
*Not Just Numbers: A Canadian
    Framework for Future Immigration,*
    30, 63, 69–70, 72–76, 86
Nunziata, John, 112

Official Languages Act, 108
Official Languages Program, 134
OHIP, 84
Okin, Susan Moller, 120
omnibus anti-terrorism bill, 85
Ontario Council of Agencies Serving
    Immigrants, 73, 84
Ontario Human Rights tribunals, 153
Ontario Public Service, 144

Pacific Rim, 155
Pal, Leslie, 108
Papademetrio, Demetrios, 94
Pearson, Lester B., 47, 107
people of colour, 30, 171
    advocacy groups, 130
people-smuggling, 94
people with disabilities, 11, 129, 137,
    140, 147, 158, 166, 171
    employment equity, 131
People's Summit, 177
Phillips, Susan, 25, 27
points system, 43–44, 78–79, 171
    domestic worker program, 54
    gender bias, 50–51, 73, 81, 88
    labour market and, 55, 65, 72
    racial/ethnic bias, 47–49
    refugees and, 46
political rights, 44
power, 13, 15–16, 27, 137, 147, 156
    nation state, 167
    relations, 19, 23, 26, 51, 118
private sector, 141–44
    equity initiatives, 155
    initiatives, 170
    Ontario, 152
    workplaces, 132
privatization, 172
Progressive Conservatives (Ontario).
    See Harris conservatives

Prosperi, Paolo, 114
public service, 142, 144
  employment equity, 138–39, 155

Quartiers en Crise, 95
Quebec City, 2001, 177–78
Quiet Revolution, 107

racism, 15, 38–39, 68, 72, 83, 109–10,
  118
  anti-racism, 110, 117, 121, 123
  race/ethnicity, 13–15, 29, 39, 49, 63,
    167, 171, 173
  racial and ethnic discrimination, 43
  racial inequality, 156
  systemic, 109, 168
Rae, Bob, 141
Razack, Sherene, 92, 120
Rebick, Judy, 88
recession
  employment equity and, 145
Reform Party, 63–64, 69, 72, 111, 118,
  151
  Bill c-64 and, 149
refugees, 44, 46, 78, 97, 167, 171
  asylum, 93–94
  bogus refugees, 64, 84
  categories, 66
  Cold War, 54
  gender persecution, 92
  intake, 45
  landing tax, 68–69
  legislation, 46
  negative stereotypes, 83–84
  safe third country, 93
  screening, 85
  UN protocol, 169
Reid, Tim, 155
right-of-landing fees, 67, 71, 96
  head tax, 38
  for refugees, 68–69
Robillard, Lucienne, 70
Royal Commission on Bilingualism
  and Biculturalism, 107–8, 124,
  134
Royal Commission on Equality in
  Employment. See Abella commission
Royal Commission on the Status of
  Women, 135–36

Sassen, Saskia, 61
Saul, John Ralston, 15

Seattle, 178
security, 41, 54, 62, 76, 83–85, 90–91,
  123
security perimeter. See North American
  security perimeter
September 11, 62, 83 84, 86, 90 91
Setting the Stage for the Next Century:
  The Federal Plan for Gender
  Equality, 26
sexual division of labour, 23, 50, 132
  in home, 146
Sifton, Clifford, 39
Simmons, Alan, 48
social equity, 142, 155
  and global competitiveness, 145
social impact analysis, 26
social justice, 20, 29, 114, 130–31, 141,
  143, 158, 166, 171, 174, 178
social rights, 20–21, 45, 51, 68, 73, 96
  of citizenship, 74, 131, 136
Social Sciences and Humanities
  Research Council (SSHRC), 95
solidarity, 21, 131, 150, 170–71
special interest groups, 21, 114, 150,
  166, 171, 177
special treatment, 111, 145, 147, 158
sponsorship, 51, 65, 72
  common-law couples, 71, 81
  default, 67
  domestic abuse and, 52
  duration, 82, 88
  enforcing, 79
  extended family, 53, 71
  same-sex couples, 53, 71, 81, 88
state
  and culture, 168
  feminism, 88
  funding, 170–71
  intervention, 148, 158, 172
  labour market regulation, 133, 136,
    140, 144, 148
  and market, 25–26, 132
  power, 91
  role of, 20–21, 79, 169–70, 172
state sovereignty, 18, 21, 61, 91, 93, 96,
  165
  borders and border control, 17–18,
    62, 76, 85, 167
  globalization, 16–17
  refugee field, 93
Status of Women Canada, 27, 87–88,
  117, 136, 150, 170
stereotypes, 83–84, 93, 155

and national divisiveness, 112
Strategy for Change Convention, 135

technology, 61, 85, 119
terrorism, 62, 83
  anti-terrorism, 76, 85–86, 91
  war on terrorism, 90
"The Immigration and Refugee
  Protection Act," 63, 75–76
The Metro Toronto Chinese and
  Southeast Asian Legal Clinic, 72
Third Way, 175–76
Third World, 92, 109
Thomas, R. Roosevelt, 153
Tiannamen Square, 17
Trempe, Robert, 69
Trinity Group, 155–56
Trudeau, Pierre Elliott, 11, 105, 108,
  134, 136, 170
Trudeau Liberals, 110, 123, 136

Ukrainian Canadian Congress, 115
Ukrainians, 107
UN Conventions, 23
UN Human Development Index, 171
UNESCO, 95, 122
United Nations High Commission for
  Refugees, 92
United Nations' International Day for
  the Elimination of Racial
  Discrimination, 117
United Nations World Conference on
  Women, 117
United Nations Year of Women, 157

visible minorities, 11, 15, 136–37, 140
  advocacy groups, 134
  earnings, 130
  employment equity, 131, 136
  market, 154
  workers as, 129
volunteerism, 114

Watson, Matthew, 19, 176
Weber, Max, 13
welfare state, 20–21, 25–26, 45, 55, 67,
  73, 108, 130–32, 142, 166–67,
  169–70, 175
Whitaker, Reg, 39, 41
white settler society, 30, 42
Williams, Paul, 150–51
Wilson, Michael, 49
Winnipeg General Strike, 39

Witmer, Elizabeth, 146–47
women, 30, 166, 170–71, 173. See also
  feminists and feminism; gender
advocacy groups, 130, 134
barriers, 72
as bearers of culture, 119
caring work, 24, 26
Chinese, 38
of colour, 68
and cuts to family class, 66
dependency, 52, 67, 82, 88
devaluation of women's work, 50–51
as domestic workers, 53
employment equity, 11, 131, 136–37,
  140, 147
exclusion, 150
in the family class, 97
family responsibilities and work, 133
federal funding, 134
franchise, 42
globalization and, 19
immigrant and minority, 89, 118–20
language training, 52
and new markets, 154
as non-contributors, 66
non-government workplaces, 132
points system and, 47
private sphere, 119
racialized, 28, 43
refugee, 89
as second-class citizens, 43
as special interest, 21
Third World immigrant, 119
unpaid labour, 25–26
work, 50–51, 66, 129
Women's Bureau, 150
Women's Educational and Action
  Fund, 150
women's organizations, 89, 115, 147
  community activism, 25
  government funding, 45, 87
  post-war economic boom, 132
"Working Towards Equality," 142
"Working Woman Barbie," 129
World Trade Organization, 22, 178
World Wide Web, 17, 178

xenophobia, 83